Pittsburgh
STEELERS

THE COMPLETE ILLUSTRATED HISTORY

Pittsburgh STEELERS

THE COMPLETE ILLUSTRATED HISTORY

Lew Freedman

Foreword by Dick Hoak

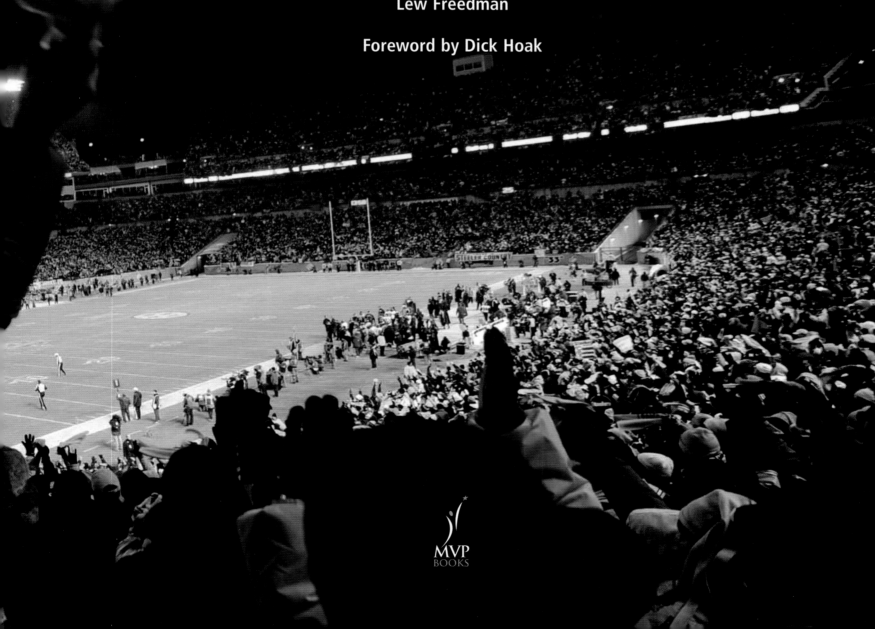

MVP
BOOKS

Half title page: Quarterback Ben Roethlisberger is fondly called "Big Ben" by Steeler fans and has now led the team to two Super Bowl titles.
Jamie Squire/Getty Images

Title page: Fans of the Pittsburgh Steelers wave their Terrible Towels during the American Football Conference championship game against the Baltimore Ravens, January 18, 2009 at Heinz Field in Pittsburgh. The Steelers' 23–14 win propelled Pittsburgh into Super Bowl XLIII.
Rob Tringali/Sportschrome/Getty Images

Right: Wide receiver Santonio Holmes during Super Bowl XLIII.
Donald Miralle/Getty Images

First published in 2009 by MVP Books, an imprint of MBI Publishing and the Quayside Publishing Group, 400 First Avenue N, Suite 300, Minneapolis, MN 55401 USA

MVP Books are also available at discounts in bulk quantity for industrial or sales-promotional use. For details write to Special Sales Manager at MBI Publishing Company, 400 First Avenue N, Suite 300, Minneapolis, MN 55401 USA.

To find out more about our books, visit us online at www.mvpbooks.com.

Library of Congress Cataloging-in-Publication Data

Freedman, Lew.
  Pittsburgh steelers : the complete illustrated history / Lew Freedman ; foreword by Dick Hoak.
    p. cm.
Includes bibliographical references and index.
ISBN 978-0-7603-3645-8 (hb w/jkt)
1. Pittsburgh Steelers (Football team)—History. I. Title.
  GV956.P57F74 2009
    796.332'640974886—dc22   2009015276

ISBN 978-0-7603-3645-8

Printed in China

CONTENTS

FOREWORD
BY DICK HOAK

Pittsburgh Steelers halfback Dick Hoak as a player in 1970.
NFL/Getty Images

I never really thought about playing pro football. It was a lot different in the 1950s and early 1960s than it is now. Pro football wasn't nearly as big as it is today. I had a great high school coach and I admired him and wanted to coach high school football and teach after I went to Penn State.

Now every football player who goes to college thinks he wants to be a pro. Nearing the time I was finishing college I was sent postcards from different teams asking if I was interested in playing pro football. That's how they did it. I never saw a scout. But I wrote down "Yes."

Penn State played in the Liberty Bowl and I had a great day. Then the National Football League had its draft and I was a seventh-round pick of the Steelers in 1961. I got off a plane in Las Vegas for an All-Star game and that's when I heard about it. Harry Gilmer, the old quarterback, who was a Pittsburgh assistant coach, was there and told me I was drafted. I said, "Drafted by who?" He tried to sign me right then.

Pittsburgh was right near my home and I talked to my father and my brother and decided to try it. I just thought I would go to training camp, which was at Slippery Rock College, and give it a try. There was no way that I could imagine that I would spend most of my life with the Pittsburgh Steelers. No way at all.

We had been there for about a week and they gave us a Saturday night and Sunday off. Home was only an hour or so away. I went home and told my brothers I was not going back. I was about the sixth or seventh running back and I never got a chance to do anything. The coach was Buddy Parker and he didn't use me. My brothers talked me into going back. My life would have been very different if I had not returned to training camp. It so happened that the next week I got a chance to start doing things for the team.

The Steelers were playing the Baltimore Colts in an exhibition game. I think it was in Roanoke, Virginia. Tom Tracy was in for about six plays and he got hurt, so I went in. I played the rest of the game and the next game I started against the Detroit Lions. And I ended up staying for 45 years. It's amazing.

I was 5 feet 11 inches and weighed 195 pounds, and there was always a rap against me that I was too small and too slow. Every year the Steelers would bring in a No. 1 draft choice or a No. 2 draft choice, but after three or four games I was back starting. I played for 10 years and I rushed for 3,965 yards, I caught 146 passes and scored 33 touchdowns. I made up my mind to retire about the fourth game of the 1970 season. I told my wife "This is it." With four games left I got hit and knocked out. I had a concussion and most people think that's why I retired, but I had made my mind up already.

I talked the doctor into letting me go in just to hold for extra points and field goals. It so happened that the center hiked the ball over my head on one of the field goals. I chased the ball down, picked it up, got hit, and got another concussion. The second concussion put me into the hospital.

The Steelers have always been in the hands of the Rooney family. Art Rooney was the founder and he was called "The Chief," and later his son Dan took over. When I was in the hospital, every day, The Chief came to visit me first thing in the morning. He brought me the newspaper and then before I went to bed he was there. That's the way he was. I wasn't the only one he did things like that for. He was an extraordinary owner. The Rooneys have been great for the Steelers and for Pittsburgh.

The Chief used to come down to the locker room all the time and talk to the players. He would walk around and shake hands with all of the players. Art II and Dan do it, too. And yet they stay out of the football end. They don't tell a coach who to play or what plays to run.

This story will tell you what type of man The Chief was. In 1968, I was having a good year and we used to go to the office to pick up our paychecks in downtown Pittsburgh every two weeks. It was eight or nine games into the season and I stopped in to see Fran Fogerty, who was the guy who wrote the checks. He said, "Art wants to see you." So I went into Art's office and he said, "Here, take this." I opened up the envelope and there was a check for an extra $10,000. He said, "We're having a lousy year, but you're having a good year. I want you to have this." Just like that.

After the last game that year when I had a separated shoulder, I went to the doctor's office to be checked out. It was across the street from the Steelers' offices, so I went in to say hello. Dan Rooney called me into his office and gave me an envelope. It was another check for $10,000. I said, "You know, your dad gave me one of these four or five weeks ago." He said, "I know, but my dad says he wants you to have this." They didn't have to do that.

I was very surprised, but I'm not the only one they've done that for. That's how the Rooneys are. The Chief lived on the north side and sometimes he walked home. Some of those streets weren't very safe, but nobody bothered him. Sometimes, he just handed out money to people, older guys who were just hanging around whom he knew needed a buck.

When I retired I returned to the idea of coaching high school and teaching. For one year. The University of Pittsburgh called me, and Chuck Noll, who had taken over as coach of the Steelers, called me and each of them asked if I was interested in being an assistant coach. I was supposed to interview for both jobs on the same day. But I accepted the job as Steelers' backfield coach. My first year was 1972 and I stayed for 35 years. I played for Chuck Noll two years and then I went back and coached for him. He's an amazing man. He's responsible for a lot of the good feeling between the Steelers and the community, too.

We won four Super Bowls in six years in the 1970s and 1980, and I coached Franco Harris and Rocky Bleier. That was a pretty good one-two punch for a while. I don't know if those Steelers were the best team of all time, but I do know it's going to be pretty tough for any team to match that record. We'd go into some games knowing we couldn't be beat. And I was still there when the Steelers won their fifth Super Bowl in January of 2006. It meant a lot to me because I knew I was getting ready to hang it up.

The Super Bowl teams of the 1970s established the real connection to the community. That's when it started. The Steelers weren't quite as loved before that. Sometimes I'm not sure they were even liked. But the link began then and it's lasted since then. They hadn't had a winner in so long before 1972.

There were so many great players and Hall of Famers. And they had things going like the Terrible Towel. The announcer Myron Cope, started that, and it just took off. There was Gerala's Gorillas for kicker Roy Gerala, and Franco's Italian Army for Franco Harris. We could go to away games and fans were waving the gold and black Terrible Towels. You would look in the crowd and there were as many people with the Terrible Towels as there were fans wearing the other team's colors.

I've got some Terrible Towels. My grandkids use them. And I keep some folded up that are never used. I've got a few of them. And I watch the Steelers every Sunday. There's no question where my allegiance is.

Dick Hoak as a coach, prior to a Steelers-St. Louis Rams game in 2003. Hoak spent 45 years in the Pittsburgh organization.
Scott Boehm/Getty Images

INTRODUCTION

The Pittsburgh Steelers were born in 1933 when local sports enthusiast Art Rooney invested $2,500 in their founding. But like Moses, they wandered in the wilderness for 40 years before their efforts were truly recognized.

Although the Steelers are one of the oldest teams in the National Football League, they did not join the league's elite until the 1970s. The confluence of great talent and great leadership vindicated four decades of the Rooney family's suffering with an also-ran to produce some of the best teams in NFL history.

By winning four Super Bowl titles in six years, the Steelers became Pittsburgh's favorite franchise and developed a national following. Their defensive front four was christened with the catchy nickname "The Steel Curtain," and one terrific player after another was drafted by future Hall of Fame coach Chuck Noll, who presided over Steeler fortunes for 23 seasons.

Noll's coaching and personnel guidance (with the able assistance of the Rooney family, as beloved as owners as anyone in league annals) made the team not only a Pittsburgh, but a national favorite, as well.

The Steelers were a work in progress for decades, featuring the occasional star like Bill Dudley, Bobby Layne, and Ernie Stautner. But the 1970s Steelers had a star-studded cast. Pittsburgh could field all-stars at almost every position, from quarterback Terry Bradshaw and his receivers Lynn Swann and John Stallworth, to running backs Franco Harris and Rocky Bleier. Behind stalwarts like Mean Joe Greene, Jack Lambert, Jack Ham, and Mel Bount, the defense was feared in all quarters.

The good old days of the 1970s were characterized by Bleier, a decorated Vietnam War veteran, the creation of the Terrible Towel by broadcaster Myron Cope as a fan accessory, the award-winning Joe Greene Coca-Cola commercial, and a national lovefest for the Rooneys as the Steelers superseded the Dallas Cowboys as America's Team. The Steelers made the phrase "Immaculate Reception," perhaps the greatest play in NFL history, part of household lexicon.

Once the most downtrodden team in the NFL, with a resume littered with last-place finishes and mediocre won-loss records, the Steelers' emergence as a league power was popular in all quarters—except in the cities whose teams were defeated in various Super Bowls. Year after year the Steelers paid their dues and finally were able to collect their due.

Although dynasties do not last forever, the Steelers' decade-long run for glory uplifted the club permanently. The four Super Bowl trophies collected in the lobby of the team offices serve as reminder to all visitors where the Steelers have traveled. They are permanent testimonials to the greatness of an era.

When Chuck Noll retired he was replaced by Bill Cowher, who maintained the winning tradition his predecessor established. The Steelers were often in the hunt for another Super Bowl championship and the pursuit of the coveted title became known as "one for the thumb," meaning a fifth championship ring for the team.

After the 2005 season, culminating the Cowher era, the Steelers brought home that fifth trophy, that fifth ring, equaling the largest number of Super Bowls captured by a single franchise. Once again, the Steelers had become a team of victors, of first-rate players, hard-working men who jelled at the right time to pull off a startling conquest.

This Super Bowl triumph belonged to Cowher, his sturdy, veteran running back Jerome Bettis, receiver Hines Ward, and a young, emerging quarterback named Ben Roethlisberger, who was maturing before his time.

Many years had passed since the Steelers had distinguished themselves with such an able and talented cast in the 1970s. Founder Art Rooney had passed away, but the team's fortunes still rested in Rooney hands. Son Dan, like his father a Hall of Famer, joyfully accepted the Vince Lombardi Trophy emblematic of pro football supremacy.

As additional proof of the 1970s Pittsburgh dominance, Steeler after Steeler was voted into the Pro Football Hall of Fame in Canton, Ohio, the birthplace of the NFL. Both Rooneys were elected. So was Noll. Defensive tackle Greene, linebackers Lambert and Ham, receivers Swann and Stallworth, quarterback Bradshaw, defensive back Blount, running back Harris, and center Mike Webster, were all enshrined. Others equally as deserving are still under consideration.

Through canny drafting, trading, and coach selection, the Steelers have cleverly maintained a position at or near the top of the American Football Conference and the NFL for decades now. They have made three straight fairly unconventional hires as head coaches, from Noll and Cowher to present coach Mike Tomlin. Although all three were highly regarded assistant coaches, none had a minute's worth of NFL head coaching experience when the Steelers tapped them for their most important job. All succeeded admirably and indisputably.

The hiring of Tomlin for the 2007 regular season paid immediate dividends. In just his second year at the helm Tomlin led the Steelers to their sixth Super Bowl triumph in February 2009, the most of any team in the league. Steering a team that improved throughout the season, Tomlin made the most of the skills of playmakers like Roethlisberger, linebacker James Harrison, the NFL's defensive player of the year, and star defensive back Troy Polamalu.

The victory solidified the Pittsburgh Steelers' reputation as one of the most successful and popular teams in the NFL. The black and gold reigned supreme again and gave their home city something special to celebrate once again. It is often said that everyone loves a parade, but parades in support of championship teams seem just that much sweeter than the average Fourth of July march.

Lew Freedman

1930s
GETTING STARTED

In a one-year period between July 1932 and July 1933, Art Rooney contributed to the birth of two Pittsburgh institutions that have affected the people of the Steel City ever since.

His son Dan was born in 1932 and his football team was born in 1933. Dan grew up to become president of the Pittsburgh Steelers, and the Pittsburgh Steelers grew up to become the favorite sports franchise of Western Pennsylvania. Dan, who matured into chairman of the board of the prominent National Football League team, and became one of the city's most prominent citizens, says he has been around the football team for his entire life, and he isn't joking.

The story of the Pittsburgh Steelers is the story of the Rooney family. Art, a one-time boxer and semi-pro football and baseball player, was always a gambling man, open to taking risks (promoting boxing and playing the horses), and committed to endeavors that would improve his beloved hometown.

Dan was the oldest of five Rooney sons, and took the greatest interest in the football team. Art Rooney Jr. was very active as well. "My father used to tell us boys," said Art Jr., "'Treat everybody the way you'd like to be treated. Give them the benefit of the doubt. But never let anyone mistake kindness for weakness. He took the Golden Rule and put a little bit of the [rough-and-tumble side of Pittsburgh] North Side into it.''

One of the NFL's enduring myths is that Art Rooney had a big day at the races and the payoff was his down payment on the Steelers. The story is off the mark. Rooney was quite wealthy enough to afford the minimal franchise fee of $2,500 in 1932, with assistance

from a pony's long-shot finish. However, over two race sessions at Empire Race Track and Saratoga Race Track in New York he did cash in big, beating the odds to collect $250,000 in winnings. That blessed event did not occur until 1936 when the Steelers were already part of the family's holdings.

As a young man, Rooney was a superior fighter. He won a national AAU welterweight title and was slated to be the United States representative in that weight class at the Olympics in Belgium in 1920, but he chose to stay home in Pittsburgh immersed in various business ventures. As a young man and forevermore, Rooney was an all-around sports fan who identified strongly with his Irish heritage and Catholic beliefs.

Decades later, Dan Rooney spoke at a dinner about his father's background and upbringing. "My dad was an Irishman," said Dan, the eldest of Art's children. "His dad was a barkeeper. They grew up in Pittsburgh's first ward. That's on the North Side and it's located right where Three Rivers Stadium stands today. Dad's family lived upstairs over the bar. Every Saturday night the place was packed with a lot of drunken Irishmen looking for a fight. My dad said his father would come upstairs three or four times to change his torn shirt and wash the blood off his face. He would tell his sons, 'Lads, when you grow up and make your fortune, go back to Galway, Ireland to see what makes these harps tick. They are all nuts.' Dad and his brothers were real tough guys. Dad said his brother Dan had more knockouts than Jack Dempsey and most of them were outside of the boxing ring."

Adults in the Rooney family wanted Art to take a

reliable, paying, career job in a steel mill. He tried it briefly, but realized he could make more money playing semi-pro baseball and have more fun. He played at Indiana University of Pennsylvania and in the minors in Wheeling, West Virginia.

Eventually, Rooney operated a couple of semi-pro football teams, one called the J.P. Rooneys. Football appealed to the hard-working, blue-collar families of the Pittsburgh area, who grew up forging steel and drinking a beer called Iron City.

The game's historical roots run deep in Western Pennsylvania. Researchers claim that the first game involving a professional player dates to 1892, when Pudge Heffelfinger was paid $500 to play for the Allegheny Athletic Association against the Pittsburgh Athletic Club. In later years, the region was regarded as the cradle of great quarterbacks, with Johnny Unitas, Joe Namath, Dan Marino, and Joe Montana hailing from the western portion of the state. The founders of the United States, Thomas Jefferson, Benjamin Franklin, and John Adams, gathered in Philadelphia, but many of the classiest progenitors of the T-formation served an apprenticeship near Pittsburgh.

In 1920, the National Football League was founded in an automobile showroom in Canton, Ohio, which proudly embraces its role as the birthplace of the modern game. The Decatur Staleys, which quickly morphed into the Chicago Bears, and the Racine Cardinals, which became the Arizona Cardinals, were there at the beginning, and the Green Bay Packers formed right alongside them. Teams with big ideas and small bank accounts came and went with now-you-see-them, now-you-don't speed. Teams teetering on the brink were wiped out when the Great Depression swamped the nation's economy.

Commissioner Joe L. Carr fought to stabilize the league and keep it afloat. He was not sad to see small-town teams disappear and wanted big-city ownership as replacements. He approached Art Rooney and asked for a $2,500 entry fee to join the league. Although a paltry sum by modern standards, not many entrepreneurs had a couple of thousand bucks to spare during the Depression. Count me in, Rooney told Carr, and on July 8, 1933 he and his Pittsburgh club were on board. To Rooney, owning a pro football team sounded like a reasonable sporting proposition. An important incentive was the fact that Pennsylvania rescinded its restrictive blue laws that banned play on Sundays when the NFL convened. No one foresaw an era when NFL football on Sundays would be practically a religion unto itself.

Like many early football team owners seeking to make a mark with a new sport dominated by the local major league baseball franchise, Rooney cast his lot

with the familiar name of the hometown Pirates who featured Paul and Lloyd Waner and Pie Traynor. Besides, he was a big fan of the ball club. It was only in 1940, after running a contest accepting public recommendations, that Rooney changed the name of the team to the Steelers.

The economic climate was not advantageous for a new business venture. The stock market had dropped lower than the Dead Sea, and banks and businesses were failing at a rapid rate. The wealthy became poor

Founding Pittsburgh Steelers owner Art Rooney during the 1930s.
NFL/Getty Images

BACK ROW— PEARLMAN, BILL GALLAGHER, NOWLAND, KRAMER, PIRT, RED GALLAGHER, McNICHOLS
FRONT ROW— BROWN, LAWLER, McNAMARA, WHILE, D. ROONEY, NOVAK, A. ROONEY.

The 1924 Pittsburgh Lyceum Football Team. Art Rooney is kneeling at the far right, in the front row. Rooney organized and operated Western Pennsylvania semi-pro grid teams before 1933 when he purchased the Pittsburgh NFL franchise. Rooney was inducted into the Pro Football Hall of Fame, class of 1964.
Pro Football Hall of Fame/NFL/Getty Images

and the poor became destitute.

Rooney established team offices in the Fort Pitt Hotel and used it as his base for years. Selling tickets was a major challenge. Rooney, just 33, and with limited ties to high level football, was no genius at spotting talent and did not work at ferreting it out, either. He couldn't field a winner and lost $21,000 during the 1937 season alone. Throughout the 1930s, Rooney had no marquee players and the Pirates were perpetual losers. They could not crack .500 even once during that decade.

The Pirates took the field for their first game against the New York Giants on September 20, 1933, and lost 23–2. That would become a habit. Some 25,000 Pittsburgh fans turned out at Forbes Field, however, which did not prove to be a habit. The first Pirates/Steelers were coached by Forrest Jouds, a player-coach at tackle, from Washington & Jefferson University.

The first Pittsburgh thrower was Angel Brovelli, out of St. Mary's College in California, even though his position was listed as fullback. When Brovelli signed with Pittsburgh, the news was given a paragraph's

"We played in Forbes Field and we didn't draw flies."
—*Angelo Brovelli, the Steelers' first quarterback in 1933, on the team's lack of attendance.*

worth of play in the local press. When he was traded to the Boston Redskins, he got two paragraphs worth of farewells.

Ray Kemp, a 215 pound graduate of nearby Duquesne, was Pittsburgh's first black player. A tackle, he was edged out of the lineup by Jouds and then cut. There were only two African-American players in the NFL that year and none for the next 13 seasons as the league that had once had no qualms signing black players temporarily became a closed shop.

Rooney made Kemp a personal acquisition for his roster after meeting him at a sports banquet, but would not step in and rescue him from Jouds' axe. Rooney was the most genial of men, who was, by all accounts, color blind, but throughout his long

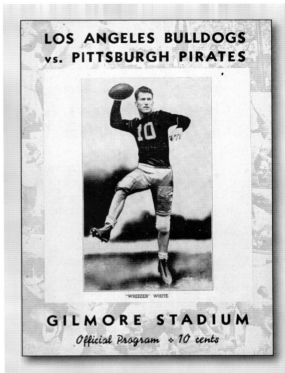

LOS ANGELES BULLDOGS
vs. PITTSBURGH PIRATES

"WHIZZER" WHITE

GILMORE STADIUM
Official Program ÷ 10 cents

Program for a Pacific Coast League game pitting the Pittsburgh Pirates against the Los Angeles Bulldogs at Gilmore Stadium, Los Angeles, in 1938.
Pro Football Hall of Fame/NFL Photos/Getty Images

THE TEAM NAME

Younger fans of the fabled Pittsburgh Steelers probably have no idea that their beloved team was founded as the Pittsburgh Pirates. When founding owner Art Rooney introduced his pro football team to the Steel City in 1933, he adopted the same nickname as that being used by the local major league baseball team.

There was no copyright on nicknames, and in the 1930s baseball was the only pro team sport that mattered in the United States. Baseball was the National Pastime and it was not uncommon for fledgling teams in pro football to attempt to ride the coattails of the established club in their town.

The New York football Giants were named after John McGraw's National League baseball club. At one time or another during National Football League growing pains years, or when upstart leagues challenged the NFL, there were also pro football teams called the New York Yankees and the Brooklyn Dodgers.

In 1940, the Pittsburgh football franchise ran a contest seeking a new name to replace Pirates. A young man named Joe Santoni, who worked in a mill for Pittsburgh Steel submitted the name "Steelers" and his recommendation was selected by Rooney. Santoni was given season tickets for one year and he renewed them for decades, until shortly before his death in 2003.

The Pittsburgh football team first played as the Steelers in 1940. The goal may have been partly to erase memories of a 1930s decade during which the team never posted a winning season.

The brand new Forbes Field exterior after a baseball game in Pittsburgh appears in a color postcard from 1909.
Mark Rucker/Transcendental Graphics, Getty Images

Forbes Field and the surrounding area in 1955.
Charles "Teenie" Harris/Corbis

what type of man Rooney was, who even complimented him on the way out the door. Kemp spent three decades as a coach and athletic director at predominantly black schools and never doubted that his pro career was cut short because of discrimination. He experienced the bad, but recognized the good. "It wasn't too bad in the sense that everywhere I went I had white people befriend me," Kemp said. "Like Elmer Layden and Art Rooney. I always felt that someone had to pay the price for being a pioneer, and I tried."

There was no sophisticated scouting in the NFL in the 1930s. Rooney employed many members of his ex-semi-pro team as the core of the pro team, and signed other players based on word-of-mouth reports. Other teams did this as well. It's just that George Halas in the Bears' offices and Curly Lambeau in Green Bay seemed to have more knowledgeable friends providing tips. Rooney's network of contacts seemed to be limited to Pittsburgh and vicinity, and Catholic schools that featured football as part of the curriculum.

In the earliest days of the Pittsburgh pro franchise, many players were of the one-year-and-out variety. The turnover was high and the team's scores were low.

association with the Steelers, he believed in hiring underlings to do their jobs and refused to impose his opinions on them. That was true for five decades for general managers and coaches alike, whether or not Rooney agreed with their decisions.

Kemp played in college for coach Elmer Layden, one of the players famed as one of the "Four Horsemen" of Notre Dame. And he felt he knew

THE FIRST AFRICAN-AMERICAN PLAYER

Ray Kemp and Art Rooney attended the same athletic banquet being held for Duquesne University sports teams in 1932. The cigar-smoking Rooney operated a local semi-pro football team. Kemp had been an honorable mention All-American for Duquesne and planned on attending law school.

Rooney convinced Kemp to play for his outfit, and in 1933, Kemp and Rooney wrote a little bit of history together. Rooney shepherded a new team into the National Football League representing Pittsburgh, and Kemp became the first black player for the team ultimately known as the Steelers.

A smattering of black players had competed on teams across the league since it was founded in 1920, but in 1933 Kemp was one of only two black players in the NFL. Between 1933 and 1946, mostly at the urging of Washington Redskins' owner George Preston Marshall, who was building southern allegiance to his club, no NFL team employed a black player.

Although the 6 foot 1 inch, 215 pound Kemp had a good rapport with Rooney, coach Forrest Douds, who was a player-coach at tackle, Kemp's position, cut him after five games. Rooney may have had misgivings, but refused to overrule his coach's decision. Kemp's stay with the team had not always been a picnic. On a road trip he had to stay at a black YMCA instead of in the team hotel.

Kemp subsequently coached and served as athletic director at Bluefield State, Lincoln University, and Texas A&I, three primarily black colleges, for decades.

> **"I was flabbergasted when he told me I would be paid to play."**
> —*1930s kicker Armand Niccolai, on learning that the Steelers wanted him to play for them.*

Although they finished 3–6–2 in their inaugural season, the Pirates/Steelers won the second game they ever played, on September 27, 1933 defeating the Cardinals, 14–13. Kicker Chris "Mose" Kelsch booted the extra point that gave Pittsburgh the victory. Kelsch was 36 years old, hardly a fresh-faced rookie, and was known throughout the region for his exploits with semi-pro teams. The *Pittsburgh Post-Gazette's* account of Kelsch's kick was fairly melodramatic given that the winning play was only an extra point. It read in part, "The man of the hour in Pittsburgh gridiron circles this morning, the fair-haired boy whose name is on everyone's lips, is a gent who never trod a college campus, never cut a lab period or a quiz."

A little bit earlier in the fourth quarter, Marty Kottler intercepted a pass for Pittsburgh and ran it back 99 yards for a touchdown. Kottler, who played at 5 feet 10 inches and 178 pounds, served time at quarterback that season. From Carnegie, Pennsylvania, Kottler attended Centre College in Kentucky, and played in just three games in 1933, his only NFL season. Much later in life, when he retired from a job with the Avis rental car company, he was surprised at a testimonial dinner by presents that included a letter of praise from Art Rooney. Kottler called it one of his most prized possessions.

An undersized, 188 pound guard named Nick DeCarbo came to the Pirates/Steelers from Duquesne. His 11 games that year represented his only time in the NFL. But his pride in belonging to the select group from the first team manifested itself in several ways. He said he "always, always" considered himself to be part of the Steelers' organization and regularly attended team reunions.

Ray Tesser, who played his college ball at Carnegie Mellon, another in-the-neighborhood school, caught 14 passes as a 1933 rookie and was a holdover on the 1934 team.

At the time when these men made their NFL debuts, Pittsburgh was a baseball town. The Pirates had been very successful from the turn of the century, with the arrival of the "Flying Dutchman," the great shortstop Honus Wagner. Wagner was not only a phenomenal player on his way to the Baseball Hall of Fame when it inducted its first class in 1936, he was so

SCOUTING FOR PLAYERS

Unlike most of the other early National Football League teams that got their start in the 1920s and 1930s and have endured, such as the Chicago Bears, Green Bay Packers, and New York Giants, the Pittsburgh Steelers did not succeed right away. The Steelers made their debut in 1933, but did not record a winning season at any time during the decade.

The long-term strength of the Steelers' organization—family-owned and operated—was initially a weakness. For team founder Art Rooney, owning the Steelers was mainly a hobby. He supervised the franchise primarily with the notion that its existence provided a public service, and that sporting a pro football team was good for his home city.

However, Rooney did not invest money in scouting to seek out young, talented players to join his roster. An Irishman, devoted Catholic, and true believer in locally produced muscle, Rooney had a soft spot in his heart for any player who had matriculated at Duquesne, the University of Pittsburgh, Notre Dame, or Catholic University. For Rooney, who was only loosely paying attention to detail at the time, pedigree was at least as important as resume.

His outlook may have worked to the Steelers' advantage if Rooney had signed more players from Notre Dame and Pitt, but the Steelers' lineup of the 1930s featured a remarkable number of Duquesne players. Many of those Duquesne players were of little fame and were often one-and-done participants, indicating that a single season was enough to analyze their abilities.

revered that a statue of him was later built.

As a community, Pittsburgh was a city of immigrants. There were many first-generation Germans who worked hard, emerged from mines sooty, with blackened faces, and then breathed the blackened, fouled air belched from smokestacks. Men worked hard and drank hard and if they had any spare money to spend for a night out—rare during the Depression—they would have been the properly targeted fan base for a football team.

Jouds was Pittsburgh's coach for one year and his role is remembered as nothing more than the answer to a trivia question. The second-year coach, Luby DiMelio, ranks as no more important. His team finished 2–10 and he was gone after the 1934 season.

Rooney was after a winner and he thought he had found the right man to deliver it when he lured Joe Bach from Duquesne to take over the Pirates/Steelers in 1935. Bach had been a lineman at Notre Dame under Knute Rockne. The famed sports writer

Grantland Rice had christened the Irish Notre Dame backfield with the moniker, the "Four Horsemen." The others on offense who did the blocking were called the "Seven Mules." Bach was a mule.

Rooney gave Bach a three-year contract, which in terms of security at the time was about as good as anyone could find outside of Franklin Delano Roosevelt's four-year term in the White House. Bach faced about the same degree of difficulty in trying to supervise a major turnaround.

Bach's Pirates/Steelers finished 4–8 in 1935 and Bach led them tantalizingly close to a winning record in 1936 with a 6–6 mark. With one year left on his contract, Bach felt the club's first winning season ever was in reach.

Art Rooney's famous killing on the horses took place in the summer of 1936. Saratoga Springs was the place where the thoroughbred crowd from New York City vacationed with the ponies instead of their otherwise year-round haunts at Belmont and Aqueduct. In Rooney's telling of the tale, roughly 36 years later, he studied horse charts provided by Tim Mara, the bookmaker who owned the New York Giants' football club at a time when bookmaking was a legal profession. "I came close to sweeping the card," Rooney said. "In those days, they ran only eight races, maybe seven."

Rooney started his day by placing a $2,000 wager at 8–to–1 on a horse named Quel Jou. He was literally off to the races. The key bet of the day was a long shot that paid off on a $10,000 bet. Rooney won at least $250,000 that day, and it was all witnessed by a sports writer who recorded the day's events. Rooney gained so much notoriety for the astonishing winning day that one newspaper assigned a writer full-time to follow him around the track. When Rooney won, the stories were given major headlines. When he lost, the defeats were played down. Rooney acquired a reputation as a brilliant horse player. There was also a wildly exaggerated story that he sent all of his winnings to his brother Dan Rooney, a priest, for his missionary work in China. Rooney admitted sending Dan some money, but said it was never as much the papers indicated.

The legend of Rooney breaking the bank at Saratoga contains elements of truth, but not the unvarnished kind. He did make the type of profit players always dream of, and he did so in a dramatic way. He most certainly did not use the windfall to purchase the Steelers, but during the difficult days of the 1930s and 1940s he may well have plowed his winnings back into the operations of the team.

Variations of the story contribute to the myths surrounding the popular team owner, and when author Roy Blount Jr. wrote a book about the Steelers' later

A 1975 portrait of Art Rooney, the founder of the Pittsburgh Steelers, who paid $2,500 for the city's franchise rights in 1933.
Ross Lewis/NFL/Getty Images

"I've always been interested in the fortunes of the Steelers and watch them on TV every chance I get."
—Marty Kottler, reminiscing 47 years after becoming the team's first kicker in 1933.

success he referred to Rooney's brilliant betting day. He wrote, "You can talk about Man O' War and Eddie Arcaro all you want. The Chief for my money is the biggest figure in horse racing history."

Rooney would be the last one to claim he was a bigger figure in horse racing history than a phenomenal race horse or a champion jockey, but the telling of the story earned bows from every $2 bettor at windows across America.

The same year Rooney astounded horse players across the nation, the NFL instituted its draft of college players. With their first-ever, first-round selection, the Steelers chose a Notre Dame All-American back named William Shakespeare. Shakespeare never played for the team and as far as is known in literary circles, never penned a sonnet extolling the Steelers, either.

Byron "Whizzer" White was an All-American running back at the University of Colorado who later became a U.S. Supreme Court justice.
New York Times Co./Getty Images

He was, however, later inducted into the College Football Hall of Fame.

Rooney hungered for his first winning Pirates/Steelers season. While Bach may have been optimistic after the 6–6 year, he never got the chance to lead the team in 1937. Rooney, who later admitted that he made a mistake, discharged Bach from his contract early, and brought in Johnny Blood McNally as a player-coach.

In today's world, Johnny Blood (his playing alias) would eclipse Terrell Owens, Deion Sanders, and Dennis Rodman for notoriety, although he never dyed his hair, or to any football expert's knowledge, dressed in women's clothing. Blood was a night owl who drank, smoked, and caroused, hardly slept, and rarely showed the effects on the field. Decades after Blood's career ended, a Wisconsin sports reporter said that he "would have made Brett Favre seem like an introverted librarian." Blood played on four championship teams with Green Bay, but drove Packers coach Curly Lambeau batty.

Blood was wildly popular, but broke every rule but the golden rule (and if he did so, that was unintentional). If Blood got bored he left his team of the moment, jumped in a car and just drove away, or if he was broke (a regular occurrence), he joined hobos on the rails, leaping into moving freight cars. He was the ultimate spur-of-the-moment guy, but generally friendly and a rule breaker who did himself more harm than others. Rooney hired Blood in the fading days of his career for his name value. He hoped that Blood's popularity would sell tickets and that his reputation as a great back would rally the troops. He had no illusions that Blood would be a disciplinarian as a coach. Rooney didn't care if his players drank beer until 3 a.m. if they won more often on Sundays. "I suppose I must have a strong need for attention," Blood once said. "I can't explain some of the things I've done on any other basis."

In Blood's first game as Pirates/Steelers boss, he watched from the bench as the Philadelphia Eagles built a lead. Then he went in. Blood ran a kickoff back 92 yards for one touchdown and caught a 44-yard pass for another touchdown. Pittsburgh was comfortably in the lead when Blood returned to the bench, saw Rooney, and said, "There's your ballgame, Art."

During the 1938 season, the team waterboy was John Doar, a Blood relative with a rebellious streak. Blood, who had known many a day when he skirted serious violations of public indiscretion, gave the boy a pep talk. Doar grew up to be the counsel to the U.S. House Judiciary Committee during the Watergate hearings.

Blood, who was born in Wisconsin in 1903, played college ball for St. John's in Minnesota. His family owned the *Minneapolis Star-Tribune* and he was regularly encouraged by relatives to settle down and assume a full-time management position at the paper. He dabbled in newspaper work, but as he became more entrenched in his odd habits, he barely read the paper again.

A brilliant halfback, Blood was a dangerous runner, receiver, passer and defender between 1925 and 1938. He was a Hall of Fame player who seemed unlikely to survive as long as he did in the league. His antics inspired a biography called *Vagabond Halfback*, testimony to his itchy feet and urge to roam, and also the movie *Leatherheads*.

Blood always had a serious side, focusing on reading literature during his football travels at a time when his teammates were more often reading the sports page or comic books. Although he left college early to play pro football, he returned to obtain an economics degree at the age of 42. During World War II he was a cryptographer. As he put football behind him, he returned to the use of the last name McNally, prompting many football fans to wonder where Blood disappeared. At one point, Blood became a professor of economics at the University of Minnesota. Of course, at the time he was known as John Victor McNally.

Blood returned to football prominence long before his death in 1985, after being named to the NFL's all-decade team of the 1930s and being inducted into the Pro Football Hall of Fame in 1963. "I zigged and zagged on the field," Blood once said. "And I've zigged and zagged off it, too. I wouldn't trade anything, not one of my experiences in football."

Blood retained fond memories of his vagabond days. He wasn't the same reckless soul later in life, but he wasn't repentant, either. He had put considerable time and effort into excelling at something he enjoyed. "Some people have the gift for football," Blood once said. "This is what they can do. The sports business is just a great life. I've come to believe there is one major purpose for human beings on this planet. That's to maximize your emotional income."

In Blood's thoughts, taking the field to play a football game was an adrenaline high, one so satisfying and pleasurable, he said, it was just like one's wedding day. "You were doing more living per second than any ordinary day."

Blood could have made much more money in private business, but traveled where his heart led him. His curiosity may have taken side trips to remote corners of America, but his passion always led him back to the gridiron. He understood that football was not only his vocation and avocation, but appropriately enough, in his blood.

No one played football with more zest, or lived a more colorful life, than John Victor McNally, the famed "vagabond halfback." McNally assumed his "Johnny Blood" alias from a Rudolf Valentino movie title, "Blood and Sand." Blood scored 49 TDs in 14 seasons with five NFL teams.
Pro Football Hall of Fame/NFL/Getty Images

JOHNNY "BLOOD" MCNALLY
Back
1934, 1937–38

Johnny "Blood" McNally was ahead of his time. He was a colorful athlete when players were expected to say "Aw shucks" and keep their eccentricities to themselves unless they were named Babe Ruth.

McNally was better known as Johnny Blood. He and a pal had determined they wanted to earn a few bucks playing pro football while retaining college eligibility. They were walking past a movie marquee advertising the film *Blood and Sand,* and McNally said, "I'll be Blood and you be Sand." A legend was born and the alias stuck.

Blood, a 6 foot 1 inch, 190 pound all-around back, enjoyed the nightlife more than adhering to team rules, but played from 1925 to 1938. He played for Pittsburgh in 1934 and again in 1937 and 1938, and somehow convinced Art Rooney that he could be a focused, capable coach.

Counter to his joking, partying image, when Blood wasn't hopping freight trains to satisfy his wanderlust, he hung out in libraries reading Shakespeare and other literature. Still, Blood once lived up to his name by cutting his arm with a razor blade in order to sign an autograph in blood. He was the role model for the George Clooney character in the 2008 movie *Leatherheads.*

Blood would have been heir to the *Minneapolis Star-Tribune,* but didn't want to be. He was good enough at football, however, to be elected to the Pro Football Hall of Fame in 1963, the charter class.

BYRON "WHIZZER" WHITE
RUNNING BACK
1938, 1940–41

Those who knew him later in life would have been surprised how good Byron "Whizzer" White was as a football player. Those who knew him when he was young were surprised how far he traveled.

Whizzer White was a star running back from the University of Colorado and on his way to Oxford as a Rhodes Scholar when Pittsburgh Steelers owner Art Rooney waylaid him. Rooney persuaded to White to delay his study in order to play one season of pro football in 1938.

Rooney's speech was peppered with dollar signs and White could not resist accepting the league's richest offer of $15,800 to play one season in the Steel City before matriculating in England. At the time, Rooney was paying his player-coach Johnny Blood McNally $3,500 to fulfill two jobs.

The 6 foot 1 inch, 187 pound White was worth the money. He became the NFL's rookie-of-the-year and won the league rushing title with his 567 yards gained from scrimmage. True to his plan, White departed Pittsburgh for Oxford and would likely never have seen another NFL game without a ticket if World War II hadn't interrupted his studies. White played two more seasons in the 1940s, for the Detroit Lions, also leading the league in rushing in 1940.

Then White put the name "Whizzer" behind him and embarked on a serious career that culminated with the position of Justice of the U.S. Supreme Court, where he stayed for 31 years. As short as his pro football career was, White was always remembered for his talents.

White was a star athlete at the University of Colorado, a football All-American, who rushed for 1,121 yards as a senior and was an outstanding punter. Critics contended his favorable performances were the results of playing against inferior competition and that White wasn't really that good. Always the gambling man, Rooney believed it was worth taking a chance on drafting him with the Steelers' No. 1 pick. The price was high, but Rooney read his man correctly in that he could be rented for a season. "I figured I'd offer him so much money, he couldn't refuse," Rooney said.

Initially, White did refuse. But Coach Johnny Blood McNally intrigued White with some of his colorful antics and language. When White realized he could delay admission to Oxford long enough to

play the season, he called Rooney back six weeks later and signed with the Steelers. Ironically, given what was to come in future decades with multi-million-dollar contracts, Rooney was vilified by some of his co-owners for being such a spendthrift. Oh, the horrors of such a large contract.

Although the Rooney offer made White the highest paid football player in history by a long-shot, the pro game was still feeling its way. Being a pro football player was neither an esteemed line of work, nor a very secure one during the Depression era, but while White harbored loftier ambitions, he had a love for the sport. It so happened he was also intrigued by the suggestion of playing for Johnny Blood. "That character (Blood) got him so interested he had second thoughts," Rooney said. "White later told me he couldn't wait to follow Blood and see what happened."

Even star players made nowhere near the amount of money White was raking in with the Steelers, and there was some jealousy about White's earnings. After New York Giant Tuffy Leemans creamed White with a hard tackle, he sarcastically commented, "I always wondered what it felt like to get my hands on a $15,000 football player."

White played at an exceptionally high level, showing the promise that might have made him one of the all-time greats if he had stuck with the sport. But the Steelers, mired in a 1930s-long slump, were no better with White in the lineup. They finished 2–9 in 1938.

White did not intend to play football beyond his single season with the Steelers, but the world situation was stormy and he recognized he might not get the chance to complete his scheduled stay in England. "There is only one way I will come back and play football," White said. "That's if they start shooting across the pond."

Of course, that is exactly what happened. In 1940 White returned to the NFL, this time hooking up with the Detroit Lions in order to raise money for his study at Yale Law School. "I liked football and I would have liked to have played some more," White said many years later.

While serving in the Navy in the Solomon Islands, White met a soon-to-be war hero and future politician named John F. Kennedy. Fifteen or so years later, White, by then a Denver attorney in private practice, helped Kennedy obtain enough delegates for the 1960

Democratic nomination for president. In 1962, when JFK was president of the United States, he chose White to fill a vacancy on the Supreme Court. It had taken a quarter of a century, but White exchanged a numbered jersey for black robes.

One of those in attendance for White's swearing in was Johnny Blood McNally. The two had remained friends from the years of their shared Pittsburgh experiences.

In 1972, having developed a fondness and an admiration for White when they were both associated with the Steelers, Blood initiated a draft-White campaign for the Democratic nomination for president. Blood served as the blocking back on the run, but there was no serious effort put into the matter by White, who was already at home in Washington, D.C. White remained on the Supreme Court for 31 years, until 1993, the longest serving justice in the nation's history.

That was one mighty long broken field run.

Byron "Whizzer" White.
Pro Football Hall of Fame/NFL/Getty Images

> **"Kies was one of the finest men I have ever met."**
> —*Steelers founder Art Rooney, on long-time Pittsburgh player, assistant coach, and head coach Walt Kiesling.*

As was easily predicted, Blood was not a head coach with a lot of rules on his agenda when he assumed command of the Pirates/Steelers for the 1937 season. That would have been totally out of character for a one-man "come-as-you-are" party. Pittsburgh finished 4–7 that year, going backwards. In 1938, Pittsburgh was 2–9 under Blood's tutelage.

Blood's greatest contribution to Pittsburgh's future was away from the gridiron. Although he had made it clear that he planned to go to Oxford, England as a

Rhodes Scholar rather than play professional football, Colorado All-American Byron "Whizzer" White was chosen as Pittsburgh's No. 1 draft pick in 1938. Art Rooney thought offering White the unheard-of sum of $15,800 would woo him.

White said no. Rooney sent Blood to Colorado to change White's mind. There are contradictory stories about just who discovered that White could delay his scholarship to Oxford until January, after the football season. One story goes that the Pittsburgh team found out the shift was possible. Another version has it that White's brother, who was already studying in Oxford, talked school officials into allowing it.

No one really knows exactly how Blood charmed White, but White seemed enamored of Blood's story telling and the idea of playing for him as a coach helped lure the running back to Pittsburgh.

White made his mark as the top rookie in the league during the 1938 season. He led the NFL in rushing with 567 yards that autumn. If Rooney secretly hoped that White would be seduced to stick around by his positive experience in the Pittsburgh backfield, it was not to be. Promptly after the season, White departed for England. He was a one-year wonder for Pittsburgh. War erupted in Europe, ending White's studies in England, and White returned to the United States to enroll in Yale Law School. Doubtful that White would ever play pro ball again, Pittsburgh traded his rights to the Detroit Lions. White spent the 1939 season in school, but in 1940 the Lions convinced him to put on a uniform again. White decided he could use the money for tuition and he once again proved to be a standout, leading the league in rushing a second time.

The more he played, the more White seemed to enjoy football. He never took his eye off his longterm goals, but he joined the Lions for a second season and a third season overall before he joined the Navy to fight in World War II. "I liked professional football better than the college game," White said. "I enjoyed it and might have played more if the war hadn't broken out."

White, who was also an outstanding basketball player, always kept sports in perspective, but always believed participating in sports was good for a young man. "Sports is one way to get some absolute experience," White said. "You are constantly being exposed to critical situations which require performance under pressure and you have to respond."

One of the Pirates/Steelers' signings of the 1930s that did pay off with longterm dividends was the acquisition of guard Walt Kiesling. A 6 foot 2 inch, 250 pound offensive lineman, Kiesling broke into the NFL

Walt Kiesling had a 34-year pro career as a player, assistant coach, and head coach, and he was always ready to help out Art Rooney whenever and wherever he needed coaching assistance. *Pro Football Hall of Fame/NFL/Getty Images*

"My father grew up strong and tough and streetwise. A natural athlete, he loved to compete. And he played to win."
—*Dan Rooney, Steelers chairman of the board, on his father, Art Rooney, the team founder.*

PITTSBURGH
PIRATES/STEELERS
YEAR BY YEAR

1933	3–6–2
1934	2–10
1935	4–8
1936	6–6
1937	4–7
1938	2–9
1939	1–9–1

with the Duluth Eskimos in 1926. That was the fabled Duluth 11 that opened with a single game at home in Minnesota and then embarked on a protracted, season-long road trip. The Eskimos had little fan following at home, so they became a touring team, competing in 28 games spread over 111 days, covering 17,000 miles.

Kiesling joined Pittsburgh in 1937 for the final two years of his playing career. When Art Rooney tired of Blood's coaching and Blood tired of coaching mid-way through the 1939 season, Kiesling became the Pirates/Steelers' head coach — for the first time.

He retained at least a share of that capacity through World War II, when the Steelers shared rosters for two years because of a player shortage. Kiesling departed for the Green Bay Packers and was an assistant coach in northern Wisconsin between 1945 and 1948. Then he came back to Pittsburgh as an assistant coach until Rooney promoted Kiesling once again to head man for three seasons beginning in 1954. In 1957, Kiesling returned to the role of Pittsburgh assistant coach. He was still working in that role in 1962 when he died at age 58. It was clear that Art Rooney liked having the big guy around.

Although Kiesling did not compile an impressive coaching mark (24–51–1), he was a powerful lineman whose performance led him to the Hall of Fame. "Walt Kiesling didn't just watch pro football grow from the rocky sandlots," said Dick McCann, the first director of the Pro Football Hall of Fame, "he shoved it along the way. He was one of the game's truly remarkable pioneers."

Despite being an offensive lineman, the most anonymous of positions, Kiesling was one of the most recognizable Pittsburgh football figures of the 1930s. If his achievements could not easily be listed by statistics such as yards gained, he came with a reputation.

Rooney was a savvy enough businessman and a pugnacious enough competitor to realize he had taken on a large task when he determined to make Pittsburgh a pro football town. The idea had seemed a winning one from the start because he already had access to semi-pro players and he didn't think the transition to the young, but fast-improving NFL would

be a great one. And although Rooney made it all work in the long run, he may have initially underestimated the talent gap and what it took financially to run a big-league football club. "It was just a hop, skip, and a jump from semi-pro ball in those days, maybe just a hop," Rooney reminisced nearly 50 years later. "The biggest thrill wasn't in winning on Sunday, but in meeting the payroll on Monday."

Before he became an icon of the game, and a hugely influential member of the NFL's owners committee, with his wavy white hair and his trademark thick cigar, Rooney was young and dark-haired and seemed agile and athletic enough to take the field himself. Unlike his Chicago Bears' compatriot George Halas, he never did. All of his sports training left Rooney with a fearsome competitive streak. He wanted to win at all sports, but not at all costs. What endeared Rooney to future generations of Pittsburgh fans, NFL supporters, and those who passed through the Steelers' organization, was his unfailing ability to comport himself as a gentleman despite his inner feelings of disappointment when his team failed to win many game, or any championships. "I take it terribly," Rooney said. "Nobody feels any worse than I do about losing."

It was an emotion Art Rooney had to cope with for a long, long time.

1940s
A WAR FOR SURVIVAL ON AND OFF THE FIELD

Art Rooney never needed an excuse to light up a cigar. Smoking the big stogies was a trademark. But topping off a special occasion by inhaling his favorite tobacco product made it all the sweeter. And after 10 years of futility, experiencing a season when things clicked was a wonderful event. Rooney had sought to bring football joy to his favorite city, but progress had been frustrating.

Bert Bell shared ownership of the Steelers with Art Rooney for a bit and served as NFL commissioner between 1946 and 1959.
Pro Football Hall of Fame/NFL/Getty Images

The combination of a 7–4 record in the 1942 season—the first winning season in Steeler history—and the unveiling of the shifty scatback Bill Dudley (nicknamed "Bullet Bill" for his speed and elusiveness coming out of the backfield), had Rooney smoking like a chimney.

For one brief, shining moment (and it was brief) Rooney experienced the pleasure of watching a winning squad. It was a great satisfaction to the team owner that his original investment was at last showing signs of paying off, both at the box office, where more fans than usual were attending Sunday games at Forbes Field, and artistically, as well. The "Stillers," as the Steelers were called in the local dialect, were making people happy. How about that?

Over the decades of his ownership of the Steelers, right up to the fielding of his dream teams in the 1970s, Rooney adopted the role of a good loser. The portrait, perpetuated in the newspapers, was not quite accurate. Rooney, an athlete in his younger days, fiercely wanted to win. He was a simply a polite man who could accept losing in a gracious manner.

But he was a happy guy when Walt Kiesling oversaw a winner in 1942. The 1940s began as the 1930s had ended for the Steelers. As the new decade started, the Pittsburgh franchise discarded its old name, the Pirates, leaving it in sole possession of the baseball team, and embraced a fresh beginning under the Steelers name. It was an appropriate name in a steel-manufacturing town, but it didn't help much on the field. Pittsburgh finished 2–7–2. The Steelers introduced new uniforms, too. Rooney, frustrated over the steady losing despite

> **"I loved being out there, loafing with the players, and working with the team."**
> —*Dan Rooney, on being the Steelers' ball boy as a teenager in the 1940s.*

the cosmetic changes, muttered "Same old Steelers." He could not have imagined that the insult would stick to his team for more than three decades. Whenever disappointment brewed, fans and sports reporters alike discussing the black and gold would resignedly fall back on the phrase.

The next year, 1941, the Steelers played musical coaches, with Aldo Donelli, Bert Bell, and Kiesling sharing the blame for a 1–9–1 campaign. Bell was a new face on the scene in Pittsburgh, a part-owner from 1941 after administering the fortunes of the Philadelphia Eagles from 1933 to 1940. The Eagles, much like the Steelers, struggled financially at the gate. Bell, who became one of the most influential leaders in NFL history, was an unlikely patron of the gridiron. Football was his true love and it cost him.

Rooney was a boxer, a horse-player, and a man who grew up above a tavern, a grounded, blue collar Pittsburgh guy. Bell was a blueblood, who grew up on Philadelphia's Main Line, the son of the wealthy attorney-general of the state of Pennsylvania (whose brother became governor). Bell's given first name was de Benneville, but anyone who actually attempted to tease him about it was likely to get a knuckle sandwich. Everyone called him Bert and that's the way he wanted it.

Bell was an independent thinker who might have preferred attending a college a little bit farther away from home, but his father, John, often said that his boy would "go to Penn or go to hell." Bell did become a football player for the Ivy League Quakers (though he also spent a year in France during World War I). Bell's father was planning to cut off his inheritance when Bell made it clear that he going to devote his life to pro football, but instead the collapse of the stock market, at the start of the Depression, cut back his finances.

Still, Bell's wife had enough cash handy for him to borrow a sum to buy into the Frankford Yellowjackets. This occurred just in time for the team to go belly up in its old location. Bell and his co-owner decided to revive the team in Philadelphia and rename it in 1933. Eschewing Phillies and Athletics, the names of the two local baseball teams, they chose Eagles, basing the name on the symbol of one of President Roosevelt's new creations, the National Recovery Administration, which saw its own startup the same year.

Given the total lack of success by the Eagles, W.C. Fields might have suggested that Bell had chosen Penn and hell. After three seasons the Eagles were put up for auction. Bell paid $4,500 to become the sole owner. That made him owner, general manager, coach, ticket manager, and public relations chief. During this period he suggested an innovative idea to bring more parity to the NFL teams. Bell proposed the draft of college players, with the top selection going to the worst team from the season before. The draft was approved.

In 1940, in a confusing serious of maneuvers, the Steelers were sold by Art Rooney to young millionaire Alexis Thompson, who had inherited a fortune from his family's cosmetics business. Thompson, who lived in New York, planned to move the team to Boston. Rooney joined Bell in the operation of the Eagles. However, when Thompson couldn't pull off his move to Boston, he decided to leave the Steelers in Pittsburgh for a year, calling them the Iron Men. However, Rooney and Bell dickered with Thompson and took back the Steelers, while Thompson took over the Eagles because it was more convenient to his New York base.

As a footnote, merely because of his lineage, it is worth noting that one of the Steelers' players in 1940 was a back named George Kiick, from Bucknell

ARTHUR JARRETT, BAREFOOT KICKER

It In the summer of 1941, as the Steelers were gathering in Hershey, Pennsylvania, to start training camp, an apparition of a sort appeared. Concluding a 6,000-mile journey from Hawaii, Big Arthur Jarrett—a barefoot kicker in the islands—announced his intention to try out for the team's place-kicking job.

Jarrett, at 230 pounds, was also vying for a guard or tackle slot in an era when kickers could not make a pro roster for that skill alone.

Previously employed as the assistant hangman at a penal colony, the 23-year-old Jarrett knew the difference between a coconut and a pigskin and did not show up unheralded. He came highly touted for his accuracy by a one-time University of Pittsburgh student. The ex-Panther passed his evaluation on to Steelers general manager Bert Bell and Bell said to Jarrett, "C'mon on down." He did, however, warn Jarrett to bring cleats because the NFL was not prepared to allow naked toes on the gridiron. "He was recommended by a former Pitt player and if he is half as good as his record indicates, he will be one of the regulars when the National Football League season gets underway," Bell said.

Apparently, Jarrett, who obtained his unusual day job because his father was the warden of the prison in Oahu (he said he never carried out an execution), was not even half as good as expected, because he did not make the team. The tradeoff was that Jarrett saved a lot of money on shoes.

University. Kiick also played the 1945 season for the Steelers. However, his son Jim became much more famous in the sport, sharing a Super Bowl backfield during the Miami Dolphins' 17–0 season of 1972.

From 1940 to 1946, Rooney and Bell were partners in the Steelers. Bell played an active role in personnel matters and descended from the owner's box briefly to coach two games in 1941. Pittsburgh lost both. Rooney gently asked Bell, "Bert, did you ever think about changing coaches?"

No one can accuse the Steelers of scouring the nation for the best available coach after Bell fired himself. They simply turned the job back over to Kiesling for the 1942 season. Kiesling pretty much deserved the reward for all of his hard time serving the club in the bad old days.

Bill Dudley was the godsend addition to the team.

Although the Total Football Encyclopedia lists his weight as 182 pounds, other sources suggest he might have weighed as little as 176 pounds. Even in the early 1940s, there were enough skeptics who owned typewriters to question whether Dudley was too small to take the pounding of the pro game.

Much as it had been said in the 1920s of Walter Johnson's fastball that a batter couldn't hit what he couldn't see, Dudley represented the school of thought that he wouldn't get hurt if he was too fast for the tacklers to tackle him.

Dudley could do a little bit of everything well, and some things very well. He led the league in rushing, with 696 yards his rookie year, but he also excelled as a passer when called upon, a punt and kickoff returner, and as a defensive back.

It took a few weeks for the Steelers to adjust to

Players discuss strategy with Coach Steve Owen during a workout before a 1941 charity All-Star game at the Polo Grounds in New York. Left to right are Cecil Hare of the Washington Redskins, Art Jones of the Pittsburgh Steelers, Owen, Pug Manders of the Brooklyn Dodgers, and Dick Riffle of the Steelers.
Bettmann/Corbis

their new-found prosperity. They opened the season with a 24–14 loss to the Eagles, and lost by an identical score to the Redskins the next week. Then Pittsburgh ripped off four straight wins and victories in seven of their next eight games.

Dudley had faced the accusation that he was too small to play his favorite sport since he was in high school in Virginia. He began his schooling early and so was only a 105 pound freshman at age 12 when he sought to become a quarterback. The coach took one look at him and said, "We haven't even got a suit that would fit you."

It took until his senior year to make a mark. By then Dudley had become an accomplished drop kicker and understood football strategy better than any of his teammates. By graduation, Dudley's size had increased all of the way up to 5 feet 9 inches and 150 pounds, which was not impressive enough to attract football scholarships from his top choices. The University of

Virginia took a chance on him based on the belief that at least he would be an excellent extra-point kicker. By his senior year Dudley had made himself into the school's first All-American.

As a rookie with the Steelers, Dudley established immediately that he could play at any level. He also let his opinions get the best of him sometimes. If he didn't feel that teammates were putting out 100 percent in practice, he told them so, loudly. That made him some enemies on the squad. Dudley sprained an ankle in his first pro game and that was indicative of the harsh treatment he occasionally suffered when walloped by extra-large defenders.

After his impressive debut, Dudley, like so many other NFL players, became a soldier for the duration of World War II. The Steelers struggled mightily during his and his main teammates' absence. In 1943, the Steelers merged with the Philadelphia Eagles to form

Hall of Fame running back Bill Dudley of the Steelers takes off up-field in a 1946 game against the Washington Redskins.
Pro Football Hall of Fame/NFL

Earle "Greasy" Neale coached the combined Philadelphia Eagles-Pittsburgh Steelers franchise called the Steagles for one year during World War II.
NFL/Getty Images

"I think that having their wives here has the married men in a much better frame of mind."
—Steelers general manager and co-owner Bert Bell, on the unusual step of allowing women at pre-season training camp in 1943.

the Steagles simply as a way for both franchises to survive with decreased attendance and a shortage of capable players. The Steelers contributed just a half-dozen players to the roster. One player thrown into the group from the Philadelphia side was a quarterback who would become much more famous later as coach of the New York Giants—Allie Sherman. In 1944, the Steelers felt their way through another one-year merger, this time with the Chicago Cardinals.

Despite the short-term duration of the arrangements, the mixing and matching of players and coaches did not work out so smoothly in either case. In a tribute to the hard-nosed, forceful personality of Eagles coach Earl "Greasy" Neale, the first bunch finished 5–4–1, with just two home games played in Pittsburgh. No one had a crazier time of trying to make do and fit in with the Steagles than Ted Doyle, an offensive lineman who had been with Pittsburgh since 1938.

Doyle obtained full-time war-support employment, as was expected of him, in Pittsburgh. However, the Steagles practiced in Philadelphia, 300 miles east. He did not practice with his teammates that season. On Friday, at the end of the work week, he hopped on a train to Philadelphia. On Saturday, he received a brief scouting report on the opponent and was filled in on any changes his own team had made during the week. He played on Sunday and then took another train home. He was a long-distance commuter.

The Steagles were the only team in the NFL that required players to work full-time outside jobs to back the war effort. In a rather astonishing exhibition of poor taste, when the Steagles played at Brooklyn to open the season, the Dodgers' general manager Dennis Shea had the temerity to dismiss them as a "town team" rather than professionals because the players worked. He claimed that any team with players working second jobs made the league look like "Humpty Dumpy outfits." The Steagles won, 17–0.

No doubt the Steagle worker-players were much wearier than their opponents come Sunday, but in a time of war it was difficult to see the benefit of criticizing their actions. The squad's winning record, despite their double duty, was further testimony to their accomplishment.

"To this day, the complexity of this crazy deal makes my head spin."
—Steelers chairman Dan Rooney, on his family's near loss of the team in 1940.

Many of the players had been drafted and rejected as 4-F because of a physical infirmity that the Army didn't want to deal with, but that wouldn't keep them off the football field. Some had been discharged from the service. Because football was such a physical game, it was hard for average members of the public to comprehend why these apparently healthy young men were exempt from service when their own children were getting killed overseas. Members of the Steagles admitted receiving "hate mail" periodically, blasting them for these very reasons. "It was rough," said Steagles center Ray Graves.

The Steagles required the players to hold full-time jobs in munitions factories or other positions that counted as supporting the war effort. Practices were held at night after full days of work, and the half-dozen or so Pittsburgh players had to relocate to Philadelphia if they wanted to practice. Although the eastern and western Pennsylvania cities shared proprietorship of the team, only two home games were played in Pittsburgh while four were contested in Philadelphia.

Remarkably, the patched-together Steagles finished with a 5–4–1 record. In a couple of ways, the arrangement was a success. Pro football was kept alive in Pittsburgh and Philadelphia, and a winning record was achieved. But no one wanted to continue as a combined team. Shortly after the season ended, the partnership was dissolved.

In 1944, the Steelers were not any much better positioned to field a full team on their own again. In a plan spearheaded by the league so there would be an even number of 10 teams, the Steelers and Chicago Cardinals merged. If the Steagles was a turn-up-your-nose name that was at the very least awkward, there was no easy way to identify this pairing of teams. At its worst, the Steelers and Cardinals were referred to as the Card-Pitts.

Even worse than that, though, was the product on the field. Once again, co-coaches were designated, Kiesling, and Phil Handler from Chicago. They were much more compatible than Kiesling and Neale, even friendly, racetrack- and saloon-going buddies. But the team was atrocious. It really was the pits. The Pittsburgh-Chicago coupling resulted in a 0–10 season with the squad being out-scored 328–108.

That year the Steelers had three home games, but only five of their own players on the roster. Both

A BRIEF CHANGE OF OWNERSHIP

It is little remembered that for a brief period of time the Pittsburgh Steelers were not actually owned by the Rooney family. But in a dizzying series of events that almost shuffled the team to Boston, and included entire franchise sales and swaps, the Steelers never formally left town and quickly reverted to Rooney rule.

Art Rooney believed that the Steelers and Pittsburgh were perfectly matched, but by the end of the 1940 season the team had still not recorded a single winning record. The crowds that Rooney imagined flocking to Forbes Field never materialized. So in December Rooney sold his Pittsburgh team to Alexis Thompson, a New Yorker who intended to move the club to Massachusetts. Thompson, then 30, was a colorful playboy who had inherited $6 million at age 15 through his steel company-owning family.

Rooney made a $5,000 profit in 1940, but with World War II on the horizon he worried about the immediate future. "I figured if that was the best that I could do, I would have to do something about it," Rooney said.

Rooney became part-owner of the Philadelphia Eagles with Bert Bell, later commissioner of the NFL. They planned to combine the Eagles and Steelers and play four home games in each Pennsylvania locale.

However, Thompson could not pull off his Boston move. Rooney and Bell offered to trade the Eagles for the Steelers so Thompson could operate closer to his New York base. Only months after the initial sale, Rooney was back in charge of the Steelers.

Rooney and Bell shook their heads, wondering how a combination of two teams could produce a team worse than either was before. After two seasons as a hybrid club, the Pittsburgh owners had enough of sharing.

The Steelers returned to being their same old selves, finishing 2–8 under one-year coach Jim Leonard. Kiesling, who was probably scared that he would be forced into another co-coaching venture in 1945 with someone like Gen. Douglas MacArthur, fled to Green Bay as an assistant coach for Curly Lambeau. Dudley returned to the team for part of the season, but didn't make a true impact again until the next year.

On January 11, 1946, Bell was elected commissioner of the NFL. Rooney bought out his shares, returning full ownership of the Steelers to his family.

Bell, who had devoted his life to football embarked on a stormy, challenging tenure as commissioner. Just after World War II, as prosperity was returning to American society, and as his fellow owners were

WARTIME COLLABORATION

When the Japanese bombed Pearl Harbor on Sunday, December 7, 1941, pro football was being played. Soon after, the United States' involvement in World War II disrupted competition and during the bleakest years the war nearly wrecked the National Football League. The Pittsburgh Steelers suffered more than many.

President Franklin Delano Roosevelt issued a statement urging major league baseball to keep playing in order to provide some semblance of normalcy on the home front and offer entertainment to civilians working in essential wartime industries. The statement came in the form of a note written to Commissioner Kenesaw Mountain Landis and was called "the Green Light Letter." Baseball was the bellwether, the national pastime, and although no other sport was singled out, others took their cue from FDR's proclamation.

The president's declaration did not exempt athletes from serving in the armed forces. Each athlete was an individual case. Throughout the war, any professional athlete who was 4-F, yet still actively playing ball, whether it was baseball or football, was viewed suspiciously by fans. Their thinking went like this: "Why was one man's son in harm's way across the Pacific, while someone healthy enough to make his living dodging tacklers was not in the Army?"

NFL team owners debated shutting down the league for the duration of the war, but decided to play on. They reduced the size of rosters from 33 to 28 players, but many teams did not have even that many players under contract from season to season.

Teams turned over their rosters faster than they could play the

games. Overall, 683 NFL players served in the armed forces during World War II and 19 of them were killed. Given the dire circumstances facing the country, the fears insinuated into daily living, and the parade of young men departing for Europe and Japan, reduced interest in sports was expected.

As attendance declined and top players became more difficult to obtain, the Steelers nearly folded. Instead, in a novel solution, the Steelers and the Philadelphia Eagles joined forces to play unofficially as the "Steagles." The league gave its approval to the one-year experiment on June 15, 1943.

It was a shotgun wedding, a match made out of necessity, not love. The clubs merged their players, three-quarters of them from Philadelphia, and their coaches. Steeler boss Walt Kiesling and Eagles' boss Earle "Greasy" Neale, became co-coaches. They had almost nothing in common, from their play calling to their personalities.

Kiesling was associated with the Steelers for about 35 years in all, as a player, assistant coach, and head coach, and was a Hall of Fame offensive lineman. Neale was a more accomplished coach and was a versatile enough athlete to play major league baseball, as well as football. There was almost as much tension between Kiesling and Neale in their roles as there was among young recruits waiting to be sent overseas. Dan Rooney recalled that the two men couldn't even agree on what brand of coffee to drink. "At times they would argue on the field in front of all the players," said Al Wistert, one of those players, about his coaches. "It was crazy."

The manpower shortage was

A manpower shortage during World War II forced the Pittsburgh and Philadelphia teams to merge as the Steagles temporarily, but other top players like Bears quarterback Sid Luckman still took advantage of the mediocre team.
Pro Football Hall of Fame/NFL Photos/Getty Images

acute. Some played pro football with disabilities that kept them out of the service and might have kept them off the field during peacetime. End Tony Bova was a cut above. He was a good receiver who played five years with the Steelers, but was nearly blind in one eye. Some players had longstanding leg injuries that would have prevented them from marching. Some players were partially deaf. It might also be said that Kiesling and Neale were hard of hearing when it came to listening to one another.

Ultimately, in what was a far more collaborative process, a compromise was reached on how the Steagles were to be run. Bert Bell, who had owned the Eagles and was then a part-owner of the Steelers, brokered a peace treaty that allowed Neale to supervise the offense and Kiesling to run the defense.

Dan Rooney said that the only reason the Steagles were invented was "desperation" and a belief that both the Steelers and the Eagles would fail if they did not help one another. He recalled the Steagles not even being able to muster the full complement of 28 players.

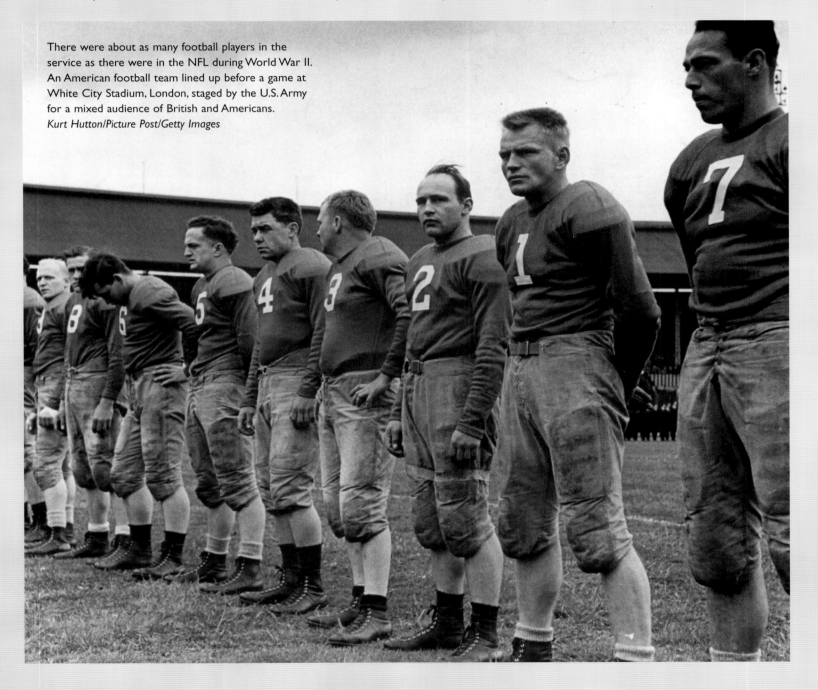

There were about as many football players in the service as there were in the NFL during World War II. An American football team lined up before a game at White City Stadium, London, staged by the U.S. Army for a mixed audience of British and Americans.
Kurt Hutton/Picture Post/Getty Images

attempting to regain their footing in their marketplaces, a new problem arose.

A fresh group of millionaires founded the All-America Football Conference, a rival league that bid for players and sought footholds in many of the NFL's prime cities. The battle raged for three years and every time someone mentioned the upstart, Bell bellowed, "We're not interested!" He refused to mention the opposition by name, either.

In late December 1949, the AAFC ran out of money, will, and energy, and the NFL absorbed its best franchises. Bell was a visionary on the importance of television to the future of the NFL, and he was probably the happiest man in America in December 1958 when the New York Giants and the Baltimore Colts engaged in the first sudden-death overtime championship game that drew a phenomenal audience. That game, since termed "the greatest game ever played," for its drama and importance to the sport, intrigued TV executives in a fresh way. From that moment forward football's future was ensured.

Pro football and the NFL were on their way to pre-eminence in the minds of American sports fans when Bert Bell died of a heart attack on October 11, 1959. At the time he was attending a game between the Pittsburgh Steelers and the Philadelphia Eagles at Franklin Field in Philadelphia. He was probably not thinking about the Steagles that day.

Art Rooney's world had always been a small one geographically. He lived and worked in a small radius of Pittsburgh and he was prejudiced in favor of anyone with Pittsburgh area football ties. With his old reliable standby coach Walt Kiesling off to Wisconsin, it was no surprise that Rooney would turn his focus on nearby college football programs to seek out a new coach. What was surprising was that Rooney could come to a deal with the famed Jock Sutherland, who had been a legend at Pitt.

Sutherland, known as "the Dour Scot," had inherited a program raised to glory status by the famed Pop Warner, and elevated it even higher in national esteem. The Pitt Panthers were one of the great football powers of the era, from the time Sutherland took command in 1925 until 1938, when he had a falling out with his old school. He actually coached the Brooklyn professional team, acquiring a taste for the style, before joining the Navy during World War II.

Sutherland, a household name in Pittsburgh, had already established his reputation in the college game and sought to see if his precepts and methods translated from teaching young men to leading older men. He well understood the Steelers' rocky results in the NFL, but was confident enough in his own abilities

**"I've never seen him caught from behind. He's a great defensive man and one of the deadliest tacklers I've ever watched."
—University of Pittsburgh coach Wes Fesler, on Steelers running back Bill Dudley.**

to believe he could turn around the perpetually losing franchise.

No one takes on a new job planning to fail, but Sutherland was staking his legacy on the fact that he could produce with the Steelers as he had with the Panthers. At his introductory press conference, he said, "I am not accustomed to coaching a loser, and I do not intend to start at this late date. We may not win the National League pennant in 1946, but the other teams will know they have been in a fight. Maybe by 1947, it will be a different story."

There is no record of any smart-mouth sports reporter jumping up to inform Sutherland that it was the baseball Pirates and not the football Steelers who were chasing the National League pennant. By all accounts, Sutherland's demeanor and comparatively limited sense of humor would not have been in evidence.

The Steelers gave Sutherland a five-year contract. Such faith was rare in the 1940s, if not unprecedented, but Sutherland wanted the security and Rooney wanted a winner to remold his organization, and to keep him on hand once that was accomplished.

As the former Naval lieutenant-commander took command of the club, Sutherland was brutally candid in his assessment of the Steelers. He announced he was going to install his favored single wing offense even though it was going out of style, with many teams favoring the new T-formation. And, Sutherland noted, a quick look at the players left over from the flawed 1945 team indicated he would be in the market for many fresh faces.

"I intend to use the system I know best," Sutherland said. "As for the Steeler roster, we will just have to start at the bottom and build. Frankly, I couldn't win with the squad which ended the past season."

The one player returning from World War II who had established himself as a popular and exceptional talent and who had participated some in 1945 was Bill Dudley. Fans felt the Bullet and Jock were going to make magic together.

Sutherland's first season at the helm of the Steelers in 1946 showed promise. They finished 5–5–1 and Dudley flashed his old form. His talent had not been

Bill Dudley was a Steeler star, but couldn't get along with coach Jock Sutherland and was sent to Detroit.
Bettmann/Corbis

"BULLET" BILL DUDLEY

Halfback
1942, 1945–46

The Depression ruined the U.S. economy in the 1930s and the Steelers' on-field results brought depression to their fans. At last, in 1942, not only did Pittsburgh record its first winning record, 7–4, but introduced a fresh star.

"Bullet" Bill Dudley was an All-American at Virginia, the school's first. He was a 16-year-old freshman and just 20 when he finished college. One newspaper termed him "the infant prodigy" after observing that he was the youngest college football captain in the nation.

Dudley was an instant sensation with the Steelers in the autumn of 1942. Slightly built at 5 feet 10 inches and 180 pounds, Dudley was not an imposing basher, but he was a slippery runner. He had no trouble overcoming sarcastic comments that he was too small for pro ball. "We expect to get a lot of service out of Dudley," said Steelers' co-owner Bert Bell upon his signing. Bell's prediction was exactly right.

As a rookie, Dudley led the NFL in rushing with 696 yards gained. He also totaled the most yards on punt returns and led the league with a 27.1-yard per play average on kickoff returns. Only one other player in NFL history led the league in three categories in one season.

Although his career was interrupted by World War II, Dudley led the league in rushing again upon his return in 1946 and intercepted 10 passes on defense to lead the NFL in that category the same season. Dudley scored 44 touchdowns in his Hall of Fame career.

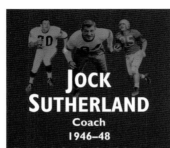

JOCK SUTHERLAND
Coach
1946–48

For Jock Sutherland, it was a fresh challenge. For Art Rooney, it was a bold stroke. Tired of the Steelers floundering around in the standings with mediocre records, Rooney wooed the native of Scotland who had established College Football Hall of Fame credentials down the street at the University of Pittsburgh.

The hiring of John Bain "Jock" Sutherland as coach represented a new era for the Steelers as the country emerged from World War II. Sutherland played on great Pitt teams under Pop Warner, one of the pioneers of the sport, and, beginning in 1925, he led the Panthers to recognition as one of the finest college elevens in the country. Pitt played in the Rose Bowl four times and was chosen as the top team in the East seven times under Sutherland.

Sutherland had strayed far from his initial ambitions. He studied to be a dentist and even worked as a professor of dentistry at Pitt. But he had long before given his heart to football. Sutherland was one of the great proponents of playing grind-it-out power football, but announced that as a pro coach, fans could expect more throwing. "You cannot depend on power plays in this professional game," Sutherland said. "The opposition is a little too rugged for that type of football alone."

Sutherland's inaugural Steelers season in 1946 produced a 5–5–1 record. In 1947, the Steelers created excitement with their best-ever 8–4 record. Then, on April 11, 1948, Sutherland abruptly died of a heart attack. He was 59.

diminished by his years at war. Dudley's 606 yards from scrimmage with a 4.1-yard per carry average led the league, and he intercepted ten passes on defense that same season. He also averaged 14.3 yards per punt return. Those were terrific numbers all around, and he was chosen as the league's Most Valuable Player.

However, Rooney was dismayed when his all-star back and his impressive new coach did not get along. Dudley retained his old habit of speaking up early and often if he didn't like the way things were going. Sutherland took each utterance as a personal affront and a challenge to his authority. This was no love match.

Sutherland had carried through with his commitment to use the single wing offense, and although Dudley was the primary offensive weapon, he felt the style exposed his smallish body to unnecessary extra hits. He was not silent on this matter, either, and Sutherland resented him speaking out. Sutherland denounced Dudley for indicating he wanted to quit. Dudley did a little two-step with semantics, saying, "I'm too small for pro football." The sports writers put their own spin on that sentence, reading between the lines. They interpreted the comment as meaning Dudley was too small to play Sutherland's way and wanted to be traded.

Later, Dudley clarified the back-and-forth. "It's true Sutherland and I didn't hit it off too well and it's also true that I took quite a physical beating playing at Pittsburgh. But I never said I wanted to quit the game. It's just that I thought it would be best for all concerned if I played elsewhere because under Jock I had to play too much for my size."

Sure enough, one season was long enough for Sutherland and Dudley to share a locker room. Dudley was shipped to the Detroit Lions, where he played three seasons. He finished his Hall of Fame career with the Washington Redskins.

Sutherland's 1947 Steeler team was the best in club history. The Steelers finished 8–4, tied with the Eagles for the Eastern Division lead. The teams met in a December 21 playoff game, with the winner to advance to the NFL title game. Philadelphia won, 21–0. But the progress made by the Steelers under Sutherland was demonstrable and provided a sense of optimism to the organization and the fans. That was something new in Pittsburgh.

Alas, less than half a year later, Sutherland died of a heart attack at age 59 while on a scouting trip. He seemed on the verge of leading the Steelers to their first championship game, but the sad setback put Pittsburgh dreams on hold indefinitely. "We respected him and feared his teams," said Bears' owner and coach George Halas. "He was undoubtedly the best coach in the league."

Halas' words were carefully chosen. Sutherland was respected and feared throughout his career. He was called the "Dour Scot," the "Silent Scot," and the Great Stone Face" because he was not a man who took things lightly. Many years later, Steelers' public relations director Ed Kiely reflected on Sutherland's commitment to football. "He was a bachelor and his players said his only mistress was football," Kiely wrote. "His practices were long and hard, almost cruel. But the end apparently justified the means. His teams were successful. His record still stands as one of the best in football."

When Sutherland joined the Steelers after World War II, he won permission from Rooney to bring along his own staff of assistant coaches. One of his favorites, and a younger man he came to rely on, was a former Pitt player, John Michelosen. Michelosen had not only played for Sutherland with the Panthers, he worked one year as an assistant coach for him at the school and two years under him with Brooklyn. He considered Sutherland his mentor and Sutherland gave him the ultimate compliment when he told Michelosen, "You know as much football as I do."

Sutherland's death stung the Steelers' organization and in hoping for continuity, Rooney took a chance appointing the 32-year-old protégé. Michelosen became the youngest coach in the league.

Whether it was the sudden change at the top, or a failure for the pupil to be able to translate what his teacher showed him, the Steelers' first team in 1948 under Michelson was a flop. From 8–4, Pittsburgh declined to 4–8. That was despite the maturing of a playmaking end named Elbie Nickel from the University of Cincinnati, who became a mainstay on the line for ten years.

Nickel was a lightweight 196 pounds as a rookie, and grew into a 220 pound tight end. He had sure hands and caught 329 passes with the Steelers, before retiring following the 1957 season. Nickel played in 11 games his first season, but was not really used as a receiver. After that, he got better and better. During his next four seasons Nickel caught from 22 to 28 passes.

But in the early 1950s, when the Steelers loosened up the offense, Nickel showed off his true worth and crowd-pleasing skills. One season he caught 55 passes. Another he caught 62, ranking second in the league. This was well before pro football teams shifted the balance of offensive power from the running game to the passing game. Nickel proved to be the perfect receiving partner for Jim Finks, the accomplished quarterback the Steelers picked up long before his Hall of Fame front office career began.

Nickel became a three-time participant in the Pro Bowl. Nickel came along well before big money trickled down to star players and said he always worked in the off-season. For players like Nickel, football was as much a labor of love as it was a profession. They almost couldn't afford to play, but didn't want to give up the game. "I always had a job," Nickel said. "It makes you appreciate playing football more and I had something to fall back on. I knew I couldn't play football the rest of my life."

Nickel was passionate about football and had fun in Pittsburgh, but played during the long stretch when the franchise couldn't put together enough victories to even reach a championship game, never mind win one. "I enjoyed my stay there," he said. "It was a good town. We didn't win too much. We were always a little short someplace."

That indeed was the story of the Steelers during the 1930s, the 1940s, and beyond. Art Rooney never despaired. He always gave his teams a chance to prove themselves. He always tried to find the players who would right the ship. True to his old boss's devotion to the single wing, Michelosen, who learned at

It was a muddy day for football when Chicago Cardinals' star Marshall Goldberg carried the ball into the end zone for a touchdown against the Pittsburgh Steelers in 1946.
Bettmann/Corbis

ELBIE NICKEL

Tight end
1946–57

When fans and experts choose all-time Steelers teams, few players from the team's early years earn favorable mention. It is the stars and Hall of Famers from the club's Super Bowl years who rightly dominate. But the one name that stands out and endures is the old-timer who excelled at tight end beginning in the late 1940s.

During an 11-year career concluding in 1957, and all with Pittsburgh, Elbie Nickel caught 329 passes, scored 37 touchdowns, and in 1949 averaged 24.3 yards per catch, leading the league. Most would agree that Nickel was an over-achiever. When the Steelers selected him in the 15th round of the 1947 draft, Nickel was not expected to blossom into an all-star.

At a time when the Steelers did not distinguish themselves often in the standings and frequently struggled to score points, the 6 foot 1 inch, 196 pound alumnus of Cincinnati, was a potent weapon. For a chunk of his career, Nickel, who bulked up to 220 pounds, was a two-way player, also lining up at defensive end.

Nickel was a successful pass catcher in an era when teams did not throw nearly as often. In his earliest seasons the Steelers had not yet even made the transition to the more explosive T-formation. "We were the last team in the NFL to play the single wing," Nickel said in 1982, "and I was the blocking end. So I was what was later called a tight end. I didn't have the speed these guys have today."

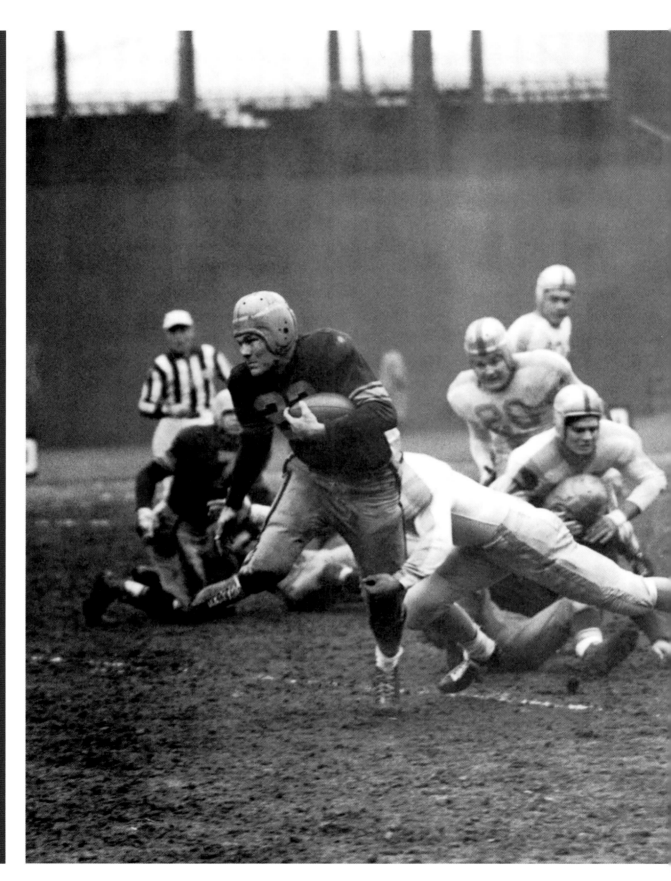

PITTSBURGH
STEELERS

YEAR BY YEAR

1940	2–7–2
1941	1–9–1
1942	7–4
1943	5–4–1
1944	0–10
1945	2–8
1946	5–5–1
1947	8–4
1948	4–8
1949	6–5–1

Sutherland's knee, stuck with the older offense.

In 1949, Pittsburgh drafted a cross-section of running backs, hoping one would emerge as a star at the key tailback slot in the offense. Bobby Gage of Clemson and Joe Geri of Georgia ended up sharing the job, and the two-headed starter combined for 772 yards rushing, 883 passing, and eight touchdowns. The Steelers finished 6–5–1 and everyone was feeling pretty darned good in Pittsburgh.

A year later Geri emerged as the man, rushing for a team record 705 yards, scoring 64 points, and being named first-team all-pro. But the team went 4–7–1 and did no better the next year. Gage's 97-yard run on December 4, 1949 against the Chicago Bears was the longest in Steelers' history. The same season Geri whacked a punt 82 yards, another record.

Those statistics were nice, but nearly 20 years after purchasing his little football team as a hobby of sorts, Art Rooney was still without a championship. He was kind of hoping that nice guys would finish first one of those days.

Steeler back Jerry Nuzum breaks free for a 6-yard gain in 1949 against the New York Bulldogs at the Polo Grounds.
Bettmann/Corbis

CHAPTER 3

1950s
TRYING TO BUILD SOMETHING TO LAST

Ernie Stautner was one of the greatest defensive players in Steeler history and culminated his 14-year career with election to the Hall of Fame.
Robert Riger/Getty Images

Ernie Stautner was the toughest, roughest Steeler since players wore leather helmets. After he was selected in the second round of the 1950 draft, the entire view of Pittsburgh's defense began to change.

Stautner was not only a great talent, but he had a built-in attitude that struck fear and doubt into the minds of offensive opponents. When runners and passers looked ahead on their schedules and saw what date their teams would be facing the Steelers, they began formulating reasons why they might have to take the day off.

A 6 foot 1 inch, 230 pound force of nature from Boston College, Stautner played meaner than his size. He was not only quick and strong, but he put the growl into a unit that had long been a pushover, as easy to bust through as a curtain of aluminum foil. That all changed when Ernie came to town.

Stautner set the new tone quickly in his 14-season, Hall of Fame career. If there was any confusion over what his objectives were when he dropped into his three-point stance prior to the snap of the ball, he explained them for eager listeners. "You've got to be a man who wants to hurt somebody," he said. "You know where I'm going for? The quarterback's face. It hurts in the face. I want him to know I'm coming the next time. I want him to be scared."

Such pronouncements, coupled with the wherewithal to carry out the mission, meant images of Stautner were soon creeping around in quarterbacks' heads like lost spiders. Or maybe they chose to picture their poison as a rampaging grizzly. Either way Stautner, who later had a long career as a defensive coaching assistant with the Dallas Cowboys, did not have many close personal friends in the quarterback fraternity. He had plenty of respect, however, among the offensive linemen trying to make their living across the line of scrimmage.

"That man ain't human," said Jim Parker, the Hall of Fame tackle for the Baltimore Colts about his run-ins with Stautner. "He's too strong to be human. He keeps coming, coming, coming. Every time he comes back,

"No matter what their records were, the Steelers still had a great defense when Ernie played."
—Hall of Fame defensive back Mel Blount, on Ernie Stautner.

he's coming harder."

Stautner represented a new generation of Steelers. Throughout the 1930s and 1940s, Pittsburgh rarely employed players who emerged as consistent all-stars. Not only was Stautner a keeper, he was a cornerstone. The Steelers were still wandering in the NFL wilderness when it came to striking gold in the way of championships, but the 1950s symbolized a breakthrough in the acquisition of talent. From 1950 on, Pittsburgh would field teams with more recognizable, more talented players.

The human roadblock recovered 21 fumbles in his career (many of them personally caused, as well), was selected for nine Pro Bowls, and established a new standard for success on the Pittsburgh defense—and in some ways, for defenses around the league. Stautner was a disrupter, a defender that foes always had to account for on the field. "Ernie was one of the NFL's first impact players along the defensive line," Dan Rooney said. "He was probably the most well-known player on the team throughout much of his career and one of the greatest players ever to wear a Steelers uniform."

In a hard-hat, lunch-bucket town, where the nine-to-five workers came home dirty enough for a shower, Stautner was a perfect symbol. He did the dirty work and those grass and mud stains splotching his uniform stood out like red badges of courage. He was an iron man in a steel city where the sky was so blackened from the mills, street lights had to be turned on at noon.

Later in his Steelers career, Stautner admitted to a secret desire to learn how to play the piano. He never got very far, though, because his fingers resembled sausages rather than the long phalanges preferred in a pianist. He also took into account the beating his fingers took grabbing and pulling other large men around a football field. "How could anyone play a piano with paws like these?" he asked. Stautner nonetheless made beautiful music for the Steelers.

As the 1950s began, Pittsburgh was still reeling from the sudden sad loss of Jock Sutherland. His successor and friend John Michelosen could not produce the same type of magic the venerable old Scotsman had. After two identically inadequate 4–7–1 seasons in 1950 and 1951, Art Rooney jettisoned the young coach.

His replacement hire was a bit of a surprise. Fifteen years after dismissing Joe Bach after a 6–6 season and later ruing his action, Rooney re-hired Bach for the 1952 season. Bach, who had been coaching one of Rooney's favorite schools, St. Bonaventure, for two seasons, was a much more seasoned coach at age 50 and brought 26 years of experience to the Steelers.

Sutherland had stubbornly clung to the single wing formation, even as other teams were achieving fresh success with the new T-formation. Michelosen's fatal mistake during his four seasons leading the club was a failure to adapt. He stuck with the single wing. Bach immediately announced that he was going to be opening up the Steelers' offense with up-to-date flourishes.

Defensive tackle Ernie Stautner played his whole career with Pittsburgh and is the only player to have his number, 70, retired by the team. He also enjoyed a long career as an NFL assistant coach. *Bruce Bennett Studios/Getty Images*

"I play to use the T-formation as a basic system, but we will have man-in-motion plays as well as end wide and flank players and all the other modern stuff," Bach said. "I expect no difficulty in molding the present Steelers into that style."

The Bach era promised more than it delivered. The 1952 Steelers finished 5–7 and the 1953 Steelers finished 6–6. Compared to the bad old days that was not so bad, but the numbers didn't lie. Pittsburgh was still mediocre. The caliber of players was improving, though, and the Steelers put on many more entertaining shows at Forbes Field.

In an unbelievable win during the 1952 campaign, the Steelers destroyed the New York Giants, 63–7. "My boys played the game I've been looking for all season," said Bach. "I knew it would happen sometime."

That was the game when kickoff return specialist

Lynn Chandnois returned two 90-yard-plus boots for scores in a row after the first was nullified by a penalty. The Steelers intercepted seven Giant passes and KO'd quarterbacks left and right, including a young man named Tom Landry (later the Cowboys' coach, who was just filling in). Quarterback Jim Finks threw for four touchdowns.

The extraordinary back-to-back returns by Chandnois were book-ended by two jokes. When the teams were lining up for the do-over, the referee teased Chandnois by saying, "Let's see you take this one back, too." Afterwards, Walt Kiesling, who never seemed to warm up to anything but the most plodding football of his youth, told Art Rooney that Chandnois had to be the luckiest guy around. "I guess I was lucky both times," Chandnois said.

At 5 feet 11 inches and 188 pounds, Finks played his college ball at Tulsa and joined the Steelers in 1949 as a 12th-round draft choice. He languished on the bench for a couple of seasons, except for defensive back work, but his breakthrough came in 1952 when he threw for 2,307 yards and 20 touchdowns, the latter a league-leading total. Finks was a T-formation quarterback in college and was the right man in the right place when Bach dumped the old offense.

Finks played his entire NFL career with the Steelers through 1955, but gained much greater fame in the second phase of his football life. He grew into an esteemed administrator, putting together winning teams in Minnesota and Chicago, and ultimately, for his work as a general manager, was voted into the Hall of Fame.

Young Finks was a daring thrower, even though NFL offenses were still rooted in the running game during his prime years. Over a four-year period when the Steelers were playing 12-game seasons, Finks attempted between 292 and 344 passes. "Jimmy was a great quarterback, not just a good one," Art Rooney said. "But we were never big winners and he didn't get the attention he deserved."

Later, Finks joked that his greatest claim to fame came at the end of his career when he beat out Johnny Unitas for the Steelers' quarterback job. He knew how ludicrous it was that then-coach Walt Kiesling never gave Unitas a chance in training camp.

After retiring, Finks joined the staff at Notre Dame as an assistant coach, stayed one year, and then became a player-assistant coach for the Calgary Stampeders in the Canadian Football League. After departing the playing field for good, Finks worked his way up to be general manager of the Stampeders and on his watch they won a Grey Cup title. Finks returned to the NFL as GM of the Vikings in 1964.

Finks died of cancer in 1994, and was selected for

Best known as a Hall of Fame front office administrator, Jim Finks was also a solid quarterback for the Steelers in the 1950s.
Pro Football Hall of Fame/Getty Images

the Hall of Fame in 1995. Paul Hornung, the Green Bay Packer star who played at Notre Dame while Finks was there, was stung when Finks died. "One hundred people just lost their best friend," Hornung said.

Hornung won the 1956 Heisman Trophy as the best player in college football the year Finks coached at Notre Dame. The achievement was even more remarkable because the Fighting Irish finished 2–8, making Hornung the only player to win the award while playing on a losing team. He and Finks teased one another about the circumstances. "Jim always said he was responsible for me winning the Heisman and I was responsible for losing eight games," Hornung said.

Finks was more responsible for winning games with the Steelers. He once rallied Pittsburgh past the favored Green Bay Packers with a three-touchdown day, while also throwing for 327 yards, mostly to Elbie Nickel and Ray Matthews.

Although his primary responsibility was at quarterback, Jim Finks (7), like many players in the 1950s, also doubled on defense. Here he leaps to intercept a pass intended for Ellery Williams (85) of the New York Giants.
Bettmann/Corbis

JACK BUTLER
Defensive back
1951–59

Jack Butler might be the best player from the past not in the Pro Football Hall of Fame.

A determined defensive back, Butler excelled for the Steelers for the entire 1950s, his career spanning 1951 to 1959. At 6 feet 1 inch and 200 pounds, Butler intercepted 52 passes, with an NFL-leading 10 in 1957, and was selected to play in four Pro Bowls.

In a 1953 game against the Redskins, Butler intercepted four passes. Overall, Butler, who came out of St. Bonaventure, returned nine interceptions for touchdowns. When the Steelers' all-time half century team was selected, Butler's name was on the list.

Despite his intentions, Butler did not graduate from the upstate New York school. Steeler official Fran Rogarty phoned Butler in 1951 and invited him to try out for the team. Butler figured it merely would be a cool experience. "I thought, 'Hey, this is a terrific way to spend my summer,'" Butler said. "'I won't make the team, but it will be a great way to pass the time.' I never went back to school."

Butler never made more than $12,000 a year playing football, but said he didn't care. "I enjoyed playing and that's enough," he said. "Pro football has been good to me. It's kept me from having to go to work."

After his playing days ended, Butler actually spent years working as a football scout, heading the multi-team scouting combine BLESTO, Inc., that provided player reports to eight teams.

The Steelers had definitely beefed up their talent level. Nickel, an excellent end, played for the team between 1947 and 1957 and caught 329 passes. One of the other new defensive faces was Jack Butler. Butler was an extraordinarily talented defensive back who broke into the league for the 1951 season and was a nine-time all-star selection. He had such great hands he intercepted 52 passes in the decade and harbored a fantasy of becoming a wide receiver. Butler did run patterns with Johnny Unitas, so he knew the young quarterback's value. "He was really accurate," Butler said. "Man, he really was."

Unitas, who was married with a young child, fretted about being cut from the team. Butler said no way that would happen. That very night Kiesling made perhaps the biggest error in team history when he dropped Unitas.

Kiesling was back in the driver's seat in 1954, his third stint as Steelers' head coach, because Art Rooney was impatient with the indifferent results produced by Bach, but mostly because Bach took ill. "Every time I see those guys practice," Rooney said, "they look like world-beaters, but when the gun goes off, something always happens."

So it was bye-bye Joe and hello to Walt again. Kiesling had not changed his spots. He still supervised a conservative offense and the Steelers couldn't win under him. In 1954, Pittsburgh finished 4–8. In 1955, the Steelers ended up 5–7. In 1956, the Kiesling-led Steelers again went 5–7. It was the ultimate running-in-place trio of years.

Art Rooney was a remarkably patient man. He was hands-off in allowing his employees to do their jobs as they saw fit. But he once reached a break point of exasperation with Kiesling. It irked Rooney that the Steelers used to always start each game the same way, calling the same run, over and over again. The handoff always went to fullback Fran Rogel who ran up the middle.

Pittsburgh Press sports writer Bob Drum began a pre-game ritual where before Pittsburgh's first possession he sang in the press box, "Hi-diddle-diddle, it's Rogel up the middle." The phrase caught on, but nothing could deter Kiesling from his set-in-concrete ways. He believed that it was important to show off superior strength on the line right away. Of course, other teams knew exactly what was coming and stuffed the play.

Finally, Art Rooney ordered Kiesling to start a game with a pass. Dan Rooney described the conversation this way: "Look, Kies, I want you to throw on first down," Art Rooney said. This behavior was so uncharacteristic of Rooney that it was as if he had marched onto the field in front of 35,000 fans at Forbes Field,

> **"Jack Butler was one guy who could have played with the teams of the '70s. He was fast, smart, and tough."**
> **—Dan Rooney, on Pittsburgh's all-star defensive back.**

blown a whistle, and taken a snap himself.

Kiesling replied, "No, you don't throw the ball on first down!" Rooney pressed the point, and before the game when the Rogel chant began, the owner promised sports writers they were about to see something different. He guaranteed that the Steelers would pass on first down. On the hike, quarterback Jack Scarbath faked the handoff to Rogel, faded back, and hit receiver Goose McClaren for an 80-yard touchdown play. However, the officials whistled an offside penalty against the Steelers and the ball was brought back. On the next play Kiesling called a Rogel up-the-middle run that gained one yard. Later, it emerged that Kiesling's response to Rooney was to order one of his players to jump offside.

The Steelers developed a new threat when they acquired Lynn Chandnois with their No. 1 draft selection in 1950. Chandnois was the most explosive kick returner of his day, twice leading the NFL in average, with yardage reaching 35 yards per attempt. It was an additional sign that the Steelers were drafting more wisely and signing better players with more versatility and improved college pedigrees. After years of growing up around football, the Rooney sons were proving to be excellent talent evaluators.

They were diplomatic when talking about Kiesling, who was well-liked by their father, had been a great player, and had helped the organization several times when needed. But it was clear that Kiesling did not have the confidence of the players and was never going to lead the Steelers anywhere. He was as old school as a one-room school house, and the club needed fresh ideas. Chandnois said Kiesling played favorites and didn't even talk to some of the players. "We had a good team, but I never cared much for Kiesling," said Chandnois, who said he felt like going right home when Kiesling replaced Bach for the 1954 season.

Despite the achievements of a player like Chandnois, who could alter the course of a game with a single return, there was much less premium placed on special teams in the 1950s than there is in the NFL of the 2000s. However, the Steelers possessed not only the best kickoff man, they also had the league's top punter on the squad, too.

Pat Brady was born in Seattle and spent time at

Bradley in Illinois after Nevada-Reno dropped football. In Nevada he blasted an NCAA record 99-yard punt. A left-footed kicker, Brady was drafted in the 13th round by the New York Giants in 1952, but became a Steeler before the season opened. He was a terrific find, booming punts 43.2 yards a crack as a rookie, and then improving dramatically in 1953. Brady averaged 46.9 yards a kick that year and 43.2 a boot again in 1954. The latter two figures were tops in the NFL.

Brady had spent his early weeks out of college with the Hamilton Tiger Cats of the Canadian Football League. He did well there, but the team had to let him go because the rules stated the clubs could carry only two non-Canadians at a time and Brady wasn't versatile enough to take up roster space. He could do only one thing—punt.

Art Rooney was tipped off about Brady, did some quick research, and signed him. He always said Brady cost the Steelers only the price of a couple of phone calls and might have been the best bargain in team history. "Never a better kicker in the National League or anywhere else for that matter," Rooney said.

Rooney was not exaggerating. When the Steelers gave Brady his tryout, his powerful punts astonished onlookers. The first kick Brady knocked with his toe traveled the length of the field with a roll. Time after

"Kies was the physical duplicate of Babe Ruth. He was big like Ruth, and a left-hander, too. Like Ruth, he played his best when he had some belly on him."
—Halfback Johnny Blood, on long-time Steeler player and coach Walt Kiesling.

time Brady put the ball into orbit, until, as Rooney tells it, Bach halted him. "He was interfering with practice," Rooney said. "The other players were standing there watching him with their mouths open."

Rooney explained that his favorite Brady punt occurred in a game against the Green Bay Packers. The Steelers were pinned back by their own goal line when they ran out of downs. Brady had to take the snap from center while standing an inch inside his own end line. When his foot connected with the ball it kept on floating downfield. The Packers' return man had to turn around and chase after the kick, finally hauling it in on the fly on his own 30-yard-line. Brady said that meant the ball traveled about 89 yards in the air, though he was officially credited with a boot of 78 yards.

Bad luck terminated Brady's career after only three

This 1954 group of Steeler players were described as "men from Mars" as they tried out special helmets to protect their faces from injuries. Left to right: Gus Craft, Jim Finks, Jim "Popcorn" Brandt, John Schweder, Elbie Nickel, Bob Goana, and Dale Dodrill.
Bettmann/Corbis

JOHNNY UNITAS: THE LOCAL BOY WHO GOT AWAY

The worst personnel decision in NFL history still haunts the Pittsburgh Steelers. The mistake of cutting hometown boy Johnny Unitas rewrote pro football history.

This was an "Oops" with a capital O. Unitas, considered by many as the greatest quarterback of all-time, grew up in Pittsburgh, but was a gangly looking player whose motion inspired no comparisons to beauty queens. All Unitas could do when he came out of the University of Louisville was zip the football and make brilliant calls.

Due to Dan Rooney's diligence, Unitas was the ninth-round pick of the Steelers in the 1955 college draft. However, coach Walt Kiesling, in a colossal error, would not even let Unitas take a snap in practice. He said Unitas was "too dumb to play."

Of Kiesling, Dan Rooney said, "When he got an idea he latched onto it like a pit bull and no one could change his mind. Unfortunately, he had made up his mind about Unitas, even before camp began."

Dan Rooney's brothers Tim, John, and Pat watched Unitas. Art Rooney's sons knew football and they told him what a great player Unitas was. They pleaded with him to keep the player.

However, as always, following his personal code to let the men he hired do their jobs, Rooney refused to interfere with his coach's decision-making. He would not issue orders in cases like this. As a result, Kiesling cut Unitas, and the Pittsburgh-born Steeler-wannabe became a Hall of Famer for the Baltimore Colts.

Above: Hall of Fame quarterback Johnny Unitas in a 1955 rookie photo as a Pittsburgh Steelers. He was cut, so he played semi-pro for a year before he was picked up by the Baltimore Colts.
NFL/Getty Images

Right: In 1956, Ted Marchibroda was a Steeler quarterback. Later generations of football fans know him better as a coach.
NFL/Getty Images

seasons. In a 1955 pre-season game, Brady jumped for a high snap, ruptured his left Achilles tendon, and never regained the strength to kick in the same manner. "When I came down, I could feel a bang," Brady said. "Before I even punted I turned around and thought the referee had kicked me in the leg." He completed his kick, which traveled just 30 yards. The injury instantly reduced Brady from the best at his craft to a below-average kicker and that marked the end of his NFL career.

Kiesling's faith in Fran Rogel was not completely unfounded, despite the "Hi-diddle-diddle" chant, which was an insult to Kiesling's lack of play-calling imagination. A pretty reliable runner, Rogel was 5 feet 11 inches and 203 pounds, and a Steeler from 1950 to 1957. His best season was 1955 when he rushed for 588 yards and was called upon to get the tough yards.

The short yardage plays were Rogel's bread and butter. Given that no player is perfect, it's possible that Rogel's memory was less than perfect after his playing days as well, but there was truth in his later statement about how good he was when the Steelers needed

"He always called me 'Star.'"
—*Kickoff return standout Lynn Chandnois, on his relationship with Steelers owner Art Rooney.*

him for short gains. "When it was third-and-one and I carried the ball," Rogel said, "we never missed a first down in my career." There was no mystery about Rogel's role. He was assigned to carry the mail. And he delivered in rain, snow or shine, 3,271 yards worth in all.

Rogel had a lengthy high school football coaching career in the Pittsburgh area after he retired, and was a close enough follower of the Steelers later on when they won championships to admire the handiwork of the offensive line and compare it to the 1950s. "They

[the holes] are beautiful," Rogel said. "I never saw them so big when I was running."

The first black Steeler player was Ray Kemp, who played part of the 1933 season. One of the first black Steeler stars seemed likely to be Lowell Perry. Perry had been a standout for the University of Michigan and was drafted with Pittsburgh's eighth-round choice in 1953 (behind second pick John Henry Johnson, who did become the team's first African-American star). But Perry had military obligations. He was released from the service in time for the 1956 season, and the Steelers used the 6 foot, 195 pound player as an end.

A mature Perry worked his way into the starting lineup after an exhibition-season 98-yard run, and caught 14 passes and scored two touchdowns. One of his pass plays went for 75 yards. Perry was also making a splash as a punt and kick returner. Once in a while, a Steeler quarterback handed the ball off to Perry from a run from scrimmage. He was a budding star and was creating a buzz around the league with his gusto and speed, already being mentioned as a potential rookie-of-the-year prospect.

On November 4, in the sixth game of the season, a tight one with the New York Giants, Pittsburgh quarterback Ted Marchibroda, later a prominent NFL coach, called for an end around play to Perry. Giant defenders Emlen Tunnell, Bill Svoboda, and Roosevelt Grier diagnosed the play and had Perry trapped. As he attempted to switch direction, Perry was hit hard and his cleats stuck in the turf.

The vicious hit produced terrible injuries. The gang tackle fractured Perry's pelvis and dislocated his hip. Perry spent 13 weeks in the hospital and his promising football career ended on the cold field.

"I went through a lot of changes lying in that hospital," Perry said. "I decided I was going to look beyond the athletic world for employment." A year later, Perry became an assistant coach working with Steelers' ends. That made him the first African-American assistant coach in the NFL after World War II. Originally, it was felt that the year on the sidelines would enable Perry to return to the Steelers' lineup in 1958. But Perry decided the risk to his body was not worth it, and he never played again. Yet once that avenue was closed to him, Perry enjoyed an extraordinary career in other fields

LYNN CHANDNOIS

**Running back, kick returner
1950–56**

Lynn Chandnois saw a lot of life before becoming a professional footballer in 1950 as the No. 1 draft pick of the Steelers. He was orphaned before high school, spent two years in the Naval Air Corps, and was married as an undergraduate while starring for Michigan State.

It didn't take long for Chandnois to star in Pittsburgh, either. During his seven seasons playing for the Steelers, ending in 1956, Chandnois was a sometimes passer, rushed for a few hundred yards a year, caught 20-something passes per season, handled punt return duties, and was a standout kickoff returner. The 6 foot 2 inch, 200 pound Chandnois was the league leader in kickoff returns, with a 32.5-yard average in 1951 and an even better 35.2 in 1952. "Lynn had everything, size, speed, and shiftiness," said teammate Jerry Nuzum.

In a 1952 game against the New York Giants, Chandnois ran a kick back 97 yards for a touchdown, only to have officials overturn it on a penalty. The teams lined up again and Chandnois returned the do-over 91 yards for a touchdown. This time it counted.

Steeler home games were at Forbes Field, the Pittsburgh Pirates' diamond. Although the grounds were re-groomed for football, the pitcher's mound still occupied a place in the middle of things. Chandnois said he used it to his advantage on kicks. "I'd use that mound to get a head start, to go downhill," Chandnois said. "Most of the guys now wait for the ball. They never catch it on the run."

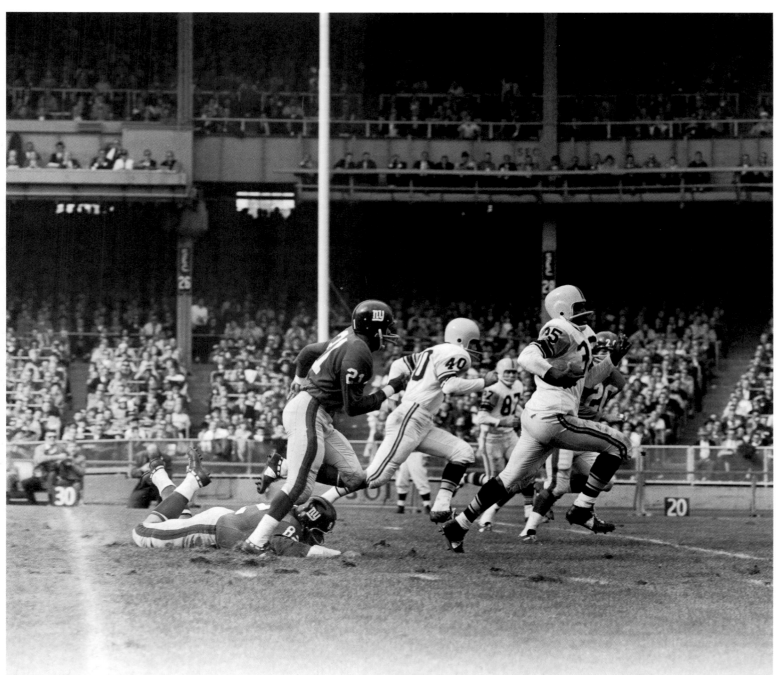

With New York's Allen Webb (21) in pursuit, fullback John Henry Johnson runs up field in a 1962 Steelers–Giants contest at Yankee Stadium. Johnson got within a foot of the end zone on the play; Pittsburgh scored shortly thereafter and went on to win the game 20–17. *Bettmann/Corbis*

Initially, Perry attended Duquesne's law school, and Art Rooney greased the way. Eventually, Perry graduated from the University of Detroit Law School. He became a clerk for a federal judge, a labor lawyer, legal counsel for the National Labor Relations Board, and then an executive for the Chrysler Corporation. When Perry was hired by CBS, he became the first black NFL broadcaster. Subsequently, Perry served as chairman of the U.S. Equal Opportunity Commission and director of the Michigan Department of Labor before dying from cancer in 2001.

"I think about it now," Perry said years after his football injury, "and I guess it would have been nice to play for a couple of years, but I think my injury was a blessing in disguise. It made me aware that there was more to life than football."

It is difficult to imagine how explosive the Steelers would have been with Perry and John Henry Johnson in the lineup together. That combination might have hastened the arrival of the long-suffering club's first championship.

Johnson, who played a few years on defense, too,

Fullback John Henry Johnson was big and fast, the prototype of the NFL back of the future during his Hall of Fame career in the 1950s and early 1960s.
Bettmann/Corbis

JOHN HENRY JOHNSON
Fullback
1960–65

John Henry Johnson's name meant toughness. He was a prototype for the great backs of the future, combining speed, strength, and agility. A muscled, dynamic, 6 foot 2 inch, 225 pound package, Johnson broke into the NFL with the San Francisco 49ers in 1954, played in the Canadian Football League and for the Detroit Lions, but was at his best during his six years with the Steelers.

Johnson twice rushed for more than 1,000 yards with Pittsburgh, compiling more than 6,800 yards on the ground overall with an average gain of 4.3 yards per carry. He scored 55 touchdowns and was chosen for the Hall of Fame.

His Steelers' coach Buddy Parker favorably compared Johnson to Jim Thorpe. "When he's running," Parker said of Johnson, "he's the best fullback in the business. He does everything a fullback should do."

Johnson was so powerful that when he collided with opponents who had malice on the brain, the other guy usually suffered the most. Either they didn't get up, or they staggered away nursing broken bones. Once, playing defense during a game in Canada, Johnson hit a kick returner so hard he broke the ball carrier's jaw in two places. When questioned about the hit, Johnson said, "Well, what did you want me to do? Kiss the guy or tackle him?"

Cleveland Browns coach Paul Brown yelled at Johnson for bloodying a player's mouth: "You've hit everybody in the league!" Johnson replied, "Then we got a tie game. Everybody in the league has hit me."

evolved into a Hall of Fame fullback and gave the Steelers one of the best ground games in the league during his prime years from the mid-1950s to the early 1960s before he finished with more than 6,800 yards rushing.

At 6 feet 2 inches and 225 pounds, Johnson was disproportionately tough. He was the offensive equivalent of Ernie Stautner. When opposing tacklers tried to bring him down, Johnson either ran right over them or just pushed them away with a straight arm. Les Richter, a rugged linebacker for the Los Angeles Rams, discovered just how forceful Johnson could be when riled. As Richter made a move to tackle Johnson, Johnson flashed out with a forearm. "Pop, my jaw was broken," Richter said.

"My greatest asset was not my speed, but my quickness in following my blockers and knowing when to cut," Johnson said after he retired. Intimidation was as much a part of Johnson's game as Stautner's. He wanted to plant doubt in the heads of would-be tacklers. "You've got to scare your opponent," Johnson proclaimed once. "It sorta upsets their concentration. I find I can run away from a lot of guys after I get them afraid of a collision with me."

A writer once observed of Johnson's determined style, "Every play to John Henry was like a battle to the death in the Colosseum."

Johnson took a bruising himself. When he was warned to take each play a little less rambunctiously, he said he couldn't do it. "I can't play any other way. Out there, it's either me or him. And I always dish out more than I can take." Johnson, who played in the NFL for 14 seasons, until 1966, added a ferocious element to the Steelers' attack, changing the team's image from a group of pussycats who could not compete with the elite, into a team on the rise that could duel with anyone.

Raymond "Buddy" Parker coached the Chicago Cardinals in the 1940s and became head man of the Detroit Lions in 1950. He was an effective leader and championship coach for the Lions, winning two world titles in the early 1950s, and three Western Division crowns. As the 1950s wore on, it appeared he might stay in Detroit for life.

Then, acting out a surreal performance, while speaking at a "Meet the Lions" annual banquet just two days before Detroit was scheduled to start the 1957 season, Parker went haywire. He badmouthed his team and in front of an audience of 600 supportive fans, he abruptly quit. Following the introduction of players, he said, "I can't handle this team anymore. It is the worst team I've ever seen in training camp. They have no life, no go. Just a completely dead team."

The startling resignation took place on August 12, but Parker did not stay unemployed long. When the

> **"The worst thing that can happen is guys telling you things in the huddle. You can't concentrate on the down, the situation, and the score with somebody else yapping."**
> —*Hall of Fame quarterback Bobby Layne, on why he didn't want to hear anyone else's voice in the huddle.*

Steelers kicked off the 1957 season on September 29 with a 28–7 victory over the Washington Redskins, the new coach was present.

The Pittsburgh Steelers' "Buddy Parker Era" began with a 6–6 record. The following years were a rollercoaster, with the volatile Parker often arguing with the Rooneys about personnel, and dumping players with no warning, but his methods did produce some success.

Parker turned pro in 1935 as a quarterback for the Detroit Lions, and then played for the Chicago Cardinals; he was a perfectionist. He expected his Steelers to avoid silly mistakes, and if they did not perform to his expectations, Parker threw a tantrum and exiled players to the waiver wire. With little forethought he might shout that a player was gone.

Parker complained incessantly to Dan Rooney and was sometimes disconsolate because things weren't going better. He blamed the Rooneys for not giving him players he felt he needed. Dan Rooney wearily talked Parker out of quitting several times.

Parker's philosophy of seeking perfection caused clashes. He had no faith in rookies, so he was constantly trading away the Steelers' draft picks for veterans. He figured the older guys were less prone to make the mistakes that enraged him. In 1959, Parker disposed of the Steelers' first seven draft picks in trades. "It drove me nuts," said Dan Rooney. "Parker believed if you go with the veteran, you'll win today. Go with a rookie and you might win tomorrow."

One of Parker's first drastic acts to show the Steeler players that there was a new sheriff in town, was cutting running back Lynn Chandnois—an obvious mistake. It was Kiesling's last revenge. On his way out of the coach's office, as he transferred to a role as a special advisor to the team, that's what Kiesling recommended. Parker realized his error, but was too proud to recall Chandnois. Dan Rooney watched those rash moves with dismay.

"He could be a tyrant, especially when he was drinking," Rooney said of the coach. "Not that he drank often, only after games and whenever he had to make a speech. His axe could fall on luckless players on the bus or plane while coming home from a game."

Parker's hesitation in relying on young players cost him at times. The Steelers drafted Len Dawson out of Purdue in 1957 and treated him almost as egregiously as they did Johnny Unitas. Dawson sat on the bench for three years, in that time attempting 17 passes in total. It took until 1962, when he joined the Kansas City Chiefs of the American Football League, for Dawson to right his career and he grew into a Hall of Famer.

One of Parker's personnel moves that Steelers' faithful did not complain about was turning to his favorite veteran quarterback for help. Bobby Layne was a rapscallian, a cowboy from Texas who almost never parked his horse, but when the opening kickoff was booted, he was ready to ride.

Layne, another Hall of Famer, guided the Lions to their championships. At nightclubs till the wee hours of the morning, the hard-playing Layne played hard on the football field, too. He was a field general par excellence, the type of leader labeled a winner wherever he went. It is possible that Layne could have made a living as a talk show host or comedian, but he chose the job he loved the most. Layne was superior in the clutch, routinely rallying his teams to come-from-behind victories.

In 1957, after Parker walked out on the team, the Lions rolled all of the way to the NFL title. Layne led them there, but he broke his leg near the end of the season and watched as Tobin Rote performed the quarterbacking duties in the victory. Layne contemplated retirement, but Parker told him he was needed in Pittsburgh and that they could work magic again.

Given Layne's loose training habits, his devotion to 80-proof beverages, and his general disdain for rules and discipline, Layne's playful contempt of authority would not have been tolerated under many coaches. Parker understood Layne and didn't interfere with his lifestyle.

On December 13, 1958, Layne threw for a team-record 409 yards against the Chicago Cardinals, and that record stood for 44 years. The most remarkable aspect of Layne's record is that he was up most of the night partying at the Brentwood Hotel, where witnesses ascertained that he spent part of his time personally directing the jazz band. Layne could dance and drink till dawn, but it never interfered with his outlook on the field. "He was 100 percent competitive," said Pittsburgh star defensive back Jack Butler. "He played one way—all out."

The Steelers of the late 1950s acquired a certain amount of veteran talent, but just didn't have enough depth to break out with big winning years. Bill McPeak, a three-time Pro Bowl defensive end, became a player-coach in 1957, and later became an NFL head coach.

> **"He asks you to do something and you go out and break your neck to do it."**
> **—Steelers guard John Nisby, on quarterback Bobby Layne.**

Frank Varrichione was an outstanding offensive tackle, five times a Pro Bowler. John Nisby, who studied judo, was a solid guard. And despite Parker's inclinations, the slight (5 foot 11 inch), but elusive end Jimmy Orr earned rookie-of-the-year honors in 1958.

Hall of Fame quarterback Bobby Layne was as old school as they come. In this 1959 game, Layne's wearing no facemask, no thigh pads, and no knee pads.
NFL/Getty images

BOBBY LAYNE
QUARTERBACK
1958–62

Bobby Layne was everyone's pal in a saloon, but nobody's buddy except his teammates' on the football field. He could swagger sitting down and in his 59 years on Earth he crammed two lifetimes into his allotted time, not the least because he never seemed to sleep.

Layne was a born quarterback, a player who teammates followed and believed in, even if he did scream at receivers that dropped passes. When the clock was ticking down and the situation looked hopeless, he could still inspire hope. For Layne, practice was an inconvenience, and curfew was irrelevant, but the tenser the circumstances, the more likely he was to deliver. Layne practically invented the two-minute drill for quarterbacks rallying their teams from behind.

He was as Texan as tumbleweed, raised in Lubbock, but Layne was attracted to big-city lights and did much of his best work after dark. Compared to Layne, Joe Namath was a wallflower. Layne just came along before the big money and the crazy NFL media attention. He played his way into the Hall of Fame by uplifting his followers to championships—at least in Detroit. In a 2002 article in the NFL's *GameDay* magazine, Layne was vividly described. "Bobby Layne's concept of the breakfast of champions was a large measure of alcohol with a pinch of Wheaties on the side."

Layne was blue-eyed, with blond hair, stood 6 feet 1 inch and weighed 208 pounds. He was the darling of the Longhorn nation as quarterback at the University of Texas, but his attitude that it was always New Year's Eve didn't sit well with his first pro football owner, the Chicago Bears' jut-jawed George Halas.

Halas' mistake in cutting Layne loose was the Lions' gain. Layne led the NFL in just about every passing category for a couple of years in the early 1950s and cajoled Detroit to three championships. The first was registered in 1952, well before championship rings were in vogue. "We got a $9 blue blanket that said, 'World Champions,'" Layne said.

He sat out the third title game with a broken leg in 1957, his most demoralizing moment. The coach who let him run wild on and off the field was Buddy Parker, soon to resurface with the Steelers and who, in 1958, immediately procured Layne's hard-nosed game for Pittsburgh.

Bobby Layne was a Lone Star State legend for his phenomenal play at the University of Texas long before he became a pro. *Bettmann/Corbis*

"We needed a leader before we were going anywhere," Parker said. "Bobby Layne is the greatest leader I've ever been associated with. He'll set the pace for the rest of our players."

In a 15-year pro career, Layne threw for 196 touchdowns, then the NFL record, and more than 26,000 yards, and ran for 25 more touchdowns and nearly 2,500 yards. Layne broke Sammy Baugh's record for touchdown passes of 186 in dramatic fashion, with a four-touchdown performance against the Redskins in Washington in 1961.

Scouts tend to evaluate tangibles. They admire speed, size, and strength, and in quarterbacks they tend to look down on a thrower whose passes are not picture-perfect beauties. Layne was not that type of quarterback. He didn't have the type of zip on his passes that modern-day bullet tossers feature. Instead, Layne was the king of intangibles. He kept the huddle loose, cracked jokes, and got the job done, even if the play-by-play might be dissected as flawed. Somehow it all worked. "When he went on the field,

Bobby Layne was in charge," Dan Rooney said. "In charge. There was no question of that from the first minute."

Lou Creekmur, a former Layne teammate with Detroit, compared Layne's demeanor to another well-known leader of the 1950s. "What a general," Creekmur said. "The MacArthur of the National Football League."

Layne was the Steelers' field boss for five years. Although Pittsburgh never duplicated the Lions' success, Layne provided thrills and entertainment. A man who loved to tell stories and jokes, Layne was colorful copy for sports writers when not carrying the team across the goal line in Forbes Field.

The most prominent Steeler of his day, Layne had more than a passing acquaintanceship with trouble, in addition to his passing connections to receivers Buddy Dial and the like. At a pool party on a road trip to San Francisco, several Steelers, including Layne, linebacker John Reger, and running back Tom Tracy, gathered to imbibe. At least one reporter was thrown in the pool. The manager called the police and Layne soaked the employee with a martini. Afterwards, the errant quarterback said, "How'd I know he wanted beer?"

Once, in Detroit, Layne was arrested for drunk driving. A police officer testified that Layne was so drunk he couldn't talk. Layne's defense attorney suggested that the officer was not familiar with Texas speech and that Layne was guilty merely of having a twanging accent very different in nature to the local speech patterns. Layne beat the rap, and some with a sense of humor created buttons reading, "Ah ain't drunk. Ah all am frum Texas."

Layne once celebrated a Steeler victory over the Dallas Cowboys by playing the piano and trumpet, though not simultaneously.

Doak Walker, the famous halfback who is the namesake of the award presented to the best college runner each season, was another Texan who shared a huddle with Layne. He saw early the qualities that would make Layne special.

"He was the best winner," Layne said. "Nobody hated to lose more than Bobby. He never was erratic, always cool. It didn't matter if we were ahead by 20 points or behind by 20, he was the same."

Layne retired after the 1962 season at age 36. He said he had almost retired in 1957 when the busted leg kept him out of the title game. There was some speculation that Layne would become a coach—and also what type of rules he might have for his players.

Layne died in 1986 and his passing was deeply lamented, especially by his old Steeler road roommate, Hall of Fame defensive end Ernie Stautner. "He had more best friends than anyone I've ever known," Stautner said.

On the sideline and in the huddle, Bobby Layne was a leader for the Steelers during the last five seasons of his Hall of Fame career. *NFL/Getty Images*

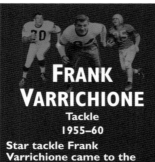

FRANK VARRICHIONE

Tackle
1955–60

Star tackle Frank Varrichione came to the Pittsburgh Steelers in 1955 with the strangest of nicknames: he was known as "Fainting Frank." Lest he be confused with a damsel in distress tied to the railroad tracks, Varrichione earned his moniker while playing for Notre Dame under Frank Leahy.

A five-time all-star with the Steelers, the 6 foot 1 inch, 235 pound Golden Domer was complicit in a sneaky play during the 1953 season when the Fighting Irish played Iowa. Trailing by a touchdown, with the clock running out, Varrichione faked an injury. The clock stoppage gave Notre Dame one last play, the Irish scored a touchdown, and tied the contest.

The nickname followed Varrichione throughout his 11-year pro career, six of them with Pittsburgh, but he said he never minded. "It was planned," Varrichione said. "We'd practiced it right along. Every team in football does the same thing. It was my assignment to fake the injury in case it was necessary."

Much later, after Varrichione had been traded to the Rams for defensive end Lou Michaels, his teammate, running back Jon Arnett, needled him about the incident. When the duo played ping-pong, Arnett said, "Every time I'm beating Frank, he faints."

Varrichione was probably the Steelers' best offensive lineman of the 1950s and he once graded out perfectly against Baltimore's exceptional defensive end Gino Marchetti who said, "Frank was among the best I ever faced. He may not have been the very best, but one thing I know, he was the most persistent."

Orr, a 25th-round draft pick of the Los Angeles Rams, was a surprise. He caught just 33 passes, but averaged a shocking, league-leading 27.6 yards per catch. He was also the team's punter that year. Although Orr was only with the Steelers for a couple of seasons, he caught 400 passes in his career and averaged nearly 20 yards per catch.

Injuries unreasonably offended Parker. Orr recalled that Parker rampaged through the trainer's room when John Henry Johnson was treating an injury in a whirlpool bath. "He just walked over to Johnson, turned over the whirlpool, and dumped John Henry right on the floor," Orr said. "Then he ordered everybody out of the training room, took a hammer, and nailed boards across the door. Then he put up a sign that said, 'There will be no more injuries. In the future, players will use Pepto Bismol for internal injuries and iodine for external ones.'" It's not clear if those prescriptions could cure broken bones, but Parker ran his team as he saw fit.

When Steeler quarterback Bobby Layne (22) got the ball in the closing minutes of a game, he was deadly. He practically invented the two-minute drill and he always thought he could win no matter the odds.
Fred Roe/NFL/Getty Images

During his Steelers' years, Bobby Layne was the last player in the NFL to play without a face mask on his helmet. He had developed a slight pot belly, possibly because Layne spent more time drinking than doing sit-ups. And he perfected the two-minute drill before anyone had a name for it. He provided flavorful copy for the sports writers and entertained Steeler fans.

Although he was a 30-some veteran, Layne hosted beer parties for Steeler rookies to make them feel part of the team. He was equally renowned as a clutch thrower and a big tipper. Layne's reputation for his generosity with waitresses, barmaids, bartenders, and nightclub bands led "Dandy" Don Meredith, another Texas quarterback, to say if he came back in another life he wanted to be Layne's chauffeur.

One exploit that made Layne a Texas football hero in his home state, was accounting for all 40 points in the University of Texas' 1946 Cotton Bowl win over Missouri, with his arm, legs, and foot. For the Steelers, he threw for 20 touchdowns in 1959 and led the Steeler offense with passion every second he was on the field.

Later, when Bobby Layne was inducted into the Pro Football Hall of Fame, a journalist recounted a barber shop discussion about the player's overall athletic abilities. Someone said Layne just didn't seem to have the natural gifts of others.

"His name is in the win column, ain't it?" another observer noted.

It usually was.

PITTSBURGH
STEELERS
YEAR BY YEAR

1950	4–7–1
1951	4–7–1
1952	5–7
1953	6–6
1954	4–8
1955	5–7
1956	5–7
1957	6–6
1958	7–4–1
1959	6–5–1

Gunslinger quarterback Bobby Layne liked to test young receivers by seeing if they could catch up to his deepest passes.
Bettmann/Corbis

1960s
A TEAM OF CHARACTERS

Buddy Parker came to Pittsburgh to win. With his successful track record in Detroit, the Rooneys gave Parker carte blanche to reorganize and reinvigorate a franchise that had never even won a division title since its founding in 1933.

What they didn't know was that Parker was prone to rages, impatience, and bouts of dictatorial mania. He was in love with players who had a track record and he despised letting his fate rest with rookies and newcomers. He had no patience for player development.

Pittsburgh fans had been patient for 27 years as the 1960s dawned and certainly no one demonstrated more tolerance for coaches and their foibles than the Rooney family. But Dan Rooney, whose responsibility was growing within the club's administration, did not want to be as hands-off as his father. Art Rooney was guilty of too much faith in coaches who made poor personnel moves. Dan argued with Parker and sometimes overruled him. Parker grew petulant and threatened to resign if he did not get his way. Dan Rooney usually backed down and let the man hired to bring Pittsburgh a winner have his way.

The acquisition of Parker's old pal, quarterback Bobby Layne, was a solid move for the Steelers, even if he was into his 30s. But while the Steelers showed more promise at many positions, they did not have depth and the results did not materialize on the field.

And speaking of the field, even that changed. With the exception of the 1958 season, when they played at the University of Pittsburgh stadium, the Steelers had always shared Forbes Field with the Pirates. In 1963,

the Steelers moved to Pitt for the rest of the decade.

Layne filled a need and did his job well. He was flamboyant and a firm field leader. Wherever Layne traveled, in college and in Detroit, championships followed. But not in Pittsburgh. He put on a good show, however.

Layne was Hollywood handsome when he broke into the league and was Hollywood craggy-faced when he joined the Steelers in the late 1950s after parting ways with the Lions. He may not have been as spry, but he could still burn any defense that took him for granted. "I never lost my enthusiasm," Layne said as he readied himself for his 15th year in the NFL. "A lot of people think football never changes, that you should lose interest. It changes like the automobile changes. You got to enjoy it."

During Parker's first five years of Steeler leadership, the team finished at .500 or better three times. By Pittsburgh standards that was a miracle. Then, in 1962, the Steelers finished 9–5. It was the best record since the team's inception. The hiring of Buddy Parker was looking very good. For the first time, there were actually expectations for the Steelers in the 1963 season.

A major blow to Pittsburgh's optimism, however, was the sudden death of star defensive tackle Big Daddy Lipscomb. "He was as good as tackles come," said Steeler runner Tom Tracy. In May of that year the 300 pound giant was found dead in an apartment, the autopsy showing he had died from an overdose of heroin. Despite Lipscomb's friends' doubts of that conclusion, nothing else was ever proven. While it was

"Defense is the biggest thing in football. Winning simply comes down to having a defense."
—Steelers head coach Buddy Parker.

wildely known that Lipscomb drank heavily, even Dan Rooney was perplexed by the heroin report. Lipscomb, he said, had undergone a thorough physical only two weeks earlier and showed no signs of needle marks on his body or of ingesting the drug. Some of Lipscomb's friends and relatives suggested that he might have been injected with the fatal dose while sleeping or passed out. The long-time NFL star had a funeral attended by more than 1,000 people. "How do

you begin to replace a tackle like him?" said Art Rooney.

After Layne's retirement, Parker anointed Ed Brown as the new starting quarterback. Brown was another veteran who had put in a long apprenticeship with the Chicago Bears. The Steelers traded punter Bobby Joe Green for Brown in 1962. Brown had led the NFL in passing in 1956, but he was also a solid punter, so he was available for double duty. Brown threw for 2,982 yards and 21 touchdowns in 1963, but he also threw 20 interceptions.

That year marked the end of George Tarasovic's long association with the Steelers. The 6 foot 4 inch, 245 pound defensive end-linebacker had been with the team since 1952 except for a couple of years in the service. During the off-season, Tarasovic worked as

Pittsburgh's "Big Daddy" Lipscomb (76) tries to fend off a blocker to reach New York Giant ball carrier Alex Webster in 1962. *Bettmann/Corbis*

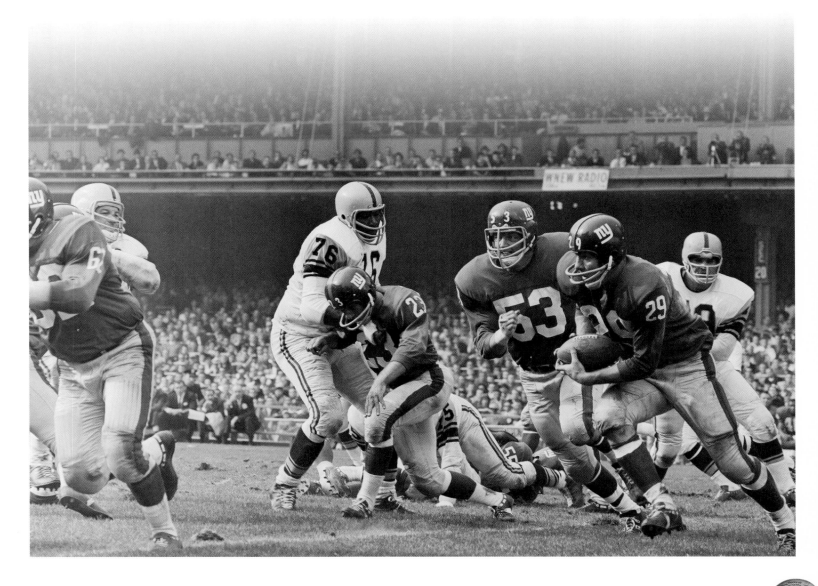

EUGENE "BIG DADDY" LIPSCOMB
DEFENSIVE TACKLE
1961–63

The story of Eugene "Big Daddy" Lipscomb is compelling, mysterious, and colorful. He was a man who lived large. Heck, he was a man who was large. But more than 45 years after his death, his demise remains perplexing.

Big Daddy grew up in Detroit and never went to college. When he broke into the NFL with the Los Angeles Rams in 1953 as a ferocious defensive tackle, he was pretty much the biggest guy in the league. By the time he was 16, he was an orphan. He never knew his father and after the police informed him that his mother was murdered, having been stabbed 47 times, he was ready to join the Marines and the Rams found him at Camp Pendleton.

Lipscomb stood 6 feet 6 inches and at various times his weight was listed as between 280 and 300 pounds. In those days the offensive tackles he faced typically weighed 240 pounds. He wore a distinguished mustache that enhanced his handsome features, as did his night life uniform that included a diamond pinky ring, alligator shoes, a feather in the brim of his hat, a red tie, and a white silk shirt.

Lipscomb, who had tremendous speed to complement his superior power, was as rugged as they come on the field and as jovial as it gets off the field. He moved from the Rams to the Colts, and was part of Baltimore's championship teams of the late 1950s. He joined the Steelers in 1961 for his final two years of football—and life.

When Big Daddy was in his prime, he was a terrific pass-rusher. He was probably the first of the monstrous defensive tackles who uttered a variation of a mini-speech credited to Bubba Smith and others. When asked about his effectiveness, Lipscomb said he bulled into the enemy backfield, gathered everyone up, and when he got to the one with the ball, he kept him.

Sometimes, Lipscomb played possum along the line of scrimmage, letting offensive lineman believe he was blocked. Then, as the running back tried to cut by, Lipscomb shoved the lineman aside and grabbed the runner, saying, "Where you going, little man? This is Big Daddy and once Big D puts the clamps on you, you're dead."

Johnny Sample, a Steeler defensive back, shared a house with Lipscomb in Pittsburgh and said Lipscomb was really a softy off the field. "Despite his size and enormous strength," Sample said, "Big Daddy was one of the nicest, friendliest cats in the world. Everybody loved him and he loved everybody. He might try to kill an opponent on the football field, but he was the kind of guy who would dig in his pocket and give you his last dollar if you needed it."

Big Daddy would have been the king of talk-show circuit if he had come along later, and fans adored him. "The fans pay their money because they want a show," Lipscomb said. "And the more show you put on, the more money you're going to make."

Lipscomb understood the great American publicity machine, but his primary nature never changed. He tackled anyone who came near him with the ball, but repeatedly said he was not a mean man. He once talked about knocking New York quarterback Y.A. Tittle out of bounds. "That's what they're paying me for," Lipscomb said, "to tackle people, and if my mother was out there, I'd tackle her, too."

As an off-season job from his regular assignment of putting half-nelsons on quarterbacks, for a little while Big Daddy, with his ready-made nickname, dabbled in professional wrestling. He wanted to play in the Eastern Basketball League, but NFL commissioner Pete Rozelle forbade him because the league employed players disgraced in college betting scandals. In 1962, he announced he wanted to be America's first man on the moon.

"I want to be one of them astronauts," Lipscomb proclaimed. "I'd like to get up on the moon, look around, wave the American flag, and get a little glory for Big Daddy, too." He said he would even lose weight for the chance, maybe drop to 260.

Big Daddy was a character in many ways. If thirsty, he could guzzle a case of soda in a day. For breakfast he might eat a dozen eggs, a pound of bacon, and wash the solids down with a pint of booze.

He was not reticent about discussing other favorite appetites. "I'm a B and B man," he said, meaning booze and broads. Given that he was divorced three times, he was not apparently satisfied with one lady at a time. There were probably two reasons why the Rams put him on waivers for $100. Lipscomb had not yet matured into the great player he was to become. And they wearied of trying to bail him out of the types of difficulties that came with being married to two women at one time.

Nothing slowed Lipscomb, though. Whenever Big Daddy traveled on the road with his team, a party followed. Whenever Big Daddy was home for any length of time, he threw a party.

Big Daddy was traded to the Steelers in time for the 1961 season in a two-for-two swap, with Pittsburgh's main contribution receiver Jimmy Orr. After two seasons in Pittsburgh, Lipscomb died tragically.

He was found dead at the age of 31 in an acquaintance's apartment on May 10, 1963. According to the police, he had three puncture holes in his right arm and had overdosed on heroin.

Friends refused to believe the report, saying Lipscomb was terrified of needles, never took drugs, and was right-handed, so he would not have injected himself with his left hand. Even doctors said Lipscomb was no addict. The apartment's owner was tried on drug charges, but there was no conviction.

More than a 1,000 people mourned Lipscomb at his funeral in Baltimore. About six months later, Big Daddy's gold Cadillac was auctioned off for $4,400. It was the last public symbol of a fun-loving man's out size life.

One of the game's first 300-pounders, defensive tackle Eugene "Big Daddy" Lipscomb loomed large on the gridiron for a decade. Here he overwhelms a Dallas Cowboys offensive lineman as he goes after quarterback Eddie LeBaron for a sack. *Robert Riger/Getty Images*

Defensive tackles Ernie Stautner and "Big Daddy" Lipscomb look to recover on a pass play in a 20–13 win over the Los Angeles Rams in 1961.
Vic Stein/NFL/GHetty Images

an insurance salesman, but he also developed an interest in politics, serving as a suburban democratic committeeman in the town of Dormant, which was overwhelmingly Republican. Like some of his other teammates who were so fascinated by the law, Tarasovic decided in 1963 to run for justice of the peace in his community. Alas, Tarasovic not only lost the election, he lost his spot on the Steelers, and was shipped to the Eagles. He did not appear crushed by the transfer. "I don't want to put the knock on anyone because that always sounds like sour grapes," Tarasovic said, before putting the knock on Parker. "Let's just say Buddy Parker and I had some differences of opinion. I know I'm a better defensive end than I am a linebacker."

It was also the beloved Ernie Stautner's final year of his 14-season career. The 235 pound Stautner was as stout a defender as the Steelers had in their first four decades of their existence, but when he came back for one last season in 1963, his body was aching and threatening to fail him.

As an undersized tackle right from the start of his pro career in 1950, Stautner was determined to be the meanest player on the field. Reporting for a game against the Cleveland Browns in 1958 with an injured

> **"There's only one way I can stick around. I gotta be mean."**
> **—Defensive end Ernie Stautner, near the end of his 14-season career.**

shoulder, Stautner accepted a shot of Novocain prior to kickoff. When the pain didn't wear off the doctor injected another. It was only after Stautner grew dizzy that it was ascertained he had accidentally been shot up with a large amount of the painkiller Demerol by accident. He was rushed to a hospital and drifted in and out of consciousness.

"I almost died," Stautner said. "I was close enough to death to receive the last rites from the Catholic Church." When a priest asked for his confession, Stautner said, "Lookit, father, I don't have much time. I can only hit the high spots."

Yet Stautner recovered. "I survived and went on to play a lot of games over the next few years," he said.

He coached in even more of them, immediately joining the Steelers as an assistant for two years, and in all coaching for 30 years in the NFL, and another two for the Frankfurt Galaxy in NFL Europe. Before the end of the 1960s, Stautner was inducted into the Pro Football Hall of Fame. "What a thrill," he said. "But I'm glad I played when I did. I don't think I could stand the pounding today's guys get every week."

Although the Steelers were still not championship material, they finished 7–4–3 and seemed tantalizingly close to a breakthrough. Even though Parker would have been happy not to carry any rookies on the team, the Steelers did try to add fresh, young blood whenever a draft choice wasn't disposed of in a trade.

Dismissing commentary that he was too small at 5 feet 11 inches and 195 pounds, and too slow, Dick Hoak, a seventh-round draft choice out of Penn State, spent 10 years in the backfield from 1961. The Steelers were forever trying to replace him with a faster model, but after tryouts, the fill-in always got shipped off to Siberia or Green Bay, and Hoak was retained.

Once, during one of those we-can-do-better-than-Hoak periods, linebacker Myron Pottios spoke up. "How come Dick Hoak's not playing?" Pottios said. "He's too good a football player to be sitting on the bench."

Hoak rushed for 3,965 yards during his career and scored 58 touchdowns on the ground and receiving. After becoming well established as a hard-nosed contributor who could block as well as tote the ball, Hoak wearied of hearing the barrage of criticism about being slow-footed. He finally asked a Pittsburgh sports

Ernie Stautner, a 1969 selection to the Pro Football Hall of Fame, earned his fame during 14 seasons on the Steeler defensive front line.
Pro Football Hall of Fame/NFL/Getty Images

Cleveland Browns fullback Jim Brown was always a handful for any defense. Pittsburgh's Brady Keys (on the ground behind Brown) and Bill Butler (on his back under Brown) attempt, in vain, to stop him from scoring on a 3-yard burst during a game in November 1961.
Bettmann/Corbis

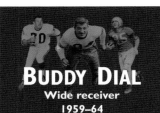

BUDDY DIAL
Wide receiver
1959–64

Buddy Dial was one of those fleet-flooted Texas receivers out of Rice that quarterbacks loved to dial up and order "Go long!"

The 6 foot 1 inch, 194 pound Dial joined the Steelers in 1959 after being waived by the Giants. When New York cut him, Dial told coach Jim Lee Howell, "Someday I'm going to make you look bad." Dial was Pittsburgh's best wide receiver in the early 1960s, before inexplicably being traded by coach Buddy Parker. Dial caught 53 passes in 1961, then 50 in 1962, and 60 in 1963.

Dial sang religious songs, but was a keep-the-clubhouse-lively joke teller, too. Yet he was no match for his quarterback Bobby Layne, the emperor of the night. The first time Dial met Layne, he said, the quarterback was "drinking his breakfast."

Layne inserted Dial into the huddle his first day of practice, then tried to throw the ball deep over his head. Dial passed Layne's challenge by making the catch. "The first day Buddy worked out, he had all the moves of a pro," Layne said. "You can spot these guys right away."

Layne's judgment was accurate. Dial had sticky fingers, inspiring defensive back Jimmy Hill to say, "He catches every damn thing that comes to him."

Parker traded Dial for defensive lineman Scott Appleton in 1964. Dial's career floundered and Appleton didn't help the Steelers. "It was very much of a gamble, but still he (Parker) went out to do the best for his club," Dial said.

writer to tell the world how he felt. "You can do me a favor," Hoak said to *Pittsburgh Press* writer Roy McHugh. "Put in the paper that I'm sick and tired of hearing about this speed stuff. I'm tired of this stuff about not being fast enough, not being big enough. I'm tired of hearing about it. It's bothered me for eight years."

Guys do not make it in the NFL—and start for most of a decade—if they can't run around the corner without being caught. Hoak simply did not have the look of an Olympic sprinter, but he regularly got the job done for the Steelers. They liked him so much, in fact, that after one year away from the team Hoak returned and served for 35 more years as backfield coach. He didn't have to run match races against the draft picks, only teach them what he knew. "I knew when I was a freshman in high school that I wanted to be a football coach," Hoak said.

For a little while, football experts thought that John Baker might be the second coming of Big Daddy Lipscomb, even if he did scowl more often. Unlike Lipscomb, Baker attended college, predominantly black North Carolina Central. But like Lipscomb, Baker was a huge guy, standing 6 feet 6 inches and weighing in at 300 pounds when he entered the league with the Los Angeles Rams. Baker came to the Steelers in 1963, by then trimmed down to 275 pounds. The big man played much of his best football for the Steelers and became team captain.

"On Sunday, I work," Baker said. "I'm not loafing or lollygagging around. I've got three people back home

Not an easy catch for receiver Buddy Dial as he lands on his head with Giants defender Linden Crow looking on.
George Silk/Time Life Pictures/Getty Images

"You take all those guys with their fast feet and their long strides. Give me a half-dozen guys like Hoak, guys who like to hit."
—Hard-nosed quarterback Bobby Layne, on backfield mate Dick Hoak.

depending on me, a wife and two kids to support."

Paul Martha was another new face on defense. Parker had traded away star receiver Buddy Dial to the Dallas Cowboys with visions of installing Martha as the flanker in the offense. As the No. 1 draft pick out of the University of Pittsburgh in 1964, he was a well-known local All-American. Martha was 6 feet tall and weighed 187 pounds, not very large for the pros, and was switched to the secondary.

Martha was slow to mesh with Parker and was frequently criticized by him. His mistakes were magnified and eroded his popularity for a time, especially with his slow adjustment to the pros during his rookie year. Martha had been assigned to return punts, but lost that role when he fumbled two of them, one costing Pittsburgh a game. "The whole season has been kind of a nightmare for me," Martha said. "It's the worst season I had ever since I started playing football. I've never felt as bad as I do right now."

Martha's slow start surprised Parker. "I think he's the unluckiest kid I ever saw play," Parker said. "Of course, he's had a bad year. Everyone knows that. But I still think he's a football player. If I'm wrong on him, he'll be the only one that I scouted personally that I've ever been wrong on."

Martha did spend six years starting for the Steelers and one with the Denver Broncos, but retired at age 28. Unexpectedly, after graduating from law school, Martha, who completed his schooling while still active, experienced a sports career resurrection in the NFL and in Pittsburgh. Martha became an executive with the San Francisco 49ers and then the Pittsburgh Penguins hockey team, general manager of the Pittsburgh Maulers United States Football League team, and was on the legal team mediating NFL collective bargaining contracts.

Coincidentally, another Steeler of the same era practiced law. Offensive lineman Charlie Bradshaw juggled football and lawyering simultaneously. When he graduated from Baylor University's law school after attending part-time over a four-year period, he opened his own firm in Houston.

"I could have connected with some pretty good firms," said Bradshaw in 1965, who instead kept renting his services to the football firm of Rooney, Rooney &

Rooney. "But firms all want full-time lawyers."

Bradshaw did his best for sports writers to make comparisons between slamming other large bodies at the line of scrimmage and practicing law, or maybe he just thought that way. "The trial part of it appealed to me because it's a lot like sports," Bradshaw said. "It's like an athletic contest. You have to prepare yourself."

At the least, Bradshaw could represent the Steelers in court if a frustrated fan sued for non-support due to the team's failure to win.

As if the shocking death of Big Daddy Lipscomb had not shaken the team up enough, during a 21-21 tie with the Philadelphia Eagles that began the 1963 season, linebacker John Reger almost died on Franklin Field. Reger, a 6 foot, 225 pound veteran, who had also played college ball at Pitt, collided with the Eagles' Theron Sapp on a tackle on the last play of the first quarter, hitting his head on Sapp's knee. As time ran out on the 15-minute period, Reger was knocked unconscious and went into convulsions. Trainers and team doctors rushed onto the field and realized that Reger had swallowed his tongue and could choke to death.

Medical personnel immediately recognized the emergency. One doctor ran to obtain a knife in case he had to perform an on-field tracheotomy. Steeler officials forced a scissors into Reger's mouth and pulled loose a couple of teeth. Then they reached into his mouth, opened it wide, and pulled up his tongue to restore his breathing. Doctors said Reger's face was turning blue-black. Reger was given oxygen on the field and was held overnight at a hospital for observation.

"It scared me," said Pittsburgh guard Mike Sandusky. "I talked to a couple of other guys and they said they were scared, too."

He was not the only one. Reger said, "I was dead on the field. At first I could hear people yelling, 'Get a doctor! Get an ambulance!'" Reger said he passed out and didn't wake up again until he was in the hospital. "If there wasn't any [oxygen] in the ambulance I probably would have been dead."

In addition to the immediate threat, Reger suffered a concussion and missed five games. He said he believes Parker lost faith in him, and that's why he waived him. But Reger played three more years in the NFL as a starter with the Washington Redskins.

In the early 1960s, there seemed to be some kind of unofficial competition between players, in the media or just in conversation, about who on the Steelers was a meanie. Big Daddy Lipscomb kept telling people he was not a mean guy. Ernie Stautner said the only way he made it in the pros was to try to be the meanest player around. Then, *Pittsburgh Weekly Sports*, writing about Bill "Red" Mack, a receiver out of Notre Dame who came to Pittsburgh in 1961 called him "the meanest."

Best known for his exploits with the University of Pittsburgh and the Steelers, Paul Martha (47) finished his pro career as a Denver Broncos safety. Here he breaks up a pass intended for San Diego Chargers' wide receiver Lance Alworth.
Charles Aqua Viva/NFL/Getty Images

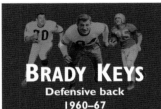

BRADY KEYS
Defensive back
1960–67

As an NFL defensive back mostly for the Steelers throughout the 1960s, Brady Keys got his fingers on a large number of enemy passes. After he retired he solicited customers by the thousands to lick their fingers in his fried chicken establishments.

Keys, a 6 foot, 185 pound All-Pro from Colorado State who beat the odds of being a 12th-round 1960 draft pick, started a business called All-Pro Chicken. Keys, also a punt and kickoff return specialist for the Steelers, is one guy who put his college degree to work beyond the football field.

In 1963, Keys averaged 15.2 yards per punt return. At various times, Keys set Steeler records with punt returns of 66, 76, and 82 yards. The irony is that Keys did not score on any of them. Twice he was caught from behind, and once he fell on his own.

Keys played nine seasons in the NFL, but after only a couple of years he was already thinking about what to do with the rest of his life. He said when he was a youngster he learned all about cooking from his mother, though he refused to do the dishes. "I'd dirty 'em up, but I wouldn't wash 'em," Keys said of his rebellious youth. "I used to get whipped for that."

When Keys started in the business he tested his spicy chicken out at a Pro Bowl party for 40. Disregarding the fact that football players will eat anything, the chicken disappeared faster than Steeler fourth-quarter leads.

They got the idea from a feature story quoting quarterback Bobby Layne, who didn't want the 5 foot 10 inch, 180 pound Mack to be overlooked in the rankings. "I mean vicious, unmanageable, consistently tough," Layne said. "I don't mean dirty. Red is a wonderful blocker and will knock guys down all day long."

Mack, whose best season catching passes (and only one in double figures) was 1963 when he nabbed 25, spent more of his time hitting people than touching the ball. Mack never had it easy. He spent time in an orphanage as a youth. He did not know what to make of Layne's praise. "If I can do everything in my power to help make a play work," Mack said. "That's the best way I know to be mean."

Mike Sandusky, a 231 pound guard who began his Steelers' tenure in 1957 and was one of the old reliables, was nearing the end of his stay in Pittsburgh, too. He overcame the rap that he was too slow and too small as sort of a Dick Hoak of the front line. Sandusky was a mainstay, a player who believed he would be wearing black and gold when the team won a title. But it didn't happen for him. Sandusky retired in 1965.

It did happen for linebacker Andy Russell, who joined the team in 1963 and stayed for 14 seasons, earning Pro Bowl mention seven times. Russell, who attended Missouri and in retirement in Pittsburgh became a merchant banker, would never have been a pro football player if parental permission slips were required as they are for high-school play. His dad frowned on pro sports as a method of making a living. "My father made me promise not to play pro football," Russell said. "He said, 'I want a son who's serious about life.'"

Russell hung around the Steelers long enough to earn a couple of Super Bowl rings and then turned his seriousness to the world of business. Russell's father had to be content to hear Steelers' chairman Dan Rooney refer to his son as "the ultimate intellectual." Maybe Rooney was comparing Russell to Buddy Parker, not Albert Einstein, but it had to do.

In 1964, Art Rooney, who had always been regarded as a gentleman and standup guy, was accorded two special honors. In January, he was the guest of honor at the Pittsburgh Circus Saints and Sinners annual banquet. Pittsburgh sports writer Lester Biederman called Rooney "perhaps one of the greatest salesmen the City of Pittsburgh ever had," because of the way he talked about the community when he traveled. "Rooney's popularity stems from one characteristic: he levels with you. He never lies. And he

likes everybody. No man ever had more friends."

That truth extended to his players, as well. Terry Bradshaw, the Hall of Fame quarterback, and a member of the team for 13 years, said, "Art Rooney is the greatest man who ever walked."

Rooney, it turned out, was held in similar esteem by football experts. The Pro Football Hall of Fame opened in 1963 with a charter class. In 1964, Art Rooney was inducted. "I never had a player on my team I didn't like," Rooney said. "I never had a player on my team that I didn't think was a star." At the time, he had 31 years invested in the Steelers and he was viewed as the Will Rogers of the football world.

The end of Buddy Parker's coaching tenure with the Steelers came suddenly. As Dan Rooney's stature grew within the organization, his skepticism of Parker's moves also grew. Trading away all of the Steelers' top seven draft picks in 1959 irked him. Parker's constant refrain of threatening to quit if his opinion was challenged got on Rooney's nerves. And his father's.

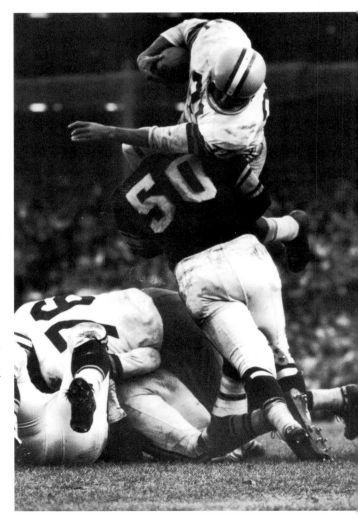

Linebacker John Reger (50) stops Green Bay's Jim Taylor as the Packer fullback tries to leap the line of scrimmage in a game at Lambeau Field. *Robert Riger/Getty Images*

Defensive back Brady Keys (26) makes a diving play to break up a pass intended for New York Giants receiver Del Shofner in the end zone during a game at New York's Yankee Stadium in November 1961.
AP Images

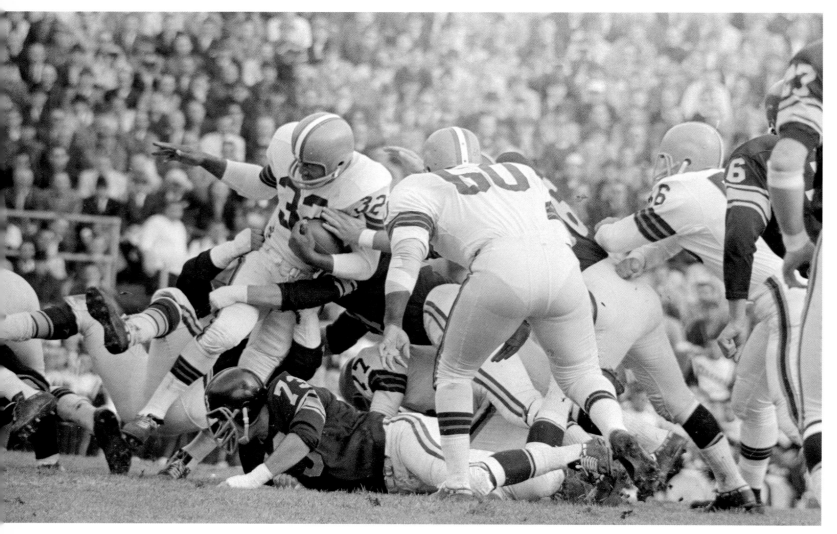

He was a hard man to stop, but here Cleveland's Jim Brown is dragged down by Steeler tackle Joe Krupa after a 1-yard run during Pittsburgh's 9–7 upset victory over the Browns in November 1963. *Bettmann/Corbis*

Right: Long-time linebacker Andy Russell (36) played through the worst and best of Steeler times. He is brought down hard by Frank Gifford of the New York Giants after intercepting a pass in this 1963 action. *Bettmann/Corbis*

Shortly before the start of the 1965 season, Parker proposed trading one of the Steelers' established defenders, Chuck Hinton or Ben McGee, for Eagles' quarterback King Hill. Art Rooney said he wouldn't do it, but told Parker, "Go ahead and do what you think would be best for the team."

Parker did not make the trade, but when the Steelers lost an exhibition game to the Colts, he suggested a different trade. Strangely, in his autobiography, Dan Rooney said it was he who had the conversation with Parker. In newspaper accounts of the time Art Rooney said he told Parker they should sleep on it. Parker wondered if the owner was questioning his competence. According to Art Rooney, he said no, he just wanted to wait till the next day. Parker quit on the spot, as he had done many times before. Echoing his abrupt departure from the Lions in 1957, also just before the start of the season, in 1965, he said he didn't think he could handle the team anymore. Rooney replied, "I don't think so, either."

Dan Rooney wrote that he talked over Parker's resignation with his father that night and they accepted it the next morning. "He quit 20 times," Art Rooney said. "He quit 20 times and I got him back 20 times. This time I didn't get him back." Mike Nixon was promoted to run the team for the 1965 season. The opener against Green Bay was a week away.

As this inner turmoil played out in the Steelers' offices, and another half-decade passed without any trophies to put on display, many other important football developments occurred.

In October of 1959, Art Rooney's long-time friend and former co-owner Bert Bell had died at 66. NFL Owners were ill-prepared to choose a successor as commissioner of the NFL, as there had been no reason to think Bell would not be in place for some time. The owners met at the Kenilworth Hotel in Miami in January of 1960 to vote for a replacement.

Art and Dan Rooney represented the Steelers. Neither of the early candidates could win a majority. The balloting went on and on. New names were put forth. At one point, it was suggested that Art Rooney become commissioner. "I'm not running for commissioner," he said. "Do you think I was born yesterday?"

Eventually, Pete Rozelle, at the time the general manager of the Rams, was chosen. On November 22, 1963, President John F. Kennedy was assassinated. It was a Friday and the NFL had a full schedule of games on tap for Sunday. Rozelle consulted with various NFL figures and after he said he got a blessing from JFK's press secretary Pierre Salinger that the president would have wanted the games to go on. Dan Rooney said when Rozelle told him, he was disappointed. "OK, Pete," Rooney said, "I disagree, but I'll support you." Rozelle had a remarkably fruitful run as commissioner, but admitted later that playing NFL games that weekend was a mistake.

Behind the scenes, the Rooneys were heavily involved in merger discussions to unify the older NFL teams and the American Football League, from 1960. The talks were difficult, but in the final breakthrough it took the Rooneys and the Steelers to make the merger reality. Against their personal inclinations, the Rooneys agreed to accept a $3 million payment to move the Steelers across the boundary into the newly

created AFC. The carrot that wooed them was an agreement to place the Steelers and their closest physically located opponents, the Cleveland Browns and Cincinnati Bengals, in the same division.

The Mike Nixon coaching experience turned out to be not so different in end results from the Richard Nixon presidency. The Steelers of 1965 collapsed to a 2–12 record. Nixon was succeeded by Bill Austin, but he couldn't cobble together a winning record in three tries, bottoming out at 2–11–1 in 1968.

Stars in the making were rare. Roy Jefferson was picked in the second round of the 1965 draft out of Utah. It took a few years, but he started to make a mark as a playmaker in 1968 with 58 catches and a league-leading 1,074 yards. He caught 67 passes the next year. "It's hard to believe that anyone has the moves of Jefferson," said Steeler rookie receiver J.R. Wilburn at training camp in 1966. "He seems to get into the open on his second step off the scrimmage line."

Jefferson was not as vociferous about the way he made magic in the open field. "I don't have speed like Bob Hayes or Homer Jones," Jefferson said. "I'm pretty sure I don't have the moves of Paul Warfield or the size of Gary Collins, but I manage to get the job done." But a schism grew between Jefferson and the Steelers and

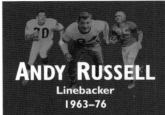

ANDY RUSSELL
Linebacker
1963–76

No Steeler player deserved a Super Bowl ring more than linebacker Andy Russell. He had to put up with a lot of losing and frustration before being rewarded. Russell was the longest lasting holdover from the 1960s when the Steelers put decades of failure behind them and began winning.

Russell, who attended Missouri, was a 16th-round draft choice in 1963. He seemed unlikely to make it out of training camp, yet became an instant regular. The 6 foot 2 inch, 225 pound Russell played in 168 consecutive games, was a seven-time Pro Bowler, and stayed with the team well into the Super Bowl glory years before retiring after the 1976 season.

"I never dreamed I'd play this long," Russell said as he approached retirement, already having earned a master's degree in business and having served in the Army as a lieutenant. "Oh, I knew that one day I'd have to get serious and go to work for a living, but I kept putting it off because it's been so much fun."

It wasn't always fun in the 1960s, but Russell made things a little bit more enjoyable for Pittsburgh fans. He had been a fullback in college, but adapted quickly to the role of pro linebacker to earn a spot on the NFL all-rookie team. Named team captain at 26, Russell held the rank for ten years.

At retirement, Russell had been a member of two Super Bowl champions. "I am very proud to be part of that amazing Steeler turnaround," he said.

Cleveland's Jim Brown steps over Steelers Bob Sherman (49) to gain 8 yards before Jim Bradshaw (24) makes the tackle.
Bettmann/Corbis

> **"This is historic. In all the years they've been playing the game, I'm the first offensive lineman who ever got booed."**
> **—Tackle Charlie Bradshaw during the 1965 season.**

soon he was trying to fit in as a Washington Redskin.

Although the flirtation with Jefferson didn't last long, a long love affair began with another player in 1968 that was unexpected, but became enduring. The Steelers made a running back out of Notre Dame their 16th-round draft pick. Few thought Rocky Bleier would make the final roster. He did make the cut, though he did not play much. After his rookie season, however, Bleier was drafted again, this time by the U.S. Army, and sent to Vietnam. The war was cruel to Bleier. On a mission in a swamp, Bleier was wounded first by a bullet through the left thigh and then by a grenade that blew off part of his right foot and spread shrapnel throughout his body. "I was afraid that I would be killed," Bleier said, "that I wouldn't make it back. Actually, I tried not to think about anything at all. But it was there—the fear—in the back of my mind."

Bleier was barely rescued and it took long rehabilitation and training work, and the generosity of the Rooneys in keeping him on injured reserve with a paycheck until 1974, until he became a major contributor. Despite the comeback from serious injuries and renown gained from winning medals at war, Bleier said the jitters of playing a game never went away, though they represented a different type of fear. "In a way, this fear is worse," Bleier said of football pre-game. "It has a focal point. "The game. You know the game is there. In Vietnam, after a while, when nothing had happened, you could almost forget the fear was there." Bleier was feted as a hero and revered for his Steeler contributions as he overcame his setbacks and helped the Steelers enjoy a new era.

By the time Bleier retired for real, with 3,865 yards gained on the ground with a 4.2 average, 136 catches, and 48 touchdowns, the entire nation knew his story and admired him.

"He's been a prime example of inspiration to this team," Harris said.

Although it was not immediately obvious at the time, the new Steeler era began when the Rooneys embarked on their first comprehensive coaching search in more than a decade. This was a pivotal moment in franchise history. The Steelers settled on a coach who was seemingly on his way to greatness at nearby Penn State. Joe Paterno had been a long-time

Bill Nunn, the Steelers' first African-American member of the front office, provided hot tips on first-rate players competing at predominantly black colleges such as Grambling, Florida A&M, and Tuskegee Institute.
George Gojkovich/Getty Images

assistant to Rip Engle for the Nittany Lions, and took over the program in 1966. He had already produced an 11–0 Orange Bowl championship when the Rooneys made him an offer to go pro. The Steelers had posted eight winning records in their first 36 years of existence and they were so sick of losing that they were ready for experimental treatments with new medications on the market. They dared to look outside the NFL.

At the time Paterno was making roughly $20,000 a year at Penn State. The Steelers reportedly offered him a five-year contract at $70,000 a year. A couple of days into the New Year, Paterno went to bed with the intent of taking the Steelers' offer. He woke up the next morning committed to Penn State, where remarkably, he remains as head coach, 40 years on.

BILL NUNN JR.
Scout

Bill Nunn Jr. was the sports editor of the black-oriented *Pittsburgh Courier* in the 1960s and he selected an All-American football team, coach-of-the-year, and player-of-the-year from the ranks of predominantly black schools. "That was the only exposure players from the black schools got," said Nunn.

Dan Rooney read the *Courier* and realized Nunn knew a lot about players the Steelers knew nothing about. Nunn considered the Steelers cold to African-Americans and essentially ignored the team that he felt was unwelcoming to him. When Rooney reached out to him, Nunn told him he thought the Steelers would always be losers.

Rooney launched a public relations campaign and hired Nunn part-time in 1967 and full-time in 1970, making him the first African-American employed full-time in an NFL front office. New coach Chuck Noll advantage of Nunn's keen judgment in finding players, and Nunn had tremendous input in the draft selection of future Steeler stars. Nunn was the king of frequent flyer miles in the organization.

"Chuck Noll was the guy who really made me feel comfortable as far as scouting," said Nunn. Among the future Steelers first spotted by Nunn as All-Americans were Joe Gilliam, Ernie Holmes, John Stallworth, Mel Blount, and Donnie Shell.

"He gave us an edge other teams didn't have," Rooney said.

ROCKY BLEIER
HALFBACK
1968, 1971–80

Rocky Bleier beat the odds in war and peace. The former Notre Dame halfback was initially considered too small and too slow to make the Steelers' roster as a 16th-round draft choice in 1968. He made the cut, but then got drafted again by the U.S. Army and sent to Vietnam.

He emerged from the war wounded, the winner of the Purple Heart, the bronze star, and several campaign ribbons, and after great struggles, an exhibit of phenomenal will, and a comeback no one felt possible, Bleier became a key cog on the Steelers' Super Bowl teams of the 1970s. Later, he became a 1,000-yard rusher sharing the backfield with Hall of Famer Franco Harris.

Bleier, who grew up in Appleton, Wisconsin, has one of the most heroic stories in NFL annals. On August 20, 1969, Bleier, then 5 feet 11 inches and 185 pounds, was part of an Army patrol ambushed in a rice paddy and cut off from help while on a grim body retrieval assignment. He was shot in the left thigh. Then, as he and his fellow soldiers were pinned down, he was wounded again and knocked unconscious by an enemy grenade that exploded at his feet.

Bleier survived because another solider rescued him, hauling him to safety with a fireman's carry, a man whose name he never learned. Reduced to tears from the pain, Bleier learned that more than 100 pieces of shrapnel were imbedded in his body. Following long rehabilitation stints overseas and in the United States, Bleier walked with a cane. Doctors told him he might never walk again and that football was out of the question.

Lifting weights and running up to three times a day, Bleier sought to return to the Steelers, but could not make the grade. Coach Chuck Noll planned to release him, but owner Art Rooney made a deal to keep Bleier on injured reserve, pay him, and offer the hope he could fight back.

"I didn't think he'd ever play," Rooney said. "But I decided to go with him until he finally said 'enough' himself. Nobody ever overcame greater odds. Nobody can imagine the misery and pain he felt."

Bleier returned to the Steelers for the 1971 season after bulking up to 220 pounds and despite playing with one size 10½ left shoe and one size 10 that was supplemented by a steel plate. He performed only on special teams until 1974 when he began earning more starts in the backfield, and the more he played, the better he got until his retirement in 1980.

Bleier said he used to laugh at newspaper stories that called him courageous and unwavering in his comeback. "I had plenty of self-doubt," he said. "Every year I played I considered retirement."

Decorated Vietnam War hero Rocky Bleier (20) was wounded in action and had trouble bouncing back in pro football, but through hard work became a backfield star for the Steelers during their Super Bowl era.
Herbert Weitman/NFL/Getty Images

> **"When I first came up as a rookie, I said to myself, 'Jeez, this guy'll never play.'"**
> **—Hall of Fame linebacker Jack Ham, on Rocky Bleier's rejoining the Steelers after returning from Vietnam with war injuries.**

"It was an awful lot of money," Paterno said. "A fantastic offer. I'd never dreamed about making that kind of money." Then, he noted, "I started thinking about what I wanted to do. I had put some things out of whack. I haven't done the job I set out to do at Penn State."

Paterno remained at Penn State and became a legend. At the end of his career he will be either first or second on the all-time list of major college football's most successful coaches.

Once rejected, the Rooneys turned to a prominent assistant coach working as defensive coordinator for Don Shula with the Baltimore Colts. A former linebacker with the Cleveland Browns, Chuck Noll was highly respected within the fraternity, even if he didn't have tremendous name recognition. That would come later.

If anyone thought that Noll had it in his power to make an instant fix-it, he proved quickly that the laying on of hands wasn't going to be enough to upgrade the roster without numerous acquisitions and savvy draft picks. Noll signed with Pittsburgh partly because he received a five-year contract.

Noll took the reins in 1969 and the Steelers finished 1–13. To many of the groaning fans it was an example of the "same old Steelers." The Rooneys may have been concerned, but they had bet the ranch on Noll. It didn't take long for Noll to prove that his Steelers were going to be the new generation of winning Steelers.

"Hiring Chuck Noll was the best decision we ever made for the Steelers," said Dan Rooney.

PITTSBURGH STEELERS
YEAR BY YEAR

1960	5–6–1
1961	6–8
1962	9–5
1963	7–4–3
1964	5–9
1965	2–12
1966	5–8–1
1967	4–9–1
1968	2–11–1
1969	1–13

Joe Paterno nearly became the Steelers' head coach in 1969, but chose to stay with Penn State. Pittsburgh hired future Hall of Famer Chuck Noll instead.
Carl Iwasaki/Sports Illustrated/Getty Images

CHAPTER 5

1970s
SUPER AT LAST

Coach Chuck Noll and quarterback Terry Bradshaw talk strategy during a 37–0 win over the San Diego Chargers.
NFL/Getty Images

In 1969, Chuck Noll came to Pittsburgh as just another in a line of coaches with the aspiration of making the Steelers into a winner. Team management asked for hope and faith. Noll brought the hope, and the unluckiest fans in football tried to maintain faith.

Noll stayed for a remarkable 23 seasons, and when he left he was feted as a brilliant architect of football, having transformed the Steelers from the most downtrodden team in the NFL, to one of its most popular. After four decades of losing, the Steelers rejoiced in Noll, the savior who presided over triumph

**"It's better to give than to receive. It's better to hit than be hit."
—Steelers' coach Chuck Noll.**

after triumph. Once lovable losers, the Steelers were now simply loved. If it was up to Pittsburgh, Noll's visage would have been carved onto Mount Rushmore. As it was, he jetted into the Pro Football Hall of Fame at Concorde-like speed.

Of course, some of his players felt Noll was a candidate for Mount Rushmore because he was stone-faced in his dealings with them. Noll sought neither celebrity nor the trappings of glitz. He did not wear Gucci or Armani, but wore his passion for winning on the sleeve of his more pedestrian attire.

After one season under Chuck Noll, those old-line Steeler fans could not be blamed for heaving deep sighs and for feeling they might have been hoodwinked by good intentions again. Noll's first team finished 1–13, the worst in the NFL. Noll was neither fan-friendly nor media-friendly in terms of issuing quips or

telling stories. Oh no, fans felt, Same Old Steelers.

When Noll could bear the repeated talk of doom and gloom no more, he snapped. "That's the trouble with this team," he said. "It's living in the past. The press is the same way. So are the fans. Everybody's perpetuating a legend of losing." If Noll had not realized it before, he knew then that it would take hard-won results on the field to change a culture of losing.

The first sign that such a break from the past was achievable could be noted in the 1969 draft. The No. 1 pick was Joe Greene. Fans may have replied, "Joe Who?" but Noll's instincts were correct. On draft day everyone is a beautiful bride. Drafts are ultimately measured by the test of time, and Noll's first draft also gave the Steelers quarterback Terry Hanratty, runner Warren Bankston, offensive lineman Jon Kolb, and defensive lineman L.C. Greenwood.

It was more of the same with the 1970 draft. Pittsburgh took quarterback Terry Bradshaw with the No. 1 pick, receiver Ron Shanklin, and defensive back Mel Blount. The Steelers improved to 5–9.

In 1971, the Steelers drafted receiver Frank Lewis,

Joe Greene was selected by the Steelers with the fourth overall pick in the 1969 draft as a relative unknown out of the University of North Texas. The defensive end would go on to have a 13-year Hall of Fame career, all with Pittsburgh.
Focus on Sport/Getty Images

"Dwight who? That's what they call me. I've been an underdog, a dark horse, all my life."
—"Mad Dog" Dwight White, an end on Pittsburgh's "Steel Curtain" defensive front four.

linebacker Jack Ham, center Gerry Mullins, defensive end Dwight White, tight end Larry Brown, and defensive back Mike Wagner. The Steelers improved to 6–8. Noll was the polar opposite of Buddy Parker. He believed in drafting young talent and developing it.

The 1972 draft produced fullback Franco Harris, defensive lineman Steve Furness, and quarterback Joe Gilliam. Gilliam, taken in the 11th round out of Tennessee State, was trying to become the NFL's first star black quarterback. In three years Noll had turned around a franchise perpetually in the dark by flipping on some very strong floodlights. That season the Steelers won their first division title ever—39 years after the club was founded—with a 10–4 record. "I've waited and waited for this club," said owner Art Rooney. "This is the best team I've ever had."

The most visible and critical position on the field is quarterback. Winning teams must have talented throwers and men of innate leadership qualities in the role. By 1972, however, Noll had a three's-a-crowd

gathering of young, hungry players, all of whom felt they should start. Bradshaw, the cannon-armed Louisianan, seemed the best suited, but as is common with young quarterbacks he was erratic. Hanratty had the poise of a player who had seen it all at Notre Dame. Gilliam had the type of swagger some like in a quarterback, and he was so sure of his gun-slinging talent that when called upon to run the offense all he wanted to do was throw.

Players got their chances, displeased Noll, and went back to the bench.

Hanratty was from Butler, Pennsylvania, so he was a local favorite. He stood 6 feet 2 inches and weighed 205 pounds. He was a savvy player, but did not have the arm strength to match Bradshaw, aka "The Louisiana Rifle." "I knew all along from day one that Terry would be the starter," Hanratty said of his competition. "You could see the talent with Terry."

Hanratty never made waves, always quietly working hard to get better. If sportswriters were used to petulance, Hanratty displayed maturity. "You mean he's acted like an adult?" Noll said sarcastically. While he was an important backup, Hanratty never really made inroads toward capturing the No. 1 role.

Gilliam did. At 187 pounds, Gilliam looked no sturdier than a match stick, but he had a powerful arm. At times, when Noll grew impatient with Bradshaw, he let Gilliam loose in the pocket. Once, memorably, Gilliam completed 31 passes for 348 yards in one

After solidifying his role as the team's regular starting quarterback, Terry Bradshaw led the Steelers offense from 1970 to 1982, taking them to four Super Bowls during the decade. *James Flores /NFL Photos/Getty Images*

TERRY BRADSHAW
QUARTERBACK
1970–83

When the Steelers made quarterback Terry Bradshaw the No. 1 choice in the NFL draft in 1970, he possessed a full head of blond hair. That may be poorly remembered by fans who have watched the four-time Super Bowl champion as a leading analyst on Sunday television pre-game shows for three decades, while making jokes about being bald all of that time.

Bradshaw was a Louisiana country boy, more familiar with farm work than skyscrapers, who probably had a right arm stronger than anyone in the world except the reigning arm wrestling titlist. He had set the national high school record in the javelin, and when he fired his passes on short routes in Steeler training camp, they came in so fast the rockets bruised receivers' chests.

Despite friction with coach Chuck Noll, and being benched in quarterback controversies involving Joe Gilliam and Terry Hanratty, Bradshaw emerged at the controls in the Steelers dynasty of the 1970s, and was one of the cornerstones of an all-around team of excellence hailed in some precincts as the best ever. An alumnus of small-school Louisiana Tech, the Shreveport boy illogically and unfortunately had to live down the nasty undercurrent of commentary that he might be too dumb to be a pro quarterback.

Bradshaw grew up rural, loved fishing, and admitted his boyhood was "a Huck Finn existence." Admittedly sensitive, Bradshaw later confessed to crying when he was booed and said he was offended and embarrassed when the Dallas Cowboys' Thomas "Hollywood" Henderson said Bradshaw couldn't spell cat if he was spotted the "c" and the "a" before Super Bowl XIII. Although he was angry, Bradshaw handled the slight cleverly, saying, "I can, too." And then he spelled cat.

Whether it was on the field on his way to a Hall-of-Fame career, or off, acting in television shows, glibly telling jokes on talk shows, and appearing in such movies as *Hooper* and *Cannonball Run*, Bradshaw proved critics wrong a thousand times over. Bradshaw probably had as much fun as anyone who ever played pro football. He and another Hall of Famer turned broadcaster, Howie Long, opened some of their shows with comedy skits. Bradshaw developed a reputation as a performer who would do just about anything, including wearing a fright wig. He eventually wrote a book called *It's Only A Game*, and maintained that attitude in his football broadcast work.

Bradshaw also became a sought-after banquet speaker, mixing homespun wisdom, motivational phrases, religious beliefs, and football anecdotes together as the recipe for his talks.

Bradshaw was a Steeler for 14 seasons, threw for 27,989 yards and 212 touchdown passes, and wanted to play longer, but ruined his right elbow. He was a 1989 Hall of Fame inductee.

"The only reason I got into the Hall of Fame is because of my rings," Bradshaw said of leading the Steelers to four championships in six years. "You can't look at my statistics and say, 'Those are Hall of Fame statistics.' It's always been about the rings."

Terry Bradshaw was the cornerstone of the Steelers in the 1970s.
Focus On Sport/Getty Images

game. But "Jefferson Street Joe" always sat himself down by throwing reckless interceptions.

At no time did Gilliam feel the object of racism from the Steelers, he said, but he did take unfortunate heat from the fans when he failed. "I was getting unpleasant vibes from the fans," he said, "at games and on the streets. Came out of practice one day and somebody had smeared yellow and blue paint on my pretty, new silver Benz. Then the threatening letters started."

Quarterback Joe Gilliam loved to pass and throw deep, but he was never consistent enough to satisfy Steelers coach Chuck Noll and could not hold onto the No. 1 job. *George Gojkovich/Getty Images*

Gilliam's flamboyance carried him only so far, and eventually the New Orleans Saints picked him up for the $100 waiver price. Gilliam made mistakes and was arrested for drug possession, carrying a pistol, and going on the lam from police. "I guess I just got buzzard's luck, but I can't get down on myself," Gilliam once told a teammate.

Gilliam was out of the NFL by 1975 and battled substance abuse problems for years. He attended the Steelers' final game at Three Rivers Stadium on December 16, 2000, but then died of a heart attack December 25, saddening ex-teammates who had seen him at the reunion.

The more the Steelers won and the more the young players blended into the team, the more excited fans got. Kicker Roy Gerala played at New Mexico State and put in two years with the Houston Oilers before joining the Steelers in 1971. In 1972, Gerala amassed 119 points.

Gerala attributed his breakthrough to a strange development. He stopped taping his ankles and found his range improved by six or so yards. Ukrainian supporters started the first Steeler fan club to cheer Gerala when the good times rolled. The club was christened "Gerala's Gorillas" and one fan dressed at games in a gorilla suit. "Frenchy's Foreign Legion" fan club was created for running back John "Frenchy" Fuqua. A "Bradshaw's Brigade" was invented. Rocky Bleier's crew was "Rocky and the Flying Squirrels."

Rookie Franco Harris was blessed with the best-known fan club. A star running back from Penn State, Harris was the son of a black father and an Italian mother. To celebrate the Italian portion of Harris' heritage, fans created "Franco's Italian Army" and wore military helmets to the games.

Tony Stagno, a baker, and Al Vento, operator of a pizzeria, were the commanding officers of the Army. Stagno was a five-star general and Vento a four-star general. They led the Army at games and their gatherings dined on pepperoni, cheese, wine, and other Italian delicacies. Harris, on his way to recording six straight 100-yard games and a 1,055-yard rookie season, was worthy of the adulation.

At one point during the season, as a stunt, members of Franco's Italian Army, in full regalia, burst onto the TV set of Myron Cope, who doubled as the Steelers' color commentator, and kidnapped him while he was on the air. The next morning, on his radio show, Cope said he was blindfolded and held for $20 ransom. The Army inducted Cope into its ranks and made him a one-star general.

The 6 foot 2 inch, 230 pound back preferred to let his legs do his talking, but after an initial shyness, Harris got a kick out of the fans. "It's a fun thing," Harris said.

> **"I came to the Steelers with one idea. I wanted to prove something to myself and to other people. Up at Penn State, they said I was only so-so."**
> **—Hall of Fame fullback Franco Harris.**

Things got even funnier when members began joining the Army from outside of Pittsburgh. Signing up the incomparable crooner Frank Sinatra was a true feather in the cap.

In December, Noll moved the team to Palm Springs to prepare for a warm-weather game against the San Diego Chargers. As the Steelers were headed West, Stagno informed Cope, "Frank Sinatra lives in Palm Springs, as you may know." Cope was given the secret mission to sign up Sinatra.

Cope was eating with a Steelers' group in a fine restaurant when Sinatra, joined by baseball manager Leo Durocher and golfer Ken Venturi, showed up at the same place. Seizing the moment, Cope wrote a note on a cocktail napkin outlining the idea of inducting Sinatra into Franco's Army the next day at practice, seeing as Franco was both Italian and from New Jersey like Frank.

An amused Sinatra, who was rooting for the Steelers that year, came over to their table, said he would do it, and then sent bottles of wine to the Steelers' contingent.

The next day Noll cornered Cope and said he heard he was planning a distraction during his practice. Cope assumed correctly that Noll was a Sinatra fan, too, and at least gave him a heads up. Sinatra turned up well into practice and Cope, while thinking that Noll would kill him, stood on the sideline hissing to Harris to come on over. Harris said, "I can't do that, Myron, I'm practicing." Noll finally thumbed Harris to the sideline, saying, "Get over there, Franco!"

Stagno and Vento, who flew to California on a redeye, presided over the ceremony. They gave Sinatra a one-star general helmet, toasted him with wine, shared salami, cheese, and whatnot, and inducted him into the Army. There were kisses on both cheeks and Harris returned to practice. A couple of weeks later, before a playoff game, Sinatra sent a "Go Steelers" telegram to Harris and signed it "Colonel Francis Sinatra." Cope thought Sinatra had forgotten his own rank, but Sinatra later told a writer, "I only wanted to be a colonel, but they made me an offer I couldn't refuse."

The son of an African-American father and an Italian mother, Franco Harris sparked a new wave of fan support when he came out of Penn State. He inspired the creation of the popular "Franco's Italian Army," which even included Frank Sinatra as a member.
Ross Lewis/NFL/Getty Images

Above: Franco Harris holds up the ball from the "Immaculate Reception" following the AFC Divisional Playoff Game, a 13–7 Pittsburgh Steelers victory over the Oakland Raiders on December 23, 1972, probably the most famous play in NFL history. With 22 seconds left in the game, quarterback Terry Bradshaw threw a pass over the middle that deflected off Raider safety Jack Tatum. Harris snatched the ball out of the air and ran it in for a miraculous 60-yard touchdown.
Morris Berman/NFL/Getty Images

Right: Officials try to clear up the confusion at the end of the AFC Divisional Playoff Game on December 23, 1972, in Pittsburgh before approving Franco Harris' miraculous touchdown.
Pro Football Hall of Fame/NFL Photos/Getty Images

Howard Cosell was then the most famous and controversial sports broadcaster in the nation, and upon assuming his position in the Army, Sinatra promised, "I'm going to court-martial Howard Cosell." Cosell proved to be out of Sinatra's jurisdiction.

By the time the Steelers advanced to the playoffs in late December 1972, two things were apparent. The first was that Bradshaw was the man. The second was that Steeler fans were delirious about this new thing called winning. Popular souvenir items included three decals for $1. One read, "Dee-Fense." Another read, "Gerela's Gorrillas." The third was an Italian flag, in color, in support of Harris.

The Steelers were slated to play the Oakland Raiders on December 23 at Three Rivers Stadium. Over the previous two decades, based on proximity, the Cleveland Browns, located about 120 miles away, were the Steelers' biggest rival. During the 1970s, the Raiders assumed the role because the teams were battling for supremacy in the American Football Conference and played some nasty games. None was more controversial than this one that featured the most famous play in pro football history, "The Immaculate Reception."

At that point, the appearance of Haley's Comet was more common than a Steeler playoff game. To say that the town was revved up would be an understatement on the scale of suggesting that Hurricane Katrina brought some drizzle to New Orleans.

Pittsburgh built a 6–0 lead on two Roy Gerela field goals. Late in the fourth quarter, the Raiders, then coached by John Madden, who ultimately became more famous as a TV football color analyst, scored on a Kenny Stabler-led drive. Oakland led 7–6.

Pittsburgh took over on its own 20–yard-line with 1 minute, 10 seconds to go. Terry Bradshaw was at the helm for the hurry-up last chance. The Steelers managed one first down, but faced fourth down on their own 40 with 22 seconds left. Steelers' owner Art Rooney headed to an elevator in order to be in the locker room and offer his condolences after the final gun.

While the Chief was gloomily descending, the Steelers were, remarkably, ascending. Bradshaw took the hike, rolled right, and threw to a streaking Frenchy Fuqua in the middle of the field. The ball, Fuqua, and defender Jack "The Assassin" Tatum intersected as if they were Pittsburgh's three rivers and everything went haywire. As the men collided, the ball shot into the air. Trailing the play was Harris. The ball bounced his way. Harris bent to his shoelaces, cupped it in his open palms, tucked it away, and ran to pay-dirt for the winning touchdown.

Officials huddled. At the time, NFL rules said members of the offense could not touch the ball consecutively. It was ruled that the ball hit Tatum, not Fuqua, however, and Harris' virtually impossible play stood. The Raiders griped, but the touchdown stood.

"I'd believed all along," Harris said, "but after today, I believe in Santa Claus, too."

It was the first playoff victory in team history. And for a team on the rise, the win represented a milestone in the rebirth of the Steelers under Noll. Many thought that team fortunes turned on the miraculous result, providing confidence for the championship runs to follow. "The glory years for the Steelers were still two years ahead," Bradshaw said, "but we buried our past that day."

The triumph over the Raiders pushed the Steelers into the AFC championship game against the undefeated Miami Dolphins. Before the game, the great golfer Arnold Palmer, who owned a country club in Latrobe, Pennsylvania, where the Steelers conducted summer training camp, announced that his followers, known for years as "Arnie's Army", were merging with Franco's Army. Palmer sent Franco's Army generals a telegram reading, "I am altering my Army to join ranks with Franco's and all of your other support forces for an all-out assault on Miami."

Alas, the Steelers lost to the Dolphins, 21–17, ending that season's magic carpet ride.

As exciting and dramatic as the season had been, it was not the culmination of a process, but a way station. The Steelers were still building. Noll recognized that more roster tweaking was needed to lift Pittsburgh from contenders to champions. The brilliant 1974 draft, the best ever for one team, did the trick. The No. 1 pick was receiver Lynn Swann, a Hall of Famer. The No. 2 pick was linebacker Jack Lambert, a Hall of Famer. The No. 4 pick was John Stallworth, a Hall of Famer. And the No. 5 pick was center Mike Webster, a Hall of Famer.

From the University of Southern California, Swann stood just 6 feet tall and weighed 180 pounds. But he was elusive, a player who astounded defenders with his leaping ability and talent for hanging onto the ball. During his first few seasons, Swann also returned punts and one season led the NFL in return yardage. He caught 336 passes in his career for a team that focused on rushing and a diversified attack.

Off the field, Swann was genial and popular for his charity work in the community. After retiring he became a network sportscaster, served as the chairman of the President's Council on Physical Fitness under George W. Bush, and later mounted a campaign for governor of Pennsylvania.

Swann the player was as graceful as a swan and stood out for it in a rugged, physical sport. Announcer Curt Gowdy called Swann, "the Baryshnikov of football," comparing him to ballet star Mikhail Baryshinikov. Announcer Howard Cosell called him, "maybe the most perfect wide receiver of his time."

In some ways, Lambert, who was a 6 foot 4 inch, 220 pound destroyer from Kent State, was the opposite of Swann. If Swann was smoothness personified, it wouldn't surprise anyone to walk in on Lambert and see him lunching on glass. There were some marvelous media headlines about Lambert that suggested he was as compassionate as a hungry lion. *Football Digest* labeled him "The Darth Vader of the NFL." A *New York Times* column was topped by the phrase, "You Don't Mess With Jack Lambert."

Buffalo Bills' coach Chuck Knox noted that Lambert was the ultimate difference-maker. "When Lambert is on the field, everything tilts in his direction." Lambert had a no-mercy way of bending things his way in terms of ruining offenses' aspirations. Opposing fans despised

FATHER JOHN DUGGAN
Team Chaplain
1971–74

Given Art Rooney's favorable outlook towards anyone Catholic and Irish, it was not surprising that in the 1970s a priest from Kilkenny named Father John Duggan studying for a doctorate at Boston College became the "unofficial chaplain" of the team.

Father Duggan befriended two of Rooney's sons when they visited Ireland, and when he came to the United States, Art Rooney borrowed his services. For three years Father Duggan attended all the games. Even though he knew little about American football he became a Steelers' fan, saying a little prayer for the Steelers.

"I have a prayer plan for the season," Father Duggan said. "I offer Mass every weekend during the season that no players be injured badly and that in all games involving the Steelers the better team win. But I must tell you, I have an understanding with God that the Steelers are the better team always."

Father Duggan admitted that football at first baffled him. "I saw four exhibition games and the Steelers won them all. I didn't know much about the game. It was confusing, especially the change of teams from offense to defense and the specialty teams."

Despite his apparent direct pipeline to the heavens, Father Duggan did not take credit when, after his final season with Pittsburgh in 1974, the Steelers won their first Super Bowl. Divine intervention was hinted at. While the Rooneys might have wanted to extend his "contract," Duggan returned to Ireland that year, saying, "I have prayed out my option."

THE IMMACULATE RECEPTION

"The Immaculate Reception" is the most famous, most significant, and most controversial play in the history of the NFL. It is not only the Steeler franchise's signature play, but represents the franchise's turning point.

Chuck Noll became the Steelers' head coach in 1969. The team showed demonstrable but slow progress under Noll for three years. But in Noll's fourth season, the Steelers catapulted to the best record in team history. They finished the regular season 11-3 and qualified for the playoffs.

The clock was ticking down to the final seconds in the December 23, 1972 American Football Conference divisional playoff game with the Oakland Raiders leading 7-6, and matters appearing hopeless for Pittsburgh.

The Steelers had led 6-0 on two Roy Gerala field goals, but after the Raiders assumed command, Pittsburgh got the ball on its own 20-yard-line with 1 minute, 10 seconds to go. Five plays later, with the ball 60 yards from the Raider goal-line, Pittsburgh faced fourth down with 22 seconds remaining.

The Raider defense chased quarterback Terry Bradshaw as he scanned the horizon searching for an open receiver. He saw Frenchy Fuqua over the middle and fired. Raider defensive back Jack Tatum had good coverage. The ball, Tatum, and Fuqua reached the same spot at the same time. The football ricocheted off bodies into the air for an apparent incompletion, sealing Pittsburgh's defeat. But before the ball landed, fullback Franco Harris streaked in. Harris plucked it out of the air inches above the ground and dashed into the end zone for the winning touchdown in a 13-7 triumph that set off delirium in Three Rivers Stadium.

The shocking denouement produced vociferous protests from the Raiders. Under NFL rules, the ball had to be touched by a defender before a second offensive player could catch it. This meant that if the ball hit Fuqua, Harris' catch was illegal. If the ball had hit Tatum, Harris' catch was legal. Officials reviewed the play and ruled in Pittsburgh's favor.

Bradshaw, who was tackled, never even saw the play until watching film, and when he heard cheers, thought Fuqua caught it. "It's impossible not to believe in the power of destiny when you review the play known as 'The Immaculate Reception,'" Bradshaw said.

The play can be watched over and over again with the answer of just which team's player was hit by the pass remaining in the eye of the beholder. Over the years, Fuqua, who says he is the only one who knows, has increasingly sought to add mystery to the moment by refusing to talk about what he feels happened.

Regardless of his other football accomplishments, the catch was the defining play of Harris' career. "I saw the ball bounce away," he said, "and I said to myself, 'Oh, no.' And then I saw it coming toward me."

The "Immaculate Reception" was subsequently named by a fan that called Pittsburgh broadcaster Myron Cope's TV show and said a friend of hers issued the clever statement. "Immaculate Reception" it has been evermore.

By 1973, the Steelers were expected to be winners, but no one really knew how far they could go because they had never gone very far. The team finished 10–4 and faced the Raiders in the playoffs again. If you wanted to get anywhere in the post-season in those years, chances were that the road led through Oakland. This time the Raiders, aching for revenge after the "Immaculate Reception," won 33–14.

When the 1974 season began, Noll knew he had all of the ingredients for full-course dining. The young talent was ready to shine. Pittsburgh went 10–3–1 during the regular season, and Oakland delivered one of the defeats.

A look at the Immaculate Reception. Running back Franco Harris (32) of the Pittsburgh Steelers runs toward the football as it bounces off of running back John "French" Fuqua (33) who was hit by safety Jack Tatum (31) of the Oakland Raiders in the AFC Divisional Playoff Game on December 23, 1972 in Pittsburgh.
Pro Football Hall of Fame/NFL Photos/Getty Images

him because he hit so hard and seemed so harsh. He insisted he only played full-blast, not dirty.

"All I want to do is to be able to play football hard and aggressively, the way it is meant to be played," Lambert said. "All the stuff upsets me because I am not a dirty football player. I don't sit in front of my locker before a game thinking about getting into a fight or hurting somebody." But he also made it clear he was going to defend himself from other big hitters or cheap shots. "I will be no man's punching bag," he said.

This attitude extended to protecting teammates. In the 1976 Super Bowl game against Dallas, Gerela missed a field goal and Cowboy defender Cliff Harris gleefully patted him. Irritated by the condescending move, Lambert memorably and visibly decked Harris for the insult.

Lambert was an outdoorsman of many stripes. He fished, watched birds, collected guns, and hunted. Geese, ducks, and deer were in his sights almost as often as ball carriers. "Mostly, it's to get out in the country and get away from things," Lambert said.

Rarely has a team simultaneously employed two receivers of the stature of Swann and John Stallworth. Stallworth, larger at 6 feet 2 inches and 200 pounds, was underexposed at Alabama A&M, but caught 567 passes for 64 touchdowns in his career. A player for 14

years, Stallworth earned a master's degree and became a successful businessman after he mastered his Steeler pass routes.

Stallworth was a major contributor during the Super Bowl years, but outlasted Swan and Bradshaw to become an elder statesman with a new core of receivers. "Lynn furnished incentive for me and others," Stallworth said of the partnership. "Every time he made a great play, I felt compelled to do the same. Now we have people who are also capable of coming up with the big play and the incentive is back. Now the young guys are watching me."

Webster, the fourth star taken in the same draft, came out of the University of Wisconsin. He stood 6 feet 1 inch, weighed 255 pounds, and was the successor to Ray Mansfield, who had manned the center position since 1964. Between the 6 foot 3 inch, 250 pound Mansfield and Webster, the Steelers basically had two centers over a 24-year stretch.

Mansfield didn't give up the snap responsibilities without a battle, holding on to his job until 1976. By 1973, Mansfield knew he was on the downside of his career, but was pleased to be part of the Steeler upswing. "It feels pretty good in one way and not so good in another," he said. "When you're the old man you know it can't be too much longer and the old

Far left: Lynn Swann was the Steelers' top pick in 1974 and he remained with the team through his entire 9-year career. The three-time Pro Bowler was inducted into the Pro Football Hall of Fame in 2001.
George Gojkovich/Getty Images

Left: Linebacker Jack Lambert's toothless grin added to his intimidating presence on the football field. Another career-long Steeler and future Hall of Famer to come out of the 1974 draft, Lambert made first-team All-Pro six times.
George Gojkovich/Getty Images

Above left: Steelers Hall of Fame wide receiver John Stallworth in 1977.
NFL/Getty Images

Above right: Long after his playing days, center Mike Webster brought attention to the plight of retired NFL players in need of assistance. He died young from dementia-related problems.
George Gojkovich/Getty Images

career will be be past. But I'm proud that I've been here longer than anyone else."

Longevity in a Steelers' uniform as the team passed from the tyranny of Buddy Parker, through the administrations of Mike Nixon and Bill Austin, and under the purview of Noll, "The Emperor," certainly gave Mansfield perspective. He was part of change for the better, outlasting the bad times and staying around long enough for the good times.

"I think the first year I really noticed it was 1970," Mansfield said. "We moved into Three Rivers Stadium and the whole surroundings changed, the whole atmosphere."

If long-term Steelers fans could barely believe the turnaround in their team's fortunes in 1975, their incredulity turned to delight again the following year, when the Steelers marched to victory once more. After finishing 12–2 in the regular season, the Steelers ran the table in the playoffs again, toppling the Baltimore Colts, the good old Raiders again, and the Dallas Cowboys, 21–17, in Miami. Kings of the world, twice in a row!

The Oakland–Pittsburgh rivalry reached new heights (or possibly depths) of bitterness, though. When the 1976 season began, the Steelers did not appear to have any weaknesses. The opening game, September 12, was against the Raiders.

Raiders' defensive back George Atkinson delivered

a vicious, unprovoked knockout blow from the forearm to Lynn Swann late in the first half while the ball was elsewhere, and Swann was turned away. Swann was blasted unconscious and missed the rest of that game and two more. The officials did not see the play, so no penalty was called. Oakland won the game, 31–28.

The next day at a luncheon, a furious Noll said that Atkinson should be "kicked out of the league" and that his type of play was evidence of "a criminal element" in the NFL. The nationally televised game prodded uncounted numbers of complaint phone calls and letters to Commissioner Pete Rozelle. Rozelle reviewed the play and fined Atkinson $1,500. He wrote the player a letter saying his miscue was the most "flagrant foul" he had seen in his 16 years on the job. Rozelle also wrote to Oakland coach John Madden and to Noll noting that their rivalry was "on the verge of erupting into something approaching pure violence" and that he would not tolerate it.

But Rozelle wrote an additional letter to Noll, saying his comments violated league rules about badmouthing opposing players, and the coach was fined $1,000. In protest, Art Rooney wrote to Rozelle, saying the fine was unwarranted because Atkinson's bludgeoning was "a cowardly act." Atkinson sued Noll for $2 million, claiming he slandered him by employing the phrase "criminal element." The case went to trial

(continued on page 96)

THE STEEL CURTAIN

Many say that the selection of little-known defensive tackle Joe Greene from North Texas State with their No. 1 draft pick in 1969 is the personnel move that signaled the new era for the Pittsburgh Steelers.

Fans shook their heads and said, "Huh?" but Steelers management knew they had chosen a special player. Although Greene did not want to play for Pittsburgh because of the team's longstanding losing reputation, the 6 foot 4 inch, 275 pound defensive tackle helped reverse that image.

A huge presence, on the field and in the locker room, Greene's dominating pass rushing and tackling earned the moniker "Mean Joe." He was the first building block in a formidable defensive front foursome that came to be known as "The Steel Curtain."

The intimidating front four, so critical to the Steelers' success in winning four Super Bowls in six years, also featured Ernie "Fats" Holmes at the other defensive tackle, "Mad Dog" Dwight White at one defensive end, and L.C. Greenwood at the other. They set the defensive tone. By December 1975, in a rare tribute, the entire foursome was featured in a cover story in *Time* magazine. A sub-headline referred to the quartet as "Half a Ton of Trouble."

Members of the unit sometimes issued bizarre statements, perhaps as misdirection plays to reporters, and sometimes confounded observers with their actions.

"There's no question that I'm schizoid," said White, who played at 6 feet 4 inches and 255 pounds. "I might be three or four people. I know I can be evil."

There was no telling just what Holmes (6 feet 3 inches and 260 pounds), was going to be at any given moment. Holmes was once charged with shooting at a helicopter manned by state police officers, flirted with professional boxing, shaved the shape of an arrowhead into his hair,

bench-pressed over his head a writer who displeased him, and boasted, "I like to eat raw meat because it makes me feel like there's a wild animal inside me." In retirement, Holmes, who died in 2008, spent time in a psychiatric facility, but eventually became a children's counselor.

Greenwood, 6 feet 6 inches and 245 pounds, grew up in Mississippi, and in retirement became a business executive. He had a voice as deep as the Grand Canyon and that aided him with radio commercials. Not as flamboyant as his linemates, he was just as effective. "I was just trying to get a job done," said Greenwood, who played in seven Pro Bowls.

Greene became beloved in the community. In 1979, Greene was in perhaps the most famous Coca-Cola commercial of all time. Weary and sweaty, trudging through a stadium tunnel, Greene was met by a small boy who offered him a Coke. Greene took a swig and as the youngster turned to go, the player yelled to him and tossed his game-worn jersey. The boy shouted, "Wow! Thanks, Mean Joe."

Years later, Greene revealed that it took 24 takes to get the 60-second commercial right and that he drank so much soda in-between he was burping and running to the bathroom.

Left: Steeler fans hold "The Steel Curtain" sign of defensive players Dwight White (78), Ernie Homes (63), Joe Greene (75), and L.C. Greenwood (68) during a 1974 game.
Heinz Kluetmeier /Sports Illustrated/Getty Images

Right: Three parts of the Pittsburgh Steelers Steel Curtain, defensive end Dwight White (78), defensive tackle Ernie Holmes (63), and Hall of Fame defensive tackle "Mean" Joe Greene (75) during a 1977 win over San Diego.
NFL/Getty Images

SUPER BOWL IX

In the playoffs, the Steelers buffaloed Buffalo, 32–14, in the opening round and dusted off the Raiders, 24–13, in the AFC championship game. Pittsburgh was on its way to its first Super Bowl. The last opponent looming was the Minnesota Vikings.

The Vikings, under coach Bud Grant, and with their "Purple People Eaters" front four on defense, were

"It took a long time, but we finally did it."
—Steelers owner Art Rooney, on the team's first championship 43 years after the team was founded.

one of the great teams of the time, but could not win the big one. On January 12, 1975, 42 years after the Steelers were founded they claimed their first championship, with a 16–6 victory in New Orleans.

The Steelers scored on a safety when Dwight White tackled Fran

Tarkenton in the end zone, on a 12-yard run by Franco Harris, and on a 4-yard pass from Terry Bradshaw to tight end Larry Brown.

Most considered White insane to play. He had been deathly ill during the week, diagnosed with pneumonia and pleurisy, and spent several days in the hospital. When Steeler team doctor John Best visited White in the hospital, he said, "You sonofabitch! I've waited all my life for the Steelers to be in a championship game, and maybe even win it. Don't you dare die on me now."

White tried to practice in mid-week, but when trainer Ralph Berlin saw how weak he was, he over-ruled that notion and sent him back to the hospital. On the day of the game, White called Berlin and said, "Come get me!"

White could barely eat at the pre-game meal. He had lost 18 pounds and was sapped. He virtually crawled into Steelers' locker room at Tulane Stadium. Steelers' team doctors, trainers, coaches, and teammates pleaded with him not to play. White ignored their entreaties. Dr. Best finally said to let White play because "he'll just pass out on the field and that'll be the end of the argument."

Only he didn't. White played a heroic game, the signature play being the safety. Between series he sat on the bench bundled up and shaking with fever. "He played like a guy going into a burning house after his family," said Steelers' defensive line coach George Perles.

White had a single-minded focus, just trudging through the Super Bowl against the Vikings. He knew it was a momentous occasion and refused to allow his body to let him down. "God takes care of fools and babies," he said. "And I wasn't a baby. The bottom line—it was too big a game to miss."

It was the single biggest game in franchise history. The losing Steelers were gone, banished. When the clock ticked down to 0:00, the Steelers were officially the best team in football. There had been many lows on the journey to greatness, and as he watched his Steelers whoop and shout, drench one another in champagne, and party, The Chief was a singular locker room presence.

Somewhat disbelieving that the long quest to become a champion was reality, white-haired Art Rooney congratulated his players. Linebacker Andy Russell presented him with a game ball. "This one's for The Chief," he said. Rooney's reply was heartfelt. "Thank you," he said. "I'm proud of you and I'm grateful to you. This is the biggest win of my life. I don't think I could top it even if we won again next year."

	Pittsburgh Steelers (AFC)			Minnesota Vikings (NFC)	
	16			**6**	
	1	2	3	4	Total
PIT	0	2	7	7	16
MIN	0	0	0	6	6

Left: Defensive tackle Joe Greene, linebacker Andy Russell, and defensive end Dwight White helped keep the Vikings scoreless for three quarters of the game.
Manny Rubio/NFL/Getty Images

Right: Coach Chuck Noll with wide receiver coach Lionel Taylor (left), Hall of Fame defensive tackle Joe Greene, and defensive tackle Ernie Holmes, during the closing seconds of the Steelers' Super Bowl IX victory.
Sylvia Allen/NFL/Getty Images

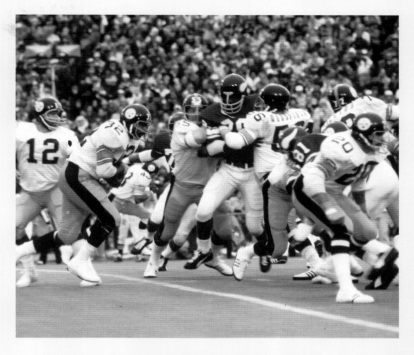

Left: Aerial view of Tulane Stadium in New Orleans, site of Pittsburgh's Super Bowl IX triumph. *NFL/Getty Images*

Top: Steeler running back Franco Harris was named the game's MVP with a Super Bowl rushing record of 158 yards.
Vernon Biever/NFL/Getty Images

Above: Terry Bradshaw scans the horizon looking for an open receiver against the Vikings. *Sylvia Allen/NFL/Getty Images*

Super Bowl X

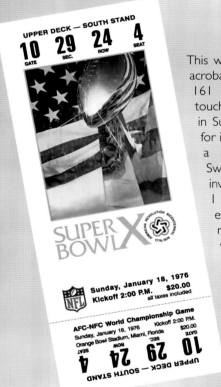

This was Lynn Swann's Super Bowl. The acrobatic receiver caught four passes for 161 yards and the game-clinching touchdown. Offense was at a premium in Super Bowl X, each yard scratched for in trench warfare. In a sense, it was a national coming-out party for Swann. "They (the Steelers) made an investment in me three years ago and I have given them more than they expected on the return of their money," he said. "I increased the value of the stock."

So did Noll. When Noll inherited the risky business of trying to make a winner out of the Steelers in 1969, the cloud cover was thick enough that no one could imagine a sunny day dawning on the hapless team. After winning two Super Bowls, Noll was earning acclaim as a genius of the gridiron. That is something he would scoff at, or ignore. Noll's idea of bright lights was turning up the high beams on his car. To him "celebrity" was a four-letter word with an extra syllable. Noll did not let either the public or the media into his mind. It became known that he enjoyed listening to classical music and cooking French food, but he cringed at the notion of being in an advertising campaign.

One thing Noll did acknowledge was that the Steelers had become champions the old-fashioned way, through diligence, by doing their homework, and with the patience needed to take their lumps. "It's like weight-lifting," Noll said of the gradual building through the draft. "You can't pick up the barbells and expect to be strong all at once. It takes time. I think we have some people who can get better and I think we have some people who played greater than anybody who has ever played this game."

The NFL realized Noll had created a monster. It might be a monster capable of pushing everyone around for a long time, too.

	Dallas Cowboys (NFC)			Pittsburgh Steelers (AFC)	
	17			**21**	

	1	2	3	4	Total
DAL	7	3	0	7	17
PIT	7	0	0	14	21

Opposite above: Ticket for Super Bowl X.
NFL/Getty Images

Opposite below: Quarterback Terry Bradshaw sprints out of the pocket trying to escape the Dallas Cowboys' rush in Super Bowl X.
Wally McNamee/Corbis

Right: The Steelers huddle on offense during Super Bowl X.
Focus on Sport/Getty Images

Below: Pittsburgh linebacker Jack Ham spies something in the Dallas offense and alerts teammates during Super Bowl X.
Vernon Biever/NFL/Getty Images

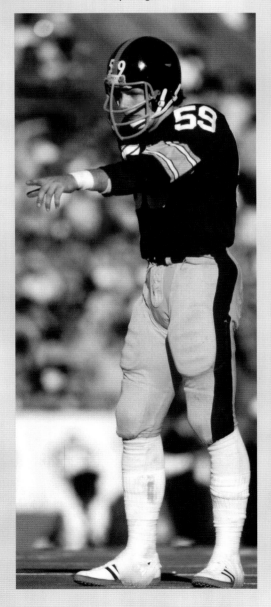

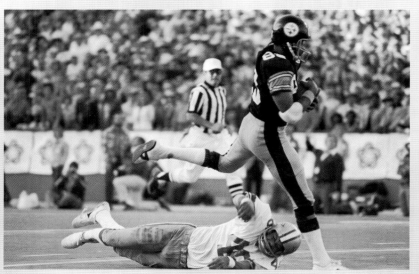

Left: Pittsburgh's Lynn Swann runs past Cowboys' Mark Washington for a fourth-quarter touchdown and the Super Bowl X win.
Bettmann/Corbis

Below: Receiver Lynn Swann hauls in a sensational catch for 53 yards. The Terry Bradshaw heave down the middle found Swann running stride for stride with Cowboys cornerback Mark Washington. Swann tipped the ball, staggered, and caught the carom falling down at the Dallas 37.
Bettmann/Corbis

Right: John Stallworth makes a tough catch with Dallas safety Cliff Harris wrapped around his waist in Super Bowl X.
Vernon Biever/NFL/Getty Images

SUPER BOWL XIII

The classic, played before more than 79,000 people in Miami, belonged to Terry Bradshaw, who threw for four touchdowns, including two to John Stallworth. Swann caught one and Rocky Bleier, who had overcome so much after suffering serious wounds in Vietnam, caught another. The Steelers built an early lead and hung on as the Roger Staubach-led Cowboys tried to snatch the win away. Instead, Pittsburgh won its third Super Bowl. Bradshaw was the MVP.

"At one time, NFL Films rated this team as the greatest in football history," Dan Rooney said. "And it's hard to dispute that claim. We had the players on both sides of the ball. We had the closeness, one of the essential ingredients in a winning team and perhaps one of the hardest to come by."

The Steelers did have everything. They had almost too many stars. In 1974, they sent eight players to the Pro Bowl. In 1976, they sent 11 players to the Pro Bowl. The Steelers were so good they were competing with themselves for all-star selections.

Above: Just toweling off. Steeler linebacker Jack Lambert catches a breather on the bench in Super Bowl XIII.
Al Messerschmidt/NFL/Getty Images

Left: Ticket for Super Bowl XIII. *NFL/Getty Images*

	Pittsburgh Steelers (AFC)	Dallas Cowboys (NFC)
	35	**31**

	1	2	3	4	Total
PIT	7	14	0	14	**35**
DAL	7	7	3	14	**31**

Inset: Steelers' then-president Dan Rooney likes what he sees during the Steelers' 35–31 victory in Super Bowl XIII.
Ross Lewis/NFL/Getty Images

Main picture: Quarterback Terry Bradshaw (12) looks to hand off during Super Bowl XIII.
Manny Rubio/NFL/Getty Images

A crowd of nearly 80,000 filled Miami's Orange Bowl for Super Bowl XIII on January 21, 1979. *Al Messerschmidt/Getty Images*

MYRON COPE
WRITER AND BROADCASTER

Myron Cope wrote for *Sports Illustrated* and other magazines before falling into broadcasting. In 1970, the motor-mouthed Cope became a radio color analyst for the Steelers and remained in the position for 35 years.

Steeler players towered over Cope, who was always explicit about his height—5 feet 4 ½ inches tall—but he was fearlessly straightforward in his pronouncements when things were going well or not.

Besides adding his voice and views to the Steeler experience for decades, Cope, who nicknamed coach Chuck Noll "The Emperor," made a notable contribution to team lore by introducing "The Terrible Towel." The orange-and-black icon became instantly identifiable as a team good-luck charm. When fans waved them, opposing players were supposed to tremble.

The Terrible Towel came into existence at the end of the 1975 season as the Steelers prepared for the playoffs. Cope's broadcast bosses ordered him to come up with a gimmick. Cope introduced the towel concept on his radio and TV shows, and then asked players what they thought. In Cope's initial tour of the locker room, linebacker Jack Ham said, "I think your idea stinks."

Too late. Cope was relieved when perhaps 30,000 fans dug out appropriately colored towels and waved them on December 27, 1975 during a game against the Colts. The phenomenon lasted, and fans can still purchase Terrible Towels from the Steelers—with proceeds going to charity.

"A piece of terrycloth will be the monument to my career," said Cope, who died at age 79 in 2008.

Myron Cope, long-time color analyst on Pittsburgh Steelers radio broadcasts and creator of the Terrible Towel (invented as a radio promotion with all proceeds to a charity), poses outside the Steeler offices at Three Rivers Stadium circa 1980.
George Gojkovich/Getty Images

"My father wanted me to accept it, but I said, 'No, this is yours, dad'."
—*Dan Rooney to Art Rooney, when the Steelers won their first Super Bowl on January 12, 1975 and were presented with the Lombardi Trophy.*

when the Steelers refused to settle—Rooney said the wrong person was being sued. After a 10-day trial, Atkinson lost the case. The incident only inflamed Steelers–Raiders feelings.

The Steelers did not make it back to a third straight Super Bowl in January, 1977. Pittsburgh finished the 1976 regular season 10–4, but lost in the second round of the playoffs to the hated Raiders. Pittsburgh went 9–5 in the 1977 regular season and lost in the first round of the playoffs to Denver, but the Steelers were back in the hunt in 1978. They rebounded and posted their finest regular-season mark of the dynasty, ending up 14–2 and crushing Denver, 33–10, and Houston, 34–5, in the early rounds of the playoffs

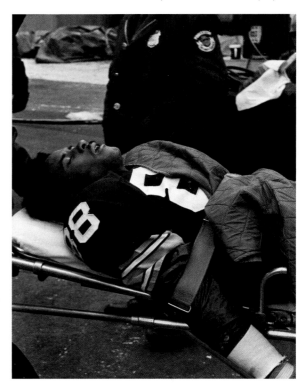

Not looking good. Injured wide receiver Lynn Swann is taken from the field on a stretcher after sustaining a concussion during the AFC Championship playoff game against the Oakland Raiders. The play infuriated Pittsburgh coach Chuck Noll. *George Gojkovich/Getty Images*

before downing the Cowboys, 35–31, in a slugfest that is considered one of the best Super Bowl games.

Defensive back Mel Blount joined the Steelers out of Southern University in 1970 and played for 14 seasons, intercepting 57 passes and being voted into the Hall of Fame. A businessman heavily involved in charity work after retirement, Blount was part of the last line of defense. He not only got his hands on the ball, he blasted receivers with hard-nosed tackles.

"A lot of cornerbacks want to be intimidators," Steeler tackle Jon Kolb said. "They go through all kinds of things to be intimidating. Mel could just walk out there, look down on the guy, and run side-by-side with him. That would be intimidating."

Coming out of a small school, Blount was not cocky, and defensive coordinator Bud Carson, the architect of Pittsburgh's outstanding unit, was a mentor. "I owe it all to Bud Carson," Blount said. "He gave me something else that nobody else on the staff ever did—he helped me believe in myself."

Penn State alumnus Jack Ham refused to be overshadowed by Lambert and also turned into a Hall of Fame linebacker, quickly learning the difference between the speed of the game at the college and professional levels. "You can make some mental errors in college and get away with it," Ham said, "but if you make any mistakes in the pros it is a long gainer or a touchdown."

Ham was 6 feet 1 inch and 225 pounds, and he had the homing instinct of radar, so he intercepted 32 passes as a linebacker. Yet Noll said he drafted Ham not because of his physical skills, but because of his intelligence. "He gets you the ball," Noll said.

Glen Edwards was not as decorated as Blount, but he was a Pro Bowler from the secondary, too. Edwards made a big-time Super Bowl hit on John Gilliam of the Vikings, causing a fumble, and kept receivers on their toes with forceful shots. "People underestimate me," Edwards said in his third year out of Florida A&M, "but I'm used to it. I've learned that the most important thing is that I believe."

Mike Wagner was primarily famous in Pittsburgh, but he also made the Pro Bowl as a defensive back. He once had a three-interception game against the Cincinnati Bengals. Wagner was such a late bloomer that he was still playing intramurals his junior year in

Always at the ready, defensive back Mel Blount was the last line of defense during his long Hall of Fame career between 1970 and 1983.
Focus on Sport/Getty Images

The Steelers defense swarms Bengals running back Pete Johnson during a game at Three Rivers Stadium.
George Gojkovich/Getty Images

Bennie Cunningham (89) helped prove to the Steelers that a tight end could be a valuable pass catcher in addition to being an important blocker.
NFL/Getty Images

high school. At Western Illinois he was briefly used as a 6 foot 2 inch, 170 pound defensive end. "I got killed," he said, "so I asked to go back to defensive back." Carson said Wagner was a self-made man. "Mike is an example of what hard work can accomplish," Carson said. "He's had to earn everything."

Several intriguing people made their living in the Steelers' secondary. J.T. Thomas, out of Florida State, played eight years with Pittsburgh. He missed the 1978 season with a blood disorder, but bounced back to play for several more years. Some used the phrase "born again" to describe Thomas because he was devoutly religious. He had plenty of time to ponder his place on Earth during the year he sat out of football. "You feel down," Thomas said. "You ask yourself, 'Why me?' But I look at it as whatever happens to me in life as a learning tree. My year sitting out, I came in touch with reality. They always say football players die two deaths, the first when they leave the game. In a sense, I've been resurrected."

In retrospect, it seems ridiculous. Donnie Shell, a Steeler for 14 years, and interceptor of 51 career passes, was not drafted by any NFL team. Pittsburgh signed him as a free-agent bargain. Shell, who played for South Carolina State, wrote his alma mater a check

for its scholarship fund as soon as he made the Steeler roster in 1974. "You know, it's not the school you go to or the size of the school that's important," Shell said. "It's what you make out of it yourself while you're there that's important."

One of the unlikeliest of keepers of the 1970s was an ex-Marine named John Banaszak, a back-up defensive end. At 6 feet 3 inches and 245 pounds, his toughness appealed to the coaching staff. Banaszak considered himself lucky to be a Steeler during his seven seasons with the team. "I'm just an average football player playing on a great football team," Banaszak said. "I wonder how an average guy like me can still be around."

Free agent Randy Grossman was another underdog who made it. The son of a butcher, Grossman is one of the few Jewish pro tight ends of all time, and one of the smallest of the last 40 years at 6 feet 1 inch and 215 pounds. His knack for pass-catching kept him around. "I've been counted out both times before I ever got to camp," Grossman said in his third year.

Hard work kept Grossman around, even after the Steelers drafted 6 foot 6 inch, 254 pound Bennie Cunningham in 1976. Cunningham caught 202 passes as a secondary receiver and primary blocker in 10 years.

Pittsburgh Steelers defensive lineman John Banaszak in 1979.
NFL/Getty Images

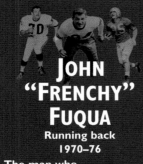

JOHN "FRENCHY" FUQUA
Running back
1970–76

The man who complemented Franco Harris and Rocky Bleier in the backfield might have suffered from an inferiority complex if he only used his given name of John. But Frenchy Fuqua had one of the catchiest nicknames in NFL history.

Fuqua, a 5 foot 11 inch runner from Morgan State, looked fine in black and gold but he preferred flashier sartorial splendor off the field. He gravitated toward much brighter colors in his ensembles, featuring capes, dashing chapeaux, and cutting-edge suits when he prowled the night life. Once, he wore a musketeer hat. Not as in Mickey Mouse, but as in the swashbuckling trio.

Fuqua was not merely a fashion plate, he was the entire buffet table. His signature item was wearing shoes with glass heels filled with water that had goldfish swimming in them. If Fuqua was a fashion consultant for an actress, she would be tabloid fodder for the rest of her life. Even Mr. GQ realized the goldfish stunt was over the top. In a later era he would have been a prime target for People for the Ethical Treatment of Animals because confined in close quarters the fish kept dying.

"There wasn't enough water," Fuqua said. "I had all type of people come up with ideas and they never worked. I had hoses in my pants. I put tubes down there. Nothing worked."

Pittsburgh was a shot and beer type of town, a blue-collar steel town, but Fuqua was embraced nonetheless, his uniqueness celebrated during the greatest winning stretch in franchise history.

"Pro football players learn to play with pain. If you can drag your sorry ass out of the grave, you play on Sunday. Even if the hearse has to drop you off on the way to your own funeral, you play on Sunday."
—*quarterback Terry Bradshaw.*

Name the position and the Steelers fielded players of note. Guards Sam Davis, Gerry Mullins, and Bruce Van Dyke were hard to move. So was tackle Jon Kolb, though as a typical offensive lineman, he was seen on film, but not heard. Kolb told the story about how his 8-year-old son disrespected him.

"He told me that Terry Bradshaw was the best player on the team," Kolb said. "I was kind of hurt, so I asked him who he thought was second best. He said Franco Harris. So I stopped. I wasn't gonna ask him who was third best. He said, 'Dad, you just don't do anything.'"

Mullins spent a couple of months as Bradshaw's road manager during one off-season when the quarterback tried to jump-start a singing career. They spent a lot of their free time drinking and fishing. Mike Webster said Mullins "could qualify as a flake." Bradshaw amended that to "free spirit." Mullins admitted that, "Football isn't my whole life. Football has always been

"He was unquestionably the player of the decade. There was no player who was more valuable to his team."
—*Linebacker Andy Russell, on Hall of Fame defensive tackle Joe Greene.*

the priority in my life, but I've just never dedicated my whole life to it."

With Franco Harris and Rocky Bleier holding down the two starting running back spots, John Fuqua could have been overshadowed. However, his nickname was

PITTSBURGH
STEELERS

1970s YEAR BY YEAR

1970	5–9
1971	6–8
1972	11–3
1973	10–4
1974	10–3–1
1975	12–2
1976	10–4
1977	9–5
1978	14–2
1979	12–4

"Frenchy" and he had a proclivity to dress as demurely as Cher. Fuqua told the world he was descended from a French count and that is why he was worthy of the nickname. He ensured he would not be overlooked, even if only because of the day he showed up for work wearing a pink lavender jump suit. Or was it the day he topped off his clothing with a cape? Or when he accessorized with white calf boots and gloves? "When I put on my count outfit I am Count Fuqua," said the running back who collected 3,031 yards on the ground. "I am not Frenchy Fuqua."

As the 1970s closed, the Steelers compiled another great season. They completed 1979 with a 12–4 record and crunched Miami, 34–14, in the first round of the playoffs. As the calendar turned to 1980, the Steelers were still alive in the post-season and on the cusp of winning a fourth Super Bowl in six years.

Chuck Noll, who had inherited the meek and conquered the Earth in ten years, was revered as an NFL god. The league faithful, who fervently hoped the Chief would one day be rewarded with a title, were now sick of the Chief winning so many titles.

Running back John "Frenchy" Fuqua (33), following blocker Jim Clack (50), was a solid ballplayer when he wasn't showing off his sartorial splendor or partying. *Diamond Images/Getty Images*

CHAPTER 6

1980s
FAREWELL TO THE CHIEF

As the calendar flipped to 1980, a new decade, it was another happy New Year in Pittsburgh. Let other American cities tune into Guy Lombardo or Dick Clark and watch the ball descend in Times Square, Pittsburgh was ready for some football.

No more bleak lonesome Januarys in Steelerland. Culminating the spillover from the 12–4 regular season of 1979, it was playoff time again. The Steelers whipped the Dolphins, 34–14, in their first-round game on December 30, 1979, and then captured the American Football Conference title by topping the Houston Oilers, 27–13, on January 6.

That meant Pittsburgh was headed back to the Super Bowl for the fourth time in six years. Once the sorriest team in the league, the Steelers were now viewed as a model franchise, admired by competitors and fans. It had been a long time coming for Art Rooney, but one of the patriarchs of the NFL was having more fun than ever in the sunset years of his life.

The victory made the club the first NFL team to win four Super Bowls. The most notable aspect of the achievement was how it had been accomplished in such a short period of time under one coach, Chuck Noll, and with the same core of brilliant players. Dan Rooney said the Steelers, from the ownership to the grounds crew, had a special closeness that provided an all-for-one intangible. "We're all in it together," Rooney said. "The management has to recruit the talent and provide the resources to win. It also has to set the tone of honesty, fairness, and integrity, because without these things, there won't be trust."

It was a grand time to be a Steelers' fan. What no

> **"Striving to be the best in every area is the secret. You never know what you can do if you keep striving. We impress that on the players."**
> **—Coach Chuck Noll, on the secret of the Steelers' success.**

one realized, amidst the wild celebration that provided the whip cream on top of the sundae following the disposal of the Rams, was that the run was over. Nothing lasts forever, and few runs in sports last as long as that of the Steelers.

A championship achieved is a mark on history. Winning again and again defies all forces of nature, sport, and business. Players age, the hunger to win dissipates, injuries intervene, and other teams catch up through wise drafting, trading, and development of their own young players. Staying at the top of the heap is a daunting challenge and in pro sports it is very much like being the best gunfighter battling for survival with everyone wanting to take a crack at No. 1.

When the Steelers topped the Rams, they recorded their second Super Bowl in a row. There were no doubts in the locker room that the same bunch of guys could do it all over again the next season. "If there's any one team that can win three in a row, we can do it," Bradshaw said.

But they could not. The 1980 Steelers finished 9–7 and missed the playoffs. If that seemed like a blip, the 1981 Steelers finished 8–8. And then the NFL began to

"I really have loved it. I enjoyed the whole trip, the whole journey. But it's come to an end."
—*"Mean" Joe Greene announcing his retirement in February, 1982.*

quiver from labor hassles. The players' union and the owners reached impasses over free agency and other critical issues. Games were lost to strikes. In 1982, the Steelers were 6–3 in an incomplete season that felt wrong from the opening kickoff.

Those aware of Steelers' history pinpointed the turnaround from losing franchise to the new gold standard to when coach Chuck Noll was hired in 1969 and he drafted Joe Greene. After the 1981 season, Greene retired. It was both a symbolic statement and a very important reality note.

Joe Greene helped change the team's image forever. Although he was as tough as players came, the secret behind his nickname "Mean Joe" was less a description of attitude than a reflection of his old college team. North Texas State was called the Mean Green. It was a fitting match.

During his 13-year career, Greene was a ten-time All-Pro defensive tackle. He announced his retirement in February 1982, at a luncheon at Three Rivers Stadium, and it was a day tinged with sadness. Greene was the heart and soul of the team and he set the tone in the locker room as well as on the field.

There were times when it appeared that Greene might shed tears, but he said he wanted his retirement to be a happy day. "What is this?" he said. "A wake? Just remember Joe as being a good football player, and not really mean." Noll rarely gushed praise, but he dug a little deeper on this occasion. "He's the best I've seen," Noll said.

Future Hall of Fame defensive tackle "Mean" Joe Greene prepares to swarm the Los Angeles Rams backfield during Super Bowl XIV.
Walter Iooss Jr./Sports Illustrated/Getty Images

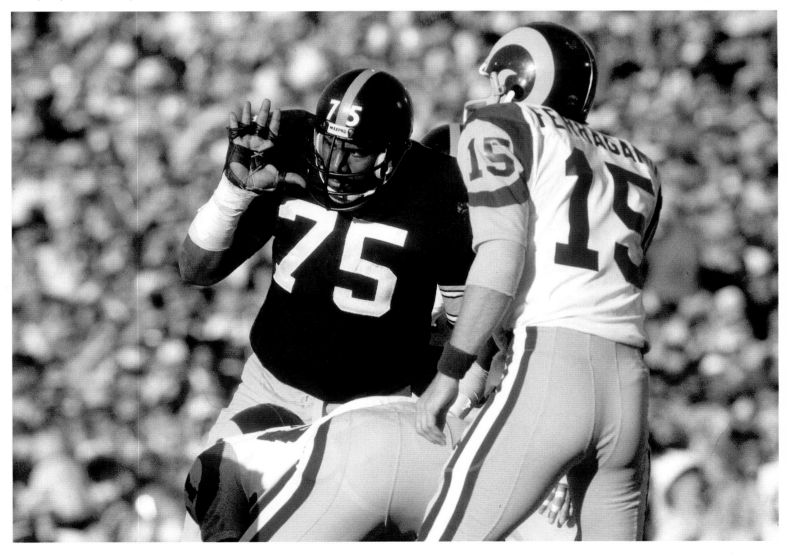

SUPER BOWL XIV

On January 20, 1980, Pittsburgh polished off the Los Angeles Rams, 31–19. At halftime, the Rams led, 13–10, and later linebacker Jack Lambert, who made a crucial, late-game interception, admitted he was worried. "I was scared," Lambert said. "They had all the momentum and our defense just wasn't playing up to par. It was just a shaky situation."

Terry Bradshaw directed the comeback. He hit Lynn Swann for a 47-yard touchdown pass and drove the Steelers to the 1-yard-line where Franco Harris plunged into the end zone.

"Beautiful catch by Swann," Bradshaw said. "He could jump like nothing you've ever seen." John Stallworth, the other Steeler wide receiver, was a huge factor in the second half and Bradshaw said he made the quarterback look good. "I looked like the hero, but the true MVP of that game was Stallworth."

Left: Ticket for Super Bowl XIV. *NFL/Getty Images*

	Pittsburgh Steelers (AFC)			Los Angeles Rams (NFC)	
	31			**19**	

	1	2	3	4	Total
PIT	3	7	7	14	31
LA	7	6	6	0	19

Below: The Pittsburgh Steeler defense did the job again against the Los Angeles Rams in Super Bowl XIV, helping provide a 31–19 victory.
Focus on Sport/Getty Images

Inset left: The Pittsburgh Steelers mascot prior to Super Bowl XIV. *Diamond Images/Getty Images*

Inset right: Pittsburgh Steelers Hall of Fame wide receivers John Stallworth (82) and Lynn Swann (88) celebrate a touchdown during Super Bowl XIV. *Manny Rubio/NFL/Getty Images*

Aerial view of the Rose Bowl in Pasadena, California during Super Bowl XIV on January 20, 1980.
Manny Rubio/NFL/Getty Images

TUNCH ILKIN

Tackle
1980–92

If Tunch Ilkin's family had stayed where he was born, there is about a one-in-a-billion chance he would have played for the Pittsburgh Steelers. There is no notable NFL presence in Istanbul, Turkey. Ilkin moved to the United States when he was two and grew into the type of specimen preferred for the favored game on this side of the ocean.

At 6 feet 3 inches and 263 pounds, tackle Ilkin attended Indiana State and was Pittsburgh's No. 6 draft selection in 1980. He represented some of the new blood coach Chuck Noll was counting on to replace aging players from the Super Bowl teams.

"There I was, a rookie, playing alongside guys who were headed to the Hall of Fame," said Ilkin, who became a Pro Bowl player later in the 1980s. Ilkin joined the Steelers at the tail end of the dynasty, and suffered through some demoralizing years when the team slumped and took some beatings reminiscent of prior decades. He said he was so embarrassed after the team was drubbed twice in a row that he asked his wife not to call him by his first, very recognizable, name in public. "When my wife and I went out to eat, I asked for a table in the back. The waiter thought I was being romantic, but I just didn't want anybody to recognize me."

Linemen are pretty anonymous, but Ilkin became more visible after he took off his helmet and began a Pittsburgh television and radio broadcasting career, sharing air time with local legend Myron Cope.

Greene retired at 35, but he did not find it difficult to explain what motivated him while playing. "There is nothing in life to compare to the Super Bowl," he said. "That's the carrot that hangs in front of you every season. That's what keeps you going through 20 games (counting exhibitions), then the playoffs."

Some Super Bowl-era players' careers spilled over into the more difficult 1980s. Bennie Cunningham, who superseded Randy Grossman at tight end, stayed with the Steelers through 1985.

Cunningham, who measured about 6 feet 6 inches and weighed 255 pounds, was the prototype model for future tight ends: bigger, stronger, and with an ability to catch passes equal to blocking techniques. "Big Bennie" was like concrete with feet. Once he got the ball, it took a crowd of defenders to tackle him. Sometimes they never did, with Cunningham shaking off a couple of hits and galloping into the end zone. "I think they're trying to do a lot of things with the tight end now," said Cunningham of how NFL teams were experimenting with the job.

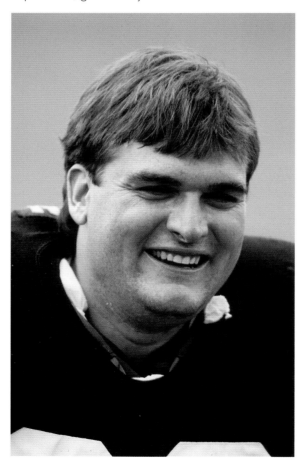

Steeler offensive lineman Tunch Ilkin (62) smiles for photographers at training camp in July 1991 in Latrobe, Pennsylvania. *George Gojkovich/Getty Images*

> **"I promised them a good week. Heck, I even brought my mother-in-law."**
> **—Terry Bradshaw, *talking about his family as he accepted the MVP award after Pittsburgh's fourth Super Bowl victory in 1980.***

For decades, the tight end was more lineman than receiver. In Cunningham's time, that was just beginning to change. But tight ends will always be asked to block and hold their own against pass rushers. "There's probably a little bit of tackle in every tight end," Cunningham said.

One of Cunningham's Steeler compadres was proof of that. Larry Brown had been an effective tight end for Pittsburgh, but got moved into the interior of the line as a tackle. He shined at both positions. Of course it took a humungous amount of calories ingested to bulk Brown up from 225 to 270 pounds.

During Noll's first years, the Steelers built themselves into a contender with savvy drafts. Some of the team's best players of the 1970s were still active and productive. Bradshaw was still running the show in the huddle. Stallworth was at the peak of his game. Harris was still available for handoffs. But the time had come to fill holes, to find new faces, to develop new stars. Yet that proved elusive.

In 1980, Mark Malone was drafted out of Arizona State as a potential quarterback of the future. Tyrone McGriff was taken out of Florida A&M with the last pick in the draft and defied the odds by making the team. In between No. 1 and No. 12, however, Steelers did not fare so well. The 1981 draft was almost a complete washout. The 1982 draft turned up running back Walter Abercrombie, but he did not turn into another Walter Payton. There were more misses than hits.

In 1983, the Steelers seemed to score big with 285 pound defensive lineman Gabe Rivera, though his selection was tinged with controversy. When Noll committed to rebuilding for a new era, he used the positive experience of going defense-first, with Joe Greene as a touchstone. However, there was one major difference involving the list of available players. By selecting Rivera, the Steelers passed on a hometown hero, Dan Marino, an All-American quarterback, from Pittsburgh, starring at the University of Pittsburgh.

The Steelers felt Terry Bradshaw would continue to play for a few years and that they had a suitable backup, Cliff Stoudt. So Marino went to the Miami Dolphins and became one of the greatest quarterbacks of all time. Pittsburgh fans have forever lamented that Marino was the one that got away.

Rivera was an All-American out of Texas Tech and when he moved right into the starting lineup, it appeared the Steelers had possibly uncovered another Joe Greene. Rivera played the first six games his rookie year and then was the focal point of one of the worst tragedies in team history.

Rivera was the driver in a head-on collision with another automobile on a rainy night after drinking some beers. He suffered a severed spinal cord and permanent paralysis that instantly ended his football career and left him relying on a wheelchair for mobility. In the hospital, Rivera said he did not recall the night of October 20 at all, never mind details of the accident. The occupant of the other car suffered minor injuries, mostly bruises. Rivera lost all feeling in his legs, had his right arm severely hurt, then caught pneumonia in the hospital. After his physical therapy, Rivera settled in Fort Worth. The Steelers, although not obligated to, paid his full salary that season.

As months passed, Rivera tried to cope with his situation and groped for a way to carve out a new life, one that might include some football coaching. "Sometimes in football," Rivera said, "you weren't motivated until that first hit, and then you'd say, 'I guess I better get going.' I guess you try to search and find it and keep it within you." As he did with many people

"Once you get to camp, all the numbers disappear. Everybody's got the same chance to be seen." —Guard Tyrone McGriff, the Steelers' No. 12 choice pick in 1980, the last player selected in the NFL draft, before making the team.

who needed assistance, Art Rooney made sure Rivera had appropriate care and covered costs that otherwise would not have been met.

The sad incident cost Rivera his career and cast a pall over the Steelers' mood, even though they finished 10–6 and qualified for the playoffs in 1983. They lost a first-round game to the Raiders by the ugly score of 38–10.

That season signaled the abrupt end of Bradshaw's career, as well, compounding the error in not choosing Marino. Bradshaw had ambitions of playing three-to-five more years, but had been experiencing arm problems and was in street clothes most of the season. He rushed his recovery and under the illusion he was fine, played in one game against the New York Jets.

Bradshaw attempted eight passes and completed five, and led the Steelers to two touchdowns.

Above: Former star defensive lineman Joe Greene (left) talks to rookie defensive lineman Gabe Rivera during training camp as Tom Beasley and John Goodman battle in 1983.
George Gojkovich/Getty Images

Left: Mark Malone (16) got his opportunities as Steeler quarterback, and had his moments in the early 1980s, but was not the long-term answer at the critical position.
Al Messerschmidt/Getty Images

GABE RIVERA

**Defensive linesman
1983**

When the Steelers made their No. I selection in the 1983 draft, some wondered if Gabe Rivera, a defensive lineman from Texas Tech, would prove to be as ingenious a pick as Joe Greene.

The powerful 285 pound player quickly earned the nickname "Senor Sack" for his Latin American heritage and knack for steamrolling quarterbacks. But Rivera's contributions were short-lived. After six games, Rivera was in a two-car, head-on collision that left him paralyzed.

Rivera, who had been drinking, received severe spinal cord and chest injuries when he was thrown through the rear window of his car after he steered across the center line of a road in Pennsylvania's Ross Township. Almost immediately, surgeons said that Rivera's football career was over and that it was doubtful he would walk again.

Rivera had the makings of a legend. His talent, combined with an outgoing personality and out-sized stories, made him a favorite in training camp. He admitted that lax eating discipline could propel him over 300 pounds and that he once ate 13 Big Macs in a sitting. When asked if he had been showing off, Rivera said, "No, not at all. I was hungry." The competitive eating circuit was not yet a glimmer in the eye of gluttons or he may have been recruited.

The injuries left Rivera in a wheelchair and he found it difficult to deal with the end of his football career. "I had everything on a silver platter," he said three years after the accident. "Now it's hard to forget about that."

Defensive tackle Gabe Rivera (69) had his career tragically cut short his rookie season when he was paralyzed in an automobile accident in 1983.
NFL/Getty Images

"My boyhood hero was Terry Bradshaw. I grew up a Steelers' fan." —*Hall of Fame quarterback Dan Marino, who went undrafted by the Steelers in 1983.*

Everyone was excited, but it was all a mirage. Unbeknownst to teammates and Noll, Bradshaw snapped a muscle in his right, throwing elbow in the game that was heralded as a comeback. He briefly hid the injury, but then had to leave the field. It was the final appearance of his 14-season NFL career.

"Deep down, I knew it was over for me," Bradshaw said later. He jogged off the field holding his arm. "No more surgery. No more shooting up the elbow with Novocain as I'd done so many times before."

Stoudt was the starting quarterback in 1983, but spent most of the season scrambling for his life. Since he was sacked a team record 53 times, Stoudt was barely living proof that the Steelers had to refurbish the offensive line. Yet great drafts seemed to be a thing of the past. The team was not only not drafting Hall of Famers in clusters, it was not even finding starters in clusters.

One wise choice was the selection of wide receiver Louis Lipps out of Southern Mississippi as the No. 1 pick in 1984. Lynn Swann retired young, aged 30, but Lipps was the right fit to replace him. Another smallish receiver, at 5 feet 10 inches and 190 pounds, Lipps was even built like Swann and had 4.4 speed in the 40-yard dash. "Louis has tremendous speed and good hands," said Steeler Mark Malone. "But what really makes a difference is that he's so dangerous after he catches the ball."

Lipps caught 45 passes as a rookie, but what truly jump-started the excitement about his potential was his eye-opening average of 19.1 yards per catch. Fans at Three Rivers Stadium soon began a "Lou...Lou...Lou!" chant. "It's really something when everyone in the stadium calls your name," he said. "It's like a cold breeze going through you. It's unreal."

Lipps was for real. He caught 59 passes his second season, inching up his average per grab to 19.2 and most importantly reeling in 12 passes for touchdowns. "When we drafted Louis we thought he had great potential with his size and quickness," Noll said. "You don't know how quickly a young player will come along, but he's advanced rapidly."

Lipps had three additional seasons with at least 50 catches and caught 359 passes in his career. That was without the benefit of Terry Bradshaw throwing to him. Part of the Steelers' ongoing adventure of the 1980s was finding a suitable new quarterback, the next reliable, long-term starter. Neither Stoudt, nor Malone,

who went on to a successful TV sports broadcasting career, was the answer.

Bubby Brister arrived on the scene in 1986, a third-round selection from Northeast Louisiana. Between Bradshaw, Lipps, who was born in New Orleans, and Brister, the Steelers seemed to have pretty good luck with players who had drawls. At one point, when Brister was throwing to Lipps, their passing game was

Still pitching. Quarterback Terry Bradshaw gets drilled near the end of his Hall of Fame career while throwing a pass against the Cleveland Browns in a 1982 game.
Dennis Collins/NFL Photos/Getty Images

111

Wide receiver Louis Lipps, a two-time Pro Bowler and the NFL's Offensive Rookie of the Year in 1984, carried on the tradition of great Steeler pass catchers.
NFL/Getty Images

Right: Bubby Brister briefly looked like Pittsburgh's quarterback of the future when he took the helm in the late 1980s.
Mitchell Layton/Getty Images

called "the Super Bayou Connection."

Brister, who was 6 feet 3 inches and 210 pounds, had been a baseball pitcher with a very strong arm. The last time Pittsburgh put its faith in a quarterback with a powerful arm who showed it in another sport was Bradshaw and that turned out pretty well. The Steelers essentially took a flyer on Brister since his track record consisted of one season leading a college team. Brister made the team, but as is the case with the majority of young quarterbacks breaking into the pros, he rode the pine for a couple of years.

The 1986 season was one of the Steelers' most frustrating in years. En route to a 6–10 finish, the Steelers lost their first three games of the season. The scores were ugly, too, a 30–0 loss to the Seattle Seahawks, a 21–10 loss to the Denver Broncos, and a 31–7 loss to the Minnesota Vikings. "You can't get any worse than we are right now," said running back Walter Abercrombie.

An Associated Press story at that point in the season offering a state-of-the-Steelers report said,

"Now the joke is that the Terrible Towels have been replaced by a terrible team."

The Steelers had not looked so clumsy on the field since the 1969 season, Noll's first, when they finished 1–13. Noll did not like what he was seeing in 1986. "The conclusion is that we've got to improve as a football team in all areas or the prospects for a single victory might be in trouble," Noll said. It was difficult to remember a time when Noll might have issued such a bleak proclamation.

In 1988, Brister proclaimed his readiness to start in training camp. "I'm the No. 1 quarterback," he said. "I'm the best quarterback here and I've earned a chance for the job. That's all I want, a chance." That turned out to be Brister's best year for the Steelers, with him throwing for more than 2,700 yards and 20 touchdowns.

But the 1980s were not a showcase for the team. The "Same Old Steelers" phrase had disappeared with the accomplishments of the 1970s, but not even Noll could keep the magic alive. He presided over two losing seasons in a row in 1985 and 1986. There was more labor unrest in 1987 when a game was lost to a strike, and the Steelers finished 8–7 before another losing campaign in 1988, this time 5–11.

Even before the first kickoff in 1988, gloom surrounded the Steelers. Art Rooney, who had founded the club in 1933, died at age 87 after a stroke during training camp in August, ending his 55-year tenure as owner. Although the club remained in Rooney hands, with Dan in charge, The Chief's absence from the premises, at the practice field and in the office, was depressing.

The white-maned Rooney, the ever-present cigar in his mouth or hand, always had a kind word for everyone connected with the team, from the lowest ranked player to the biggest star, from the field workers to the secretaries. He had always applied the common touch to his ownership, never forgetting his own roots growing up over a saloon, nor his hardscrabble pastimes of boxing and playing the horses.

Rooney supervised the Steelers for 39 years before the team won so much as a division championship in 1972. His faith paid off with four Super Bowl titles in six years near the end of his life and no one enjoyed the transformation of his team's image more. In 1975, at the age of 73, Rooney was chosen the NFL's Executive of the Year for the 1974 season. It was a just reward for 40-plus years worth of work. First prize was a flashy watch.

"Ho, ho, ho," Rooney said in response to his selection, sounding much like Santa Claus. "I'm glad to get that wrist watch. The only thing is that it's a little out of my class. I'm anything but an executive."

Thousands of Pittsburgh citizens, dignitaries, football players, and NFL officials lined up to say goodbye to Rooney at a St. Peter's Roman Catholic Church visitation and his funeral. The governor and lieutenant of Pennsylvania came. So did the mayor of Pittsburgh. So did former players like L.C. Greenwood, Roy Gerela, Franco Harris, Tom Keating, and Mel Blount.

Police estimated that more than 5,000 people attended the visitation during the day before Rooney's funeral and the service itself attracted about 2,000 people. "He was the common folks' man," said Dan Edwards, the Steelers' director of public relations at the time. "He was never too big for anyone."

Rooney did not seek publicity for his willingness to help those in the Steeler family or elsewhere, but over time the stories got out. Sometimes he reached in his pocket to pay bills for someone in distress. Sometimes he just visited a player in the hospital. "He will be remembered by all he touched for his innate warmth, gentleness, compassion, and charity," said then-NFL commissioner Pete Rozelle.

The Steelers were wrapping up their annual training

The Pittsburgh Steelers family. Dan Rooney, Art Rooney, coach Chuck Noll (each was elected the Pro Football Hall of Fame), and Art Rooney, Jr., pose with the Steelers' four Lombardi trophies in 1980.
NFL/Getty Images

Cornerback Dwayne Woodruff, a Steeler from 1979 to 1990, watches play during an NFL game.
George Gojkovich/Getty Images

"It's been a very good 12 years."
—Dwayne Woodruff, the last member of the Steelers' four Super Bowl champs, upon retirement in 1990.

camp stay at St. Vincent College in Latrobe, packing on their final day, when word reached them that Rooney had died. A pall descended on the complex. Some Steelers, such as Joe Greene, then an assistant coach, shed tears and couldn't even talk about it.

"He **was** the Steelers," said All-Pro center Mike Webster. "He meant so much to pro football through the years and to the city of Pittsburgh. Obviously, it's a tremendous void. But one thing he left us with is a lot of memories."

One of the most solid players on the club throughout the 1980s was defensive back Dwayne Woodruff. The 5 foot 11 inch, 198 pound Woodruff played college ball at Louisville—a school that retired his number—and joined the Steelers in 1979. He was good for about four interceptions a year throughout the tough times and stayed with the team for his entire NFL career, ending in 1990. Woodruff intercepted 37 passes in all.

"The thing I remember best about playing," Woodruff said later, "is just the guys. Obviously, the Super Bowl was a beautiful thing, going through that and seeing how the town got all excited and got behind the Steelers." Woodruff stayed in the Pittsburgh area and in 2005 was elected as an Allegheny County Common Pleas Court Judge specializing in juvenile matters. "I'm now in a position to continue to work with kids and to help kids."

Merrill Hoge was a 10th-round draft pick out of Idaho State in 1987. In the past, he would have represented the Steelers, demonstrating that they were just smarter than anyone else. But with the paucity of reliable picks in the 1980s their good fortune in choosing so useful a player so far down the list came off as more of a fluke.

Hoge, however, was definitely a keeper. At 6 feet 2 inches and 225 pounds, Hoge had the makings of a fullback, but could play either spot in the backfield. He was sturdy and tough and in 1988, his second season, he rushed for 705 yards. Hoge turned in four seasons with rushing totals of at least 600 yards and was also a top receiver. Coming out of the backfield he caught as many as 50 passes in a season. The popular Hoge was also twice named the Steelers' Man of the Year.

After playing out his option following seven seasons in Pittsburgh, Hoge went to the Chicago Bears. He almost immediately experienced two concussions in six weeks that ended his career. During an August 22, 1994 exhibition game against the Kansas City Chiefs, Hoge suffered a concussion. He thought he was well enough to play again, but on October 2, in a regular season game against the Buffalo Bills, he went down again. The combined effect on Hoge was scary and life-changing. When he was in the hospital, he did

"I'm at the mercy of time."
—*Running back Merrill Hoge, after suffering his second concussion in six weeks.*

Merrill Hoge, whose career was cut short by repeated concussions, runs with the ball during a game against the Denver Broncos at Mile High Stadium in 1990.
Tim de Frisco /Allsport/Getty Images

DEATH OF THE CHIEF

The Chief died happy. A devout enough Catholic to believe that his reward would come in heaven, Art Rooney lived long enough to receive a bounty of rewards on earth.

Once regarded as the most gracious of losers, even though he hated losing, Rooney's 55-year association with the Pittsburgh Steelers he founded ended in August 1988 when he died of a stroke. By then, his perpetual doormat of a team had been reinvented as perhaps the NFL's greatest club of all, champions in four Super Bowls, the toast of Pittsburgh and much of the nation, its black-and-gold uniforms popular everywhere.

Rooney had been elected to the Pro Football Hall of Fame and left the franchise in the capable hands of his sons Dan and Art Jr., and their sons, protecting the legacy of what might be Pittsburgh's most cherished institution. When he passed away at age 87, thousands attended his funeral and, symbolic of the company he kept, those who came represented the top echelons of the National Football League and its teams, ex-Steelers, the famous in public life, as well as the average Joe who recognized Rooney as one of them in spirit.

Al Davis, the living embodiment of the black and silver of the Oakland Raiders, the Steelers' fiercest rival of the 1970s title era, offered gentle testimony that the dearly departed may not have had an enemy in the world.

"He was a great man," Davis said. "He touched my family." Davis spoke of Rooney solicitousness when the Raider boss' wife was ill. "Our memories will always be great of the Steelers, but even more of Art Rooney. Great people like him never pass away. The memories will live on."

Rooney bought rights to field an NFL team in Pittsburgh for $2,500 in 1933 and sustained the team for decades out of his own pocket when the difficulties of luring spectators were at low points during the Depression and World War II. His acumen as a horse player, particularly his famed $250,000 cash-in at the race track in 1936, was the stuff of mythology and lore.

Always with a cigar jammed into his mouth, Rooney was a behind-the-scenes influence in the making of critical NFL policy, one of a group of old-line owners generous in working for the common good and not only to their own advantage.

For all of his love of his home city and his club, for decades Rooney could not provide a winner to pay off loyal fans. Year after

> **"He contributed to not only making the (NFL-AFL) merger work, but to making us feel like part of the family once we were together."**
> **—New England Patriots owner Billy Sullivan when Steelers founder Art Rooney died in 1988.**

year the Steelers finished near the bottom of the league, not winning their first division title until 1972. When the Steelers became the league's best—and maybe the best of all time—with a glowing collection of talent and four Super Bowl crowns, Rooney proved to be an equally gracious winner.

Rooney earned a reputation as a man whose word was as good as a contract and whose handshake was as binding as a government seal. He retained a human touch as just one of the boys when talking to players. He bailed out players in difficulty with cash, if that was the remedy. If they were hospitalized, he visited. There was not an arrogant bone in his body and there was not the slightest hint of snootiness in his manner. He was of the aristocracy of his city, but never forgot that he had been born into the lower class.

As an individual, Rooney was a famous ambassador for Pittsburgh, and his personal style was emblematic of the community's. Pittsburgh was a blue-collar town and Rooney was a roll-up-your-sleeves guy. The football team was his baby and it took a heap of nurturing to survive into adolescence and to ultimately perform at the level a parent would applaud for a child. Rooney lived to see it and to enjoy every minute of the grand ride of the 1970s when the team became the best.

The Steelers really were a family business. Rooney was the father not only of five sons, but of a business that employed several dozen other young men. To him, the players were more than simple hired hands—they were sons of another kind to him. If his own boys named Rooney were ball boys as youngsters and worked in the franchise's offices later, those in uniform were all special to Rooney, too. He was steeped in sentiment and once you were a Steeler, you always were, warts and all. Art Rooney was not a man to reject you because you faced some troubles. In fact, it was then he was more likely to embrace you.

"A lot of players have passed through these offices," he said once of Steeler headquarters. "And I like every one of them, even if I didn't agree with them." An attitude like that, behavior like that, translates. It set a tone for the organization and permeated the halls, the locker room, and the stadium.

"He dealt with people like no one I've ever seen," said son Dan Rooney, who became team president and then followed his father as chairman of the franchise. "He made you feel as if the most important thing he had to do was talk to you. He made you feel as if you were a friend."

The whole world was a friend to Art Rooney, who was the personification of the golden rule. Peace and harmony will not reign forever on even the friendliest of franchises, but anyone who played for the Steelers when The Chief was in charge admired his manner and thoughtfulness.

"The thing that is still amazing about that man is that he didn't care if you were Joe Greene or the guy who'd never get in the game," said Hall of Fame defensive back Mel Blount, "he treated you the same. It was contagious to all of us."

So it was no surprise how many people, and how many different kinds of people, came to pay their last respects to The Chief and speed Art into heaven.

Steeler founder Art Rooney died in 1988, but his spirit lived on with family ownership of the team and in the hearts of Pittsburgh fans. A spectator holds up a poster with a photo of Rooney at the American Football Conference championship game against the Denver Broncos in 2006.
Paul Spinelli/Getty Images 56657606

MIKE WEBSTER
CENTER
1974–88

They called him "Iron Mike" because Mike Webster never missed a game. If the Steelers were playing, so was he, even if it took a mile of adhesive tape to hold his body together.

The 6 foot 1 inch, 255 pound Webster joined the Steelers in 1974 and played with the team through the 1988 season. He was a guard at first when Ray Mansfield still held the center role, but he soon took over and it was as a center that he was elected to the Hall of Fame after a 17-year career that culminated in Kansas City in 1990. At one point, Webster had a 177-game playing streak going.

Webster was rugged and durable, became an important cog on the Super Bowl champions, and out-lasted almost all of his title-winning teammates. "There is a toughness about Webby that I like," Mansfield said. "Not a macho toughness, where you've got to strut it around, but an inner toughness. A John Wayne type."

Webster was admired for his work ethic, reliability, and strength.

"I certainly know I wasn't that athletic or fun to watch or that good of a runner," Webster said. "All I did was go to work every day and do the best I could. I think maybe there is something to be said for that."

Webster's life, however, later became a poster ad for the nightmare mix of problems former players can face. From a personal, financial, and health standpoint, Webster suffered through a downward spiral that touched Americans and the NFL's conscience.

Webster grew estranged from his wife and four children, lost his money and possessions, and ended up living on the street, or sometimes sleeping in his car. Even worse, he gradually lost his faculties and through erratic behavior alienated ex-teammates who tried to help him solve his woes. Doctors said Webster suffered from amnesia, dementia, depression, and various physical ailments from taking so many hits on the field. When Webster was elected to the Hall of Fame in 1997, his 20-minute acceptance speech was described by some as rambling and incoherent.

"I still have my championship rings," Webster announced, pointedly contradicting media reports saying that he had sold them.

Fellow lineman Craig Wolfley was especially close to Webster when they were playing and was terribly disturbed by his situation. "Mentioning Mike Webster hurts now," Wolfley said. "His problems have caused me more heartache than you can imagine. It's scary. He just looks at you now with that 1,000-yard stare. It hurts. He was my mentor. He was one of my heroes. When I was playing, I wanted to be like Mike. And that meant Mike Webster, man, not Michael Jordan."

At the end of his life, Webster was living in an apartment and being taken care of by a teenaged son. He was only 50 when he died in 2002 at a time when the public was beginning to become aware of ex-NFL players who did not live with the riches of current players and who needed assistance.

Hall of Fame center Mike Webster during Super Bowl XIII, a 35–31 victory over the Dallas Cowboys on January 21, 1979, at the Orange Bowl in Miami, Florida.
Darryl Norenberg/NFL/Getty Images

not recognize his wife and daughter. The injuries provoked retirement at age 29.

In thinking back about his Steelers career, Hoge said he treasured being taught by Noll, "one of the great coaches of our time, any time." And, "We had a playoff run there that was pretty special." Hoge went straight into a successful career as a sportscaster. In 1995, he returned to the Steelers as an analyst on their broadcasts and subsequently joined ESPN.

After the dismal mid-1980s stretch, Noll showed that he might still have rebuilding in him. The Steelers finished the decade on the upswing, with a 9–7 record in 1989. In an AFC wild-card match with the Houston Oilers the Steelers won 26–23, in overtime. It was Pittsburgh's first playoff victory since 1984.

The Steelers had trailed for most of the game, but a Hoge 2-yard touchdown run tied the contest and sent it into overtime. Then Gary Anderson, who kicked four field goals that day, booted a 50-yarder to win it. Revived, the Steelers played a fierce game against the Denver Broncos the next week in the AFC title game before losing 24–23. The Steelers were victimized by a John Elway special. The Hall of Fame quarterback led the Broncos to the game-winning score with 2 minutes, 27 seconds left.

Nearly 12 months earlier, at the beginning of 1989, Steeler management had made a bold move as an act of confidence in Chuck Noll's leadership. It was announced that Noll was granted a lifetime contract with the team. The arrangement called for Noll to coach at least one more year and then stay with the organization. It was a reward contract for all that Noll had done, and came when Noll was beleaguered by the slumping team. "He is right for the Steelers…and Pittsburgh," said Dan Rooney.

Noll said, "I always felt I would be here. I always thought security is doing the job." Then Noll went out and posted a winning mark, remarkably taking the Steelers to within one win of the Super Bowl again.

1980s PITTSBURGH STEELERS YEAR BY YEAR

1980	**9–7**
1981	**8–8**
1982	**6–3**
1983	**10–6**
1984	**9–7**
1985	**7–9**
1986	**6–10**
1987	**8–7**
1988	**5–11**
1989	**9–7**

Pittsburgh linebackers Hardy Nickerson (54) and David Little (50) and safety Carnell Lake (37) pile on Denver fullback Melvin Bratton (32) during the AFC Divisional Playoff in 1990.
MPS/NFL/Getty Images

Coach Chuck Noll of the Pittsburgh Steelers looks on during the 1989 AFC Divisional Playoff Game against the Denver Broncos at Mile High Stadium in Denver, Colorado.
Ron Vesely/Getty Images

Chuck Noll earned a lifetime's worth of respect for the way he led the Pittsburgh Steelers to fabulous heights after decades of wandering in the wilderness. But by the end of the 1980s, despite his lifetime contract from Dan Rooney, it was more difficult for The Emperor to maintain a stoical face.

Although Noll said he never paid attention, there was more and more criticism from fans on sports talk radio shows and in the media suggesting that the game had passed him by and that it was time to retire. After a 7–9 season in 1991 Noll agreed that time was up. Noll, the risky hire of 1969 that paid off so handsomely by leading the Steelers to four Super Bowl championships, stepped aside after 23 seasons.

For years after the Steelers captured their four titles in six years, providing a glitzy collection of jewelry for the winners in the way of Super Bowl rings, players such as defensive tackle Joe Greene began each season talking of winning "one for the thumb." The Steelers of the 1980s and into the early 1990s, however, could never win that fifth ring to decorate their last empty finger.

Noll believed in building a strong defense first, counting on a reliable running game, and then adding the frills of speedy wide receivers. He did not deviate from his ingrained game approaches and he could wither unwelcome questioners with a harsh stare. He admitted he was a private person (and that is why he declined commercial offers and was the only NFL coach not to host his own TV show) and not a coach who was going to deliver one-liners. "I'm not a comedian," he said, preferring to look at himself as a teacher.

"Being with Chuck for 21 years makes me proud."
—Steelers owner Dan Rooney, after coach Chuck Noll won his 200th game with the team in 1990.

Rarely did Noll admit he was wrong and rarely did he gushingly praise even the best of his players who were Hall-of-Fame bound. Yet he persevered through the longest tenure of any Steelers' coach with 209 victories. When he couldn't reach that brass ring one more time, Noll chose the moment of his retirement. "It's much easier coming in than going out," Noll said at a late December 1991 press conference. "The emotions and attachments that build up over 23 years are tough to sever."

Steelers' owner Dan Rooney said he was not surprised by Noll's decision, but that he had not lined up candidates as possible replacements. "We're not looking for a savior, (and) right now we have nobody in mind," Rooney said.

By 1993, Noll, the only coach to win four Super Bowls, had been enshrined in the Pro Football Hall of Fame. Self-effacingly, when notified of the honor, Noll said he did not deserve induction any more than the players who won the games on the field.

About three weeks after Noll retired, the Steelers introduced Bill Cowher as their new coach. Fans might well have said, "Bill Who?" because Cowher had no head coaching background. He was defensive

TRIBUTES TO THE CHIEF

To prove that team founder Art Rooney was hardly forgotten, a bronze statue of the Steelers' icon was unveiled in October 1990, two years after his death.

The statue, created by Raymond Kaskey, was placed in front of Gate 3 at Three Rivers Stadium. Rooney was sculpted sitting down. It was suggested at the time that the pose was appropriate since Rooney had not been a player throwing the ball or tackling and he was seated so visitors could "loaf" with him, using the popular Pittsburgh word for hanging out.

Pittsburgh also named a street after Rooney on the north side of the community where he lived his entire life. Duquesne University named its football field after Rooney in 1993. Also, a one-man play called *The Chief* was written about Rooney and made its debut in 2003.

A local man, John Howel, spearheaded statue fundraising, and more than 7,000 individuals contributed. There were also corporate funding events and Steeler-related contributions. On the day of the unveiling, many former players were in attendance. Former fullback Franco Harris and former linebacker Jack Lambert joined politicians in praising The Chief. "To Arthur J. Rooney, everyone he met was someone special," said Pittsburgh Mayor Sophie Masloff. "He always stopped to let you know you were important."

When Three Rivers Stadium closed and the new Heinz Field became the Steelers' home in 2001, the Rooney statue was moved to its present position, providing The Chief a new place to loaf.

A statue of Pittsburgh Steeler founding owner Art Rooney is located outside of the team's home stadium of Heinz Field, which opened in 2001. *Scott Boehm/Getty Images*

coordinator of the Kansas City Chiefs and, at 34, was the youngest coach in the league. Rooney clearly wanted to repeat the pattern that worked so well with the hiring of Noll, also an assistant coach at the time. The Rooneys did not have itchy trigger fingers. When they made a coaching hire they hoped the guy would be in the Steelers' family for a long time.

Many years later, Cowher revealed to a writer that after going through all the motions of what was expected of a new coach when introduced to the public, he had a moment of self-doubt and said to his wife, "Honey, I may have gotten myself in too deep over my head."

He hadn't. In 1992, Cowher's first season, the Steelers finished 11–5, their best regular-season mark since going 12–4 in 1979. Although Pittsburgh lost to the Buffalo Bills in the first round of the playoffs, it was an encouraging start.

Cowher proved that he could yell as loudly as Noll (and even froth at the mouth a little when berating players). He was not as funny as Robin Williams, either, but he knew how to mold a team, after years of playing in the NFL as a 6 foot 2 inch, 225 pound linebacker and as apprentice under Marty Schottenheimer with the Cleveland Browns and then the Chiefs.

Noll concluded his Pittsburgh stint with a 7–9 record in 1991. In Cowher's first year the Steelers finished 11–5. The results answered most of the basic questions and bought immediate goodwill. Rooney's gamble was a good one.

Cowher stayed with the Steelers for 15 years, took the team to the playoffs ten times, and to the Super Bowl twice, winning the championship after the 2005 season. Cowher knew how to yell, as so many

Bill Cowher became the Pittsburgh Steelers' head coach after the 23-year reign of Chuck Noll ended in 1992, and he maintained the high standards of winning Noll established. *Al Messerschmidt/Getty Images*

BILL COWHER
Coach

When Bill Cowher enters a room his chin precedes him by three steps. If ever a man's countenance lived up to the description of lantern-jawed, it is Cowher's. It suggested a look of granite in a man regarded as a disciplinary football coach who sought the respect of very large men heeding his words.

Chuck Noll retired in 1991 after 23 seasons as coach. After earlier missteps in filling its critical head coaching position, Pittsburgh struck it rich with Noll. The choice of his successor would be a sensitive, scrutinized, highly pressurized personnel decision.

The wrong choice would set the franchise back. The right choice could lead to a much-desired resurrection. Cowher was a local and he had been a player, though one whose want-to exceeded his can-do. Cowher matriculated at North Carolina State and he then scratched for an NFL job as a free-agent linebacker with the Philadelphia Eagles. He bounced between the Eagles and Cleveland Browns for five years, but became an assistant coach with the Browns in 1985.

When Cowher was hired by the Steelers, he had progressed to defensive coordinator of the Kansas City Chiefs under Marty Schottenheimer, but had no head coaching background. Cowher spent seven years working for Schottenheimer in two cities, and the older man endorsed him for the Steeler position with the caveat that no one knows if a coach is ready until he does the job.

"Cowher is an extremely bright, hard-working individual," Schottenheimer said. "He's a good teacher, very demanding. Really, the only thing that needs to happen, the only way to see how far he can go, is to do it."

Lack of experience was the first risk Dan Rooney took with hiring Cowher. The second was the fact that he was just 34 and the youngest coach in the league. If Rooney was wrong, he had left himself wide open to criticism. If Rooney was right, he had plucked a young coach on the way up at the right time, a coach who was all about winning.

"I talk high goals because I don't believe you can achieve something you don't set," Cowher said early in his tenure. "If you go in with the idea of just making the playoffs or having a winning record, when you attain that, then you feel a sense of accomplishment, and the only team in the National Football League that should feel a sense of accomplishment is the team that wins the Super Bowl."

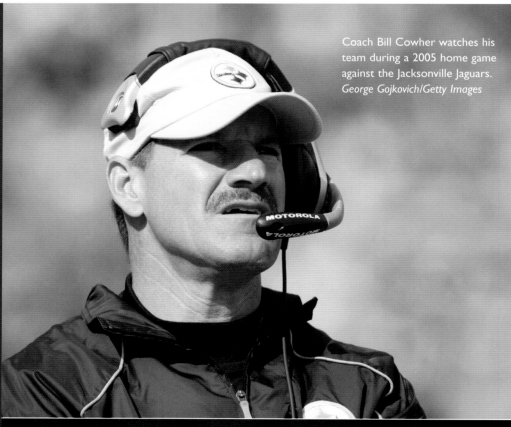

Coach Bill Cowher watches his team during a 2005 home game against the Jacksonville Jaguars.
George Gojkovich/Getty Images

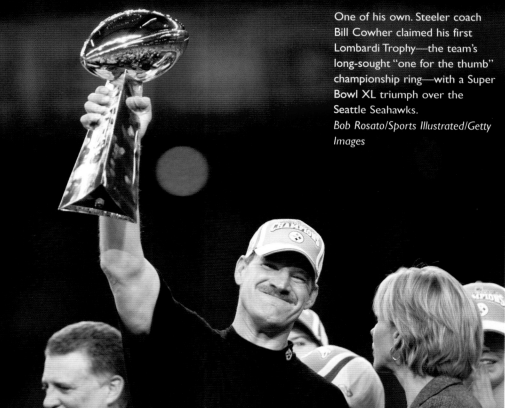

One of his own. Steeler coach Bill Cowher claimed his first Lombardi Trophy—the team's long-sought "one for the thumb" championship ring—with a Super Bowl XL triumph over the Seattle Seahawks.
Bob Rosato/Sports Illustrated/Getty Images

Above: Called "Slash" because he was a playmaker at several positions, all Kordell Stewart ever wanted to do was be a first-string quarterback.
Al Messerschmidt/Getty Images

KORDELL STEWART

Quarterback, wide receiver 1995–2002

When Kordell Stewart was taken with the No. 2 draft pick in 1995, everyone in the Steelers' organization knew they were getting a talent. The quarterback for the Colorado Buffaloes had clearly distinguished himself in college. They just didn't know what type of talent Stewart would flash.

Thus began one of the most confusing careers of any Steeler. Stewart was a quarterback by trade, but he could catch passes and run with the ball, too. He did not fit the profile of a true NFL drop-back passer, so his career became an endless series of experiments. Initially, the Steelers promoted Stewart as an all-around weapon who was unique and could hurt opposing defenses many ways. He was nicknamed "Slash," a label that implied he could make anything happen suddenly.

For a while the jack-of-all-trades could find no single one that suited him perfectly, though when Stewart became the starting quarterback in 1997, he threw for 3,020 yards and 21 touchdowns. Stewart always displayed confidence and he was explosive in that playoff year.

"He's cool, the old ice water through the veins," said lineman Jim Sweeney.

Stewart was just not always consistent, as in 1998, when he passed for 11 touchdowns and 18 interceptions. By the end of the 1999 season Stewart played nothing but wide receiver and then, defying the odds, Stewart bounced back to become the Steelers' starting quarterback again in the early 2000s.

"It's easy to give up, but it's hard to hang in there," Stewart said.

photographs illustrating his intensity showed over the years, but he proved that he knew how to coach, too.

Although the Steelers of the 1990s were not able to draft a Hall of Famer with seemingly every other pick as they had done in the 1970s, solid talent was plucked from the colleges to fortify the lineup. All-star linebacker Levon Kirkland was added in 1992, along with safety Darren Perry. In 1993, cornerback Deon Figures and linebacker Chad Brown came on board. In 1994, running back Bam Morris was a useful addition. And in 1995, tight end Mark Bruener and quarterback Kordell Stewart were the best producers.

What Cowher had to cope with that had not interfered with Noll's long-term building plans were changes in the rules governing player contracts. Players had won the right to become free agents and the eventual adoption of a salary cap made personnel planning much more challenging. Now the task of fielding a winning team could not be satisfied merely by identifying the right talent and signing the right people, but there was a need to afford and retain the right people. This musical player roster ran counter to the long-standing Steelers' policy of keeping their best and

Steeler defenders whoop it up. Linebacker Levon Kirkland (99) is congratulated by teammates Kenny Davidson (64) and Rod Woodson (26) after recovering a fumble and returning it for a touchdown in a 1993 game against the San Diego Chargers.
George Gojkovich/Getty Images

favorite players, sometimes indefinitely. It was harder to view players as members of the family if they kept saying they wanted to leave home or to get a divorce. Dan Rooney made it clear that he wanted no part of re-negotiating contracts. A deal was a deal, just as when it had been sealed with a handshake, never mind with a room full of lawyers.

In that sense, despite strong organizational backing, Cowher's task was tougher than Noll's. But the Steelers won immediately under Cowher's leadership. They were 9–7 in 1993 and 12–4 in 1994. Pittsburgh beat the Cleveland Browns, 29–9, (it was even sweeter because it was the old rival) in the first round of the playoffs, marking the club's first post-season victory since 1989. It was painful, though, when the underdog San Diego Chargers beat Pittsburgh, 17–13, to deny the Steelers a trip to the Super Bowl.

The Steelers out-gained the Chargers by a wide margin (415–226) and were threatening on the San Diego 3-yard-line as the clock ran down. With just over a minute to play, quarterback Neil O'Donnell attempted a pass to fullback Barry Foster in the end zone. The ball was batted down and the Steelers fell. When the gun sounded, the thumb was still naked.

"I'm sure everyone in our locker room is very hurt," said defensive back Carnell Lake, "and it's going to hurt for a long time."

Not as long as he might have suspected. The Steelers were back, and a year later, after an 11–5 regular season, they stomped the Buffalo Bills, 40–21, in the first round of the playoffs, out-lasted the Indianapolis Colts in a tense drama, 20–16, and did advance to the Super Bowl in Phoenix to face the Dallas Cowboys.

In the Colts game, it was the Steelers doing their best to hold on to the lead while the Colts were scratching and clawing for one last score. Indianapolis' last chance fizzled on a 29-yard pass into the end zone by quarterback Jim Harbaugh, who pretty much threw it up for grabs. Darren Perry tipped the ball, but that didn't clear it out of the way. The ball fell toward Colt receiver Aaron Bailey, who was lying on the ground, hit him in the chest, and barely squirted away. Bailey, who knew his Steelers' history, said afterwards, "It was almost another Immaculate Reception." He was right, but this one was incomplete and the Steelers won the right to play the Cowboys.

For the better part of nine years, from the moment Terry Bradshaw's right arm turned into spaghetti in 1982, the Steelers had been searching for a full-time quarterback replacement. They went along with a little bit of Cliff Stoudt, a dash of Mark Malone, some up-and-down occasions with Kordell Stewart, and some honest-to-goodness optimism with Bubby Brister, and drafted guys who didn't quite make it.

O'Donnell, a 6 foot 3 inch, 230 pound player from the University of Maryland, assumed the reins partway through the 1991 season. O'Donnell had some of his finest showings early in his career when he was still

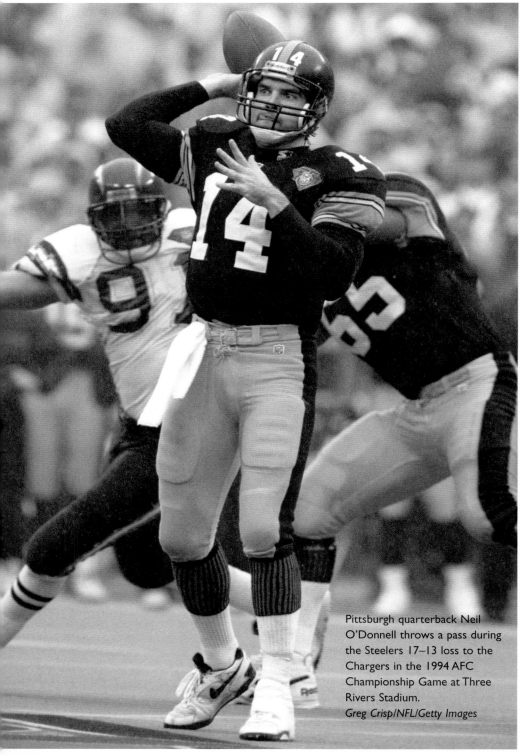

Pittsburgh quarterback Neil O'Donnell throws a pass during the Steelers 17–13 loss to the Chargers in the 1994 AFC Championship Game at Three Rivers Stadium.
Greg Crisp/NFL/Getty Images

"You can't ask for better fans than we have. Football season, people are just rockin' it like crazy. It's perfect."
—*Quarterback Kordell Stewart, on Steeler supporters.*

learning the position. He threw for 241 yards and three touchdowns in one quarter in a 1992 game against the Philadelphia Eagles, after coming off the bench at a time when his father was in the hospital undergoing brain surgery. Performances like that sent Brister to the bench and O'Donnell into the huddle.

Used to the revolving door at the position, fans apparently didn't know how to stop booing when someone played well. If O'Donnell threw an interception, members of the Three Rivers Stadium crowd called for Cowher to insert backup Mike Tomzcak.

"You pretend like you're playing a game on the road," O'Donnell said of the demanding home spectators. "You just have to tune it all out."

There were entire games O'Donnell wouldn't have minded tuning out as the Steelers tried to regroup as a contender. He was once sacked by the Cowboys nine times in a contest, including three times in a row on the Steelers' first possession of the game. He had to consider sending out an SOS to the offensive line.

There were a lot more cheers than boos during the 1995 season. When the Steelers pushed their way into the Super Bowl, O'Donnell threw for 2,970 yards (cracking 300 yards a team-record six times) and 17 touchdowns (against seven interceptions) in 12 games.

He missed four games with a broken hand. Nonetheless, teammates voted him the squad's Most Valuable Player.

It appeared that the Steelers had found a quarterback with staying power, one who was young enough at 29, to lead the team for several years. There was only one problem. After the Super Bowl, O'Donnell was no longer under contract to Pittsburgh. He was a free agent. At the end of the regular season, when the Steelers voted him MVP, O'Donnell sounded like a guy who wanted to stick around to do it all over again. He had played his best and so had the team.

As the owner of ten team records by then, O'Donnell said he could imagine being a Steeler long enough to eclipse even Bradshaw's records. "I believe so," he said. "I really do. I just think if I can stay healthy and stay right here in Pittsburgh, I guarantee I'll give you a run at almost all of his records."

Roughly eight weeks later, O'Donnell was gone, off to play for the New York Jets. The lure of a $25-million-dollar, five-year contract with a $7 million signing bonus was worth a whole lot more than the idea of displacing Bradshaw's name in selected spots in a media guide, and was a bit more than Dan Rooney budgeted to keep O'Donnell's address in Pittsburgh. The Steelers' offer was in the neighborhood of $3.5 million in a three-year deal. O'Donnell liked what the Steelers had accomplished but he still waffled.

"I gave Pittsburgh every opportunity to sign Neil O'Donnell," Neil O'Donnell said. "It was a tough decision. It really was. When you're one drive away from winning it all, you want to keep it intact."

One reason O'Donnell could entertain breaking

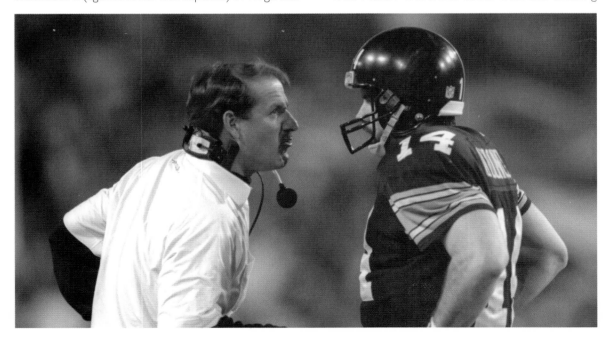

Coach Bill Cowher often yelled loud enough to get his point across to quarterbacks like Neil O'Donnell as he did during Super Bowl XXX in a 27–17 loss to the Dallas Cowboys at Sun Devil Stadium in Tempe, Arizona.
Mike Powell /Allsport/Getty Images

SUPER BOWL XXX

The Steelers and the Cowboys (self-proclaimed as "America's Team") were two of the most decorated franchises, and Pittsburgh had topped the Cowboys in two of their previous Super Bowl wins. The Super Bowl is always the most highly rated television show of the year, the sporting event with the loudest hype, and the NFL is king of the sports landscape, so the attractiveness of the match-up was a bonus.

These were the Cowboys led by coach Barry Switzer and powered by marquee players like Emmitt Smith, Troy Aikman, Michael Irvin, and Deion Sanders. Of all people, though, little-known cornerback Larry Brown won the MVP award for his two interceptions in the Cowboys' 27–17 win. Neil O'Donnell, who had emerged from the constant competition for the Steelers' quarterback job and played superbly all year, threw three interceptions and was sacked four times. Dallas was just stronger.

"It's been one great run," Cowher said. "We didn't get to the top of the mountain, but it was a great run along the way."

It was the Steelers' best finish since the 1979 team won the Super Bowl in early 1980. If Pittsburgh did not have quite the cast of legendary figures populating both sides of the ball, the defense was again considered the best in the league and the offense put points on the board.

At the line of scrimmage as the Steelers are about to hike the ball in Super Bowl XXX.
Al Messerschmidt/NFL photos/Getty Images

Pittsburgh Steelers (AFC)				Dallas Cowboys (NFC)	
17				**27**	

	1	2	3	4	Total
PIT	0	7	0	10	17
DAL	10	3	7	7	27

Above right: Yancey Thigpen doesn't need an official to tell him he has scored, after he catches a 6-yard strike from Neil O'Donnell in Super Bowl XXX.
Al Messerschmidt/NFL photos/Getty Images

Below right: Linebacker Chad Brown during Super Bowl XXX.
Peter Brouillet/NFL/Getty Images

The Pittsburgh Steelers and Dallas Cowboys get ready for the start of the second half of Super Bowl XXX.
Mike Moore/NFL/Getty Images

WHEATIES

In early 1996, it was announced that a group of Pittsburgh Steelers would adorn the outside of a special edition Wheaties box. Sports and Wheaties go together like, well, cereal flakes and milk. Being invited to appear on a box of Wheaties is as much a stamp of approval in American society as winning the Super Bowl itself.

Wheaties, made by General Mills in Minnesota, takes its motto seriously: "Wheaties: The Breakfast of Champions," and over the decades since its creation in 1922 has long favored associating with star athletes. Michael Jordan, Mary Lou Retton, decathlon champion Bob Richards, and even Lou Gehrig, appeared on the orange boxes.

Those Steelers pictured on the front of the Wheaties box were Kevin Greene, Greg Lloyd, Neil O'Donnell, Yancey Thigpen, and Bam Morris. Greene appeared a second time, on the back of the box, alongside some team history. The boxes that honored the Steelers followed the team's AFC championship victory at the end of the 1995 season. The Steelers' Wheaties boxes were not distributed nationally, however. They were sold only in Pennsylvania and in parts of Ohio.

The first tie-in with sports and Wheaties was in 1927, when the cereal makers advertised on the wall of a Minneapolis minor-league baseball park. Wheaties has become so identified with sports that its catch-line, "The Breakfast of Champions," is well established as a popular phrase in the American lexicon. By the 1990s, the Steelers certainly had a track record as champions whatever they actually ate.

Steeler running back Barry Foster on the sidelines during the AFC Divisional Playoff victory over the Cleveland Browns in 1995.

Al Messerschmidt/Getty Images

team passing records is because Cowher was a little bit more liberal with throwing frequency than Noll. Still, the square-jawed Cowher, who had grown up in the Pittsburgh area, felt running was the bread-and-butter of the offense.

Barry Foster, a 5 foot 11 inch, 223 pound battering ram, was part of the reason to adhere to that philosophy. Foster, who more resembled a fullback, had the giddy-up to return kickoffs. While Foster's rushing average was always more than four yards a carry, he was the featured workhorse back for just one full season. In 1992, he carried 390 times for 1,690 yards and 11 touchdowns. Foster recorded at least 100 yards on the ground in 12 games.

Foster had been an inside force at the University of Arkansas and was not seen as a multi-dimensional back. Yet he never lacked for confidence after assessing the competition in his first training camp.

"I didn't really worry about making the team or anything like that in camp," said the fifth-round draft pick. "I looked around and thought, 'I'm as good as the rest of the backs here.'"

An ankle injury cost Foster a large chunk of the 1993 season and then he faced a new challenge in 1994 when the Steelers drafted Byron "Bam" Morris out of Texas Tech, where he won the Doak Walker Award as the nation's best running back. Morris started the year as Foster's backup, but Foster injured his knee in mid-October. "I have all the confidence that Bam Morris will be a very solid replacement for the time frame that Barry is out," Cowher said.

Morris jumped into the lineup and accounted for more than 800 yards rushing. He topped 550 the next year, the Super Bowl season. But in the long run Morris created more problems than he solved. His woes began in earnest in March 1996 when law enforcement officials found 1.5 grams of cocaine and seven pounds of marijuana in the trunk of his car after a traffic stop.

A grand jury indicted Morris on two third-degree felony charges. Three months later, Morris pleaded guilty to a felony marijuana charge on the condition that prosecutors recommend that he receive probation rather than imprisonment. The Steelers exiled Morris barely two weeks later.

"We felt releasing Bam Morris was in the best interest of both parties," Cowher said.

Morris was fined $7,000, required to perform 200 hours of community service, and was sentenced to six years' probation. He went on to play for the Chicago Bears, Baltimore Ravens (where he served two NFL suspensions for violating the league's drug policies), and the Kansas City Chiefs. Morris was arrested again on federal drug-dealing charges and violation of parole and spent nearly three years in prison. It was the slam for Bam.

A foundation of the offense that Bill Cowher inherited from Chuck Noll was a player who didn't make either waves or headlines because he didn't carry the ball or get in trouble. Dermontti Dawson continued the tradition and lineage of terrific Steeler centers. Relying on Ray Mansfield, Mike Webster, and Dawson, who arrived in 1988 and played in Pittsburgh through the 2000 season, the Steelers essentially had no worries about who was hiking the ball for three-and-a-half decades.

Dawson's first season was Webster's last and the

Far left: Dermontti Dawson became one of the Steelers' great linemen after replacing legendary Mike Webster at center.
Rick Stewart/Allsport/Getty Images

Left: Steve Courson became a controversial figure when he revealed he took performance-enhancing drugs, then toured the country speaking about the evils of steroids to high-schoolers.
George Gojkovich/Getty Images

overlap was like obtaining a masters' degree for Dawson. "Playing with Mike was like playing with a living legend," said Dawson, who stood 6 feet 2 inches, weighed 288 pounds, and played college ball at Kentucky. "And it was great to interact with him. Usually, veterans don't like to give advice, especially to guys who play their position. Mike helped me in several ways, on and off the field."

Dawson's rookie year was Webster's final Pro Bowl year with the Steelers. Dawson received the honor seven times during his Pittsburgh career.

Cowher had enough to deal with when he was hired. He took one look at Dawson manning the middle of the offensive line and turned his attention to other issues. "He is probably one of the quickest linemen I've ever seen," Cowher said. "He allows us to do things that we otherwise couldn't do."

That is an attribute of Dawson's unusually quick feet. Ordinarily, after they hike the ball, centers require some blocking assistance from guards because they can't recover from the first action fast enough to hold off a split-second reaction from a linebacker. Dawson was quick enough to handle both tasks without help, providing the Steelers with an extra dimension to blocking. Dawson's nickname was "Dirt," because he was not afraid to get down in the dirt to fight for his position.

During the 1994 season, the soft-spoken Dawson garnered national attention when he dug down so low

"It seemed like it took forever."
—Pittsburgh defensive back Darren
"Papa Smurf" Perry, on waiting for the
ball to come down on an incomplete
Hail Mary pass that saved the AFC title
for the Steelers in January 1996.

and came up so fast that he flipped the Green Bay Packers' 350 pound Gilbert Brown on his back twice in the same game. When *Sports Illustrated* came calling to tout the accomplishments of a normally anonymous offensive lineman (about as common as a politician voting with his conscience), Dawson did not brag. "Gilbert is an excellent nose tackle," Dawson said. "Maybe he tripped."

Maybe he tripped? Twice? Right.

Dawson didn't talk a big game, but he was the Steelers' running backs' best friend.

Steve Courson was a Steelers' draft pick in 1977, at the end of the dynasty years, but didn't play until 1978, replacing Ernie Holmes in the defensive front four. He was a tenacious player, a block of concrete, who was variously listed in news reports about his exploits over time as weighing everything from 260 to 300 pounds. All of the figures might have been correct.

That's because a few years after he retired in 1985,

Courson went public with his abuse of steroids and the fact that he believed a heart condition was killing him as the result of taking the NFL-banned drugs. He had 21 inch biceps, a 58 in chest, and could bench-press more than 600 pounds. But by 1989 he had a deteriorating heart and was given two-to-five years to live by doctors unless he obtained a transplant.

Courson, who played for the Steelers Super Bowl teams in 1979 and 1980, released a tell-all book in 1991, and feeling guilty, began traveling the country to speak about the evils of performance-enhancing drugs to high school athletes at the rate of 100 schools a year. "When I took steroids, they made me moody," he said. "They make some people very aggressive. They led to alcohol abuse."

Doctors did not say specifically that steroids contributed to Courson's heart disease, but agreed it might have. "That's the crux of the whole steroids problem," said Courson. "There is so much we just don't know yet. I've gone from dominant football player to cardio invalid. I just don't know if the same chemicals helped me become both."

Courson's revelations in the book *False Glory: The Steve Courson Story* were not well-received around the league. He said he began taking steroids as an 18-year-old in South Carolina and gained an immense amount of weight, about 70 pounds, then stopped ingesting the drugs until his rookie year with the Steelers. He said he spent $1,500—characterized essentially as peanuts—to make a $300,00-a-year salary. "No athlete can be honest about their drug use without committing career suicide," Courson said. "They have to maintain the conspiracy of silence."

Courson never got the heart transplant, but non-surgical therapy advances cured him. He became a

Linebacker Levon Kirkland (99) on the sidelines watching his Steelers against the Tennessee Oilers.
Jonathan Daniel /Allsport/Getty Images

high school football coach in Western Pennsylvania and continued to speak out against steroid use, claiming the Steeler dynasty was built on them. (Team officials denied it.) In 2005, he testified before a U.S. House of Representatives committee investigating drug use in pro sports. Later that year Courson, 50, was killed in an accident when a 44-foot tree he was cutting down on his property fell on him as he moved to save his dog.

One aspect of the game that distinguished the Steelers of the 1990s, much as it had the Steelers of the 1970s, was the phenomenal defense that put the fear of God into the opposition.

Rod Woodson was one of the fastest players ever to wear black-and-gold, timed in the 40-yard dash in 4.29 seconds. He was a superlative punt and kickoff return man, but was even greater as a defensive back, winning the NFL's defensive player-of-the-year award in 1993. Woodson tackled with reckless abandon and was so quick he could close open spaces between him and the receiver in the time it took a quarterback to blink and commit his throw. Woodson's 71 career interceptions in a 17-year career rank third all-time in the NFL record book, and he was elected to the Hall of Fame early in 2009.

Woodson was a playmaker any time he got near the ball, returning it for field position, or preventing the other guys from making gains with it. As much fun as he had returning kicks, Woodson primarily got his kicks in the defensive secondary. "I'd rather be a great all-around cornerback than a good cornerback and a great specialist," he said. "I'm on the field the majority of every game as a cornerback, while I might only run back one or two kickoffs. I don't want to be remembered as a specialist. I want to be remembered as a cornerback." Woodson did not have to worry about that.

"Probably the best athlete I have ever coached," Cowher said. "The guy was an unbelievable student of the game."

Woodson had good company in the secondary with the Steelers. One of his coverage buddies was Carnell Lake. Lake was a five-time Pro Bowl player, who recorded 25 sacks to go with his 16 interceptions, recovered 17 fumbles, and scored five touchdowns on

Hall of Fame safety Rod Woodson on the sidelines during the AFC Divisional Playoff, a 29–9 victory over the Cleveland Browns in 1995.
Al Messerschmidt/Getty Images

ROD WOODSON
Defensive back
1987–1996

When Rod Woodson was born, someone was probably watching over him saying, "Football player." Woodson, a 6 foot, 200 pound defensive back offered the perfect blend of speed and strength to the Steelers.

One of the league's fastest players with a 4.29-second mark in the 40-yard dash, Woodson reveled in his nine trips to the Pro Bowl. "Every player wants to end up in Hawaii," Woodson said. "That's where I want to end up the season the rest of my career—Hawaii—and I don't want to pay for it. That's a major goal."

Coach Chuck Noll seemed as happy as a child with a new toy on Christmas morning when Pittsburgh grabbed Woodson with its No. 1 pick in the 1987 draft. "I'm in love with him," blurted Noll, who may not ever have expressed such public affection for anyone other than his wife.

A star almost from the moment he joined the team, Woodson shook up opposing teams by intercepting passes and making bone-jarring tackles defensively. Then he switched to the other side of the ball and returned punt and kickoff returns. He led the NFL in return average one year and in total returns another. At Purdue, Woodson was not only a top defender, but he also played wide receiver.

The returns represented an itch Woodson wanted to scratch by handling the ball. But defense always came first and he was named NFL defensive player-of-the-year for the 1993 season and it was his work in the secondary that got him elected to the Hall of Fame in 2009.

Woodson was confident to the point of being cocky, but he was also a player who had overcome difficulties growing up in Fort Wayne, Indiana as the son of a white mother and an African-American father. Woodson and his family were the objects of racial hatred. According to a 1994 story in *Inside Sports* magazine, the Ku Klux Klan burned crosses on the lawn of the family home, an extremist black group set the house on fire, and Black Muslims attacked his mother. Woodson said he was called "zebra," "nigger," and "yellow boy." Woodson certainly earned the right to blow off steam with his guided-missile football hits. "It makes you grow up," Woodson said of the racial taunts and hatred. "It makes you see what people are really all about." Woodson said his father taught him to never back down and he followed that advice.

As a prominent Steelers player, Woodson was called other names, too, but they had a nicer ring to them. Some teammates called him "Superman."

Woodson played for the Steelers in Super Bowl XXX, but ended up leaving the team in a contract dispute. He later competed in other Super Bowls with the Oakland Raiders and Baltimore Ravens, before concluding his 17-year pro career with 71 interceptions.

"My biggest fear is self-failure," said Woodson, who did not experience much of it in pro football. "Not living up to my abilities. I'm my own worst critic. It's scary not to be successful."

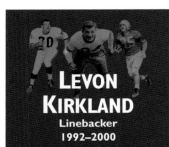

LEVON KIRKLAND
Linebacker
1992–2000

Levon Kirkland seemed like a living, breathing reincarnation of a Steelers' linebacker of the 1970s. His killer instinct, quiet work ethic and non-stop motor in pursuit of ball carriers would have fit him in neatly with the Super Bowl gang.

At 6 feet 1 inch and 265 pounds, Kirkland was the No. 2 draft pick from Clemson in 1992, and a defender who made a difference. His tackles each year could be counted in triple figures. Opposing players tried to run way from him, but Kirkland always tracked them down. His distinctive combination of large size for a linebacker and quick feet gave him the tools to deliver major-league wallops.

"Levon's change of direction and athletic ability and center of gravity and those types of things are more of what you would expect on a player who's 200–210 pounds," said Pittsburgh's respected defensive coach Dick LeBeau. "But he still hits you like a 265-pounder."

Kirkland was a late bloomer, growing up in Lamar, South Carolina, always behind an older kid on the depth chart. When he got his chance to play he showed off tremendous skill. "I always thought I could play," Kirkland said, "but I was always behind someone else. I was considered an underdog because no one knew what to expect. I just kept my faith in God. I knew with that faith and hard work you can do anything."

As a linchpin of a solid defense, Kirkland became a Pro Bowl selection in 1997 and 1998.

the defensive side. He is now an assistant coach at UCLA, where he was a college linebacker. Lake's godfather is Roy Jefferson, the old Steeler receiver from the late 1960s, so he had a Steeler connection from birth.

In his first year, Lake became a starting safety, a remarkably swift adaptation to a new position, and he said studying Woodson in training camp at St. Vincent College was a huge help. "I watched Rod Woodson like a hawk," Lake said. "I just sat there and watched everything I could and picked it up like a sponge."

Just like the 1970s, the Steelers had an amazing core of linebacker talent. Levon Kirkland, the Clemson grad, was an outsized linebacker at 260 pounds. His hits registered on the Richter Scale, just like earthquakes. Those in the know understood Kirkland's talent, but he did not make as many high-profile plays as some of his teammates because he was geared to stop the run.

"You look at outside linebackers and they get the recognition," Kirkland said, "because they get the sacks, the interceptions. My job is to make tackles and stop whoever has the ball." He was good enough at that task to be chosen for two all-star teams.

Jerry Olsavksy was the least heralded of the linebackers, but served ably between 1989 and 1997. Sometimes merely lining up wasn't so easy for the 6 foot 1 inch, 221 pound Olsavksy, who got the Steelers' attention with his play at the University of Pittsburgh. Midway through the 1993 season in a game against the Cleveland Browns, Olsavsky tore three of the four ligaments in his left knee. The injury was so serious that some doctors felt he would never play ball again.

"It was pretty ugly," Olsavsky said. "The bottom of my leg was off to one side." One of the torn ligaments was surgically stitched back together, but the other two were replaced on permanent loan from a cadaver. Olsavsky returned for the next season as a back-up. "I just like to play," he said. "I'm not a good athlete. I'm not big. I'm not strong. So many people have jobs they don't like. I have a job where I make a lot of money and I love what I do."

Kevin Greene loved to kill quarterbacks, or at least rub their faces in the turf. Greene, a 6 foot 3 inch, 247 pound monster at linebacker, is one of the greatest sackmeisters of all time. He started his career with the Los Angeles Rams and finished it with the Carolina Panthers, but the Steelers borrowed him for three years, plucking him off the free agent market for the 1993, 1994, and 1995 seasons. In those three years he collected 35.5 of his career 148 sacks. A match-up with Greene meant nightmares for linemen and fullbacks, and they hoped not more bad dreams after games.

> **"Now that I'm back, I'll do anything they say. If they want me to go out there without a face mask, I'll do it."**
> **—Linebacker Jerry Olsavsky, on his comeback in 1994 after tearing three ligaments in one knee the season before.**

Greene's father was a Vietnam War veteran and Greene was a captain in the Army reserve who was so uninhibited with his kamikaze-like charges that his own teammates just marveled at what Greene brought to the table. "Kevin Greene is from somewhere else," said fellow Ram LeRoy Irvin, who added that Greene often spoke in military terminology. "He's not from here. He's a different breed of cat."

Greene was thrilled to be part of the team that won the AFC championship and went to the 1996 Super Bowl under Cowher. "Just to know that I had the opportunity to go to the big game, you've got to give a knee and praise God about it, man," Greene said. "All of the other stuff you collect along the way, you want to go to that game and play in it."

Levon Kirkland is brought down by Kansas City Chiefs' guard Ralph Tamm after Kirkland recovered a blocked field goal in the 1999 game.
Dave Kaup/AFP/Getty Images

"We're an extension of this city and the fan who watches us play."
—Coach *Bill Cowher.*

Greg Lloyd was the Jack Lambert of the 1990s, at 6 feet 2 inches and 228 pounds defined by toughness and hunger. Some of that hunger stemmed from Lloyd coming to the pros from small-school Fort Valley State. His 1994 performance was Lloyd's signature season. He made 91 tackles, including ten sacks, and forced seven fumbles. Lloyd was voted team MVP. "It's always more meaningful when it comes from your teammates," Lloyd said of winning awards.

He won his share, being named a Pro Bowler five times, and gaining compliments from opponents such as the Atlanta coach Jerry Glanville, who said Lloyd was the toughest player in the NFL.

Lloyd didn't seem opposed to that idea. In the days leading up to a game between the Steelers and the Falcons, he wore a T-shirt that had two messages printed on it. On the front, joining a skull and crossbones picture, it read, "Caution." On the back, it read, "I wasn't hired for my disposition."

Neither was Cowher. As the 1990s ended he ran into his first potholes in the road with seasons of 7–9 and 6–10. Once again it was time for the Steelers to retool. The most recent Super Bowl appearance was receding in the rearview mirror and what-have-you-done-for-me-lately fans were getting antsy.

PITTSBURGH STEELERS
YEAR BY YEAR

1990	**9–7**
1991	**7–9**
1992	**11–5**
1993	**9–7**
1994	**12–4**
1995	**11–5**
1996	**10–6**
1997	**11–5**
1998	**7–9**
1999	**6–10**

Linebacker Kevin Greene only spent a few seasons with the Steelers, but he was one of the greatest quarterback sack specialists in NFL history.
Getty Images

Defensive end Greg Lloyd was part of a new generation of great Steeler defensive players when he suited up for the team in the 1990s.
Stephen Dunn /Allsport/Getty Images

CHAPTER 8

2000s
ONE FOR THE THUMB

Pittsburgh Steelers Hall of Fame owner Dan Rooney (right) and Director of Pro Personnel and Development Tom Donahue. *Al Messerschmidt/Getty Images*

In any sport there are cycles. Rarely do fans or owners have the patience to see the down cycles through without complaining loudly or chopping off heads, usually those of the coaches. The Steelers concluded the 1990s under Bill Cowher in a two-year slump and there was considerable pressure on him to produce better results.

Cowher offered to resign. So did Tom Donahue, the team director of football operations. Donahue lost an in-house power struggle and his resignation was accepted in 2000. Cowher stayed on. "It has to start

with me," Cowher said.

Because of the Rooney family's sense of loyalty and faith that Cowher's abilities had not diminished, Cowher resumed the quest for another Super Bowl crown. In the 2000 season, the Steelers posted a winning record again, going 9–7. And in 2001, the Steelers were great again, finishing 13–3 and besting the Baltimore Ravens 27–10 in the playoffs before running into a New England Patriots' buzzsaw in the AFC championship game.

In 2002, the Steelers finished 10–5–1, and again won a first-round playoff game. It seemed Pittsburgh was back to its station as a reliable winner in the NFL. But NFL rules encouraged parity. Under the strict rules of the team salary cap, coupled with the draft policies that benefit the weak, there was a tendency for quick turnarounds with the arrow pointing up and disappointing turnarounds with the arrow pointing down. It was harder than ever for any team to maintain excellence. In 2003, the Steelers slumped to 6–10.

More than ever it was difficult to measure what a bad year meant. Did this mean that Cowher had run his course? Did it mean that the players weren't good enough? Or did it mean that bad luck and ill-timed injuries produced an aberration? Once again the Steelers stayed the course, leaning on Cowher to lead the outfit back into contention.

It was more challenging than ever for the front office to keep a maturing, improving team together. Players sought to test free agency and often, if they received a better deal, they were gone, leaving holes in the lineup.

"They did me the biggest favor they could have done by trading me here."
—Star running back Jerome Bettis, on being sent to the Steelers from the Rams in 1996.

Coach Bill Cowher was always regarded as a fiery sideline leader, as he showed in Pittsburgh's AFC Divisional playoff against the New York Jets, in 2005.
Jason Cohn/Reuters/Corbis

"You never know what's going to happen because the years keep going by and guys are going to keep leaving," said center Dermontti Dawson. "You're not going to have the same core of guys here. It's always tough when you lose some of your better players."

That was the trick to winning in the 2000s. Teams rebuilt in a hurry and teams tumbled in a hurry. "You have to take one year at a time and try to seize the moment," Cowher said.

Teams also needed some veterans to mix with their cheaper hires. Dermontti Dawson was one of those guys, and was with the team from 1988 to 2000. Another was tailback Jerome Bettis. Bettis could lead

Pittsburgh running back Amos Zereoue dives just short of the end zone against the New England Patriots in the AFC championship game at Heinz Field in 2002.
Mike Segar/Reuters/Corbis

Steeler Stadiums

After 65 years of competing at Forbes Field, Pitt Stadium, and Three Rivers Stadium, in the late 1990s the Steelers set out to build a new home.

True to the modern way, in a move that disgruntled some long-time season-ticket holders, in 1998 it was announced that fans would have to pay up for personal seat licenses for a new stadium in 2001. Just to reserve the right to buy one 50-yard-line ticket, a fan would have to fork out over $2,700. And yes, those in the know realized that price exceeded by $200 the amount that Art Rooney paid for the rights to the entire franchise in 1933. Licenses did not buy a ticket, only the right to buy a ticket.

Ground was broken for the new stadium on June 18, 1999 in a ceremony that involved not only key team officials, but Governor Tom Ridge and NFL Commissioner Paul Tagliabue. In a turn-about, the $281 million stadium, built on the Ohio River, became not only the home field for the Steelers, but for the University of Pittsburgh's football team, as well.

The official opening was August 18, 2001 with an 'N Sync concert. The Steelers played an exhibition game against the Detroit Lions on August 25 and have used Heinz Field (the naming rights stem from the wealthy Heinz family) for games ever since.

Three Rivers Stadium opened in 1970 when cities were constructing all-purpose stadiums to be shared by their professional football and baseball teams. It was described as one of a generation of "cookie cutter" stadiums. With Heinz Field's opening, Three Rivers was imploded in a widely publicized demolition.

Heinz represented an era of football-only stadiums, with expansive and expensive luxury box space adding to team revenues. It was suggested that teams could not compete adequately without that type of cash influx.

Inset top: Forbes Field, home of the Steelers for three decades.
Bettmann/Corbis

Inset center: A crowded Three Rivers Stadium, January 1975. *Charles E. Rotkin/Corbis RT002474*

Inset below: Three Rivers Stadium stood across the Allegheny River from Three Rivers Point State Park.
Mark E. Gibson/Corbis

Main picture: Elevated view of Heinz Field at dusk, as the Pittsburgh Steelers host the New York Jets on December 12, 2004.
Jerry Driendl/Getty Images

JEROME BETTIS

Running back
1996–2006

Jerome Bettis grew up in Detroit and became a star running back at Notre Dame. At 5 feet 11 inches and 243 pounds he seemed as big as a bus, and that's one reason the nickname "The Bus" was bestowed on him and then popularized by Steeler announcer Myron Cope.

Bettis was huge, but he was also light on his feet and could make the cuts of a smaller man. Bettis, who began his 13-season career with three years on the Rams, was a fan favorite in Pittsburgh, not only because he got the job done on the field, but because he was active in charity work in the community.

A dispute with the Rams coach led to Bettis being traded to the Steelers in a lopsided deal. Dick Hoak, Pittsburgh's backfield coach, characterized it as "a steal" for the Steelers. "It was a team that wanted me and wanted to run the ball," Bettis said. "After my Rams experience, that was important."

Bettis was not an all-around athlete in major sports. His second favorite sport was bowling. He also coped with asthma throughout his career that started in 1993 and culminated with the joy of the Steelers' fifth Super Bowl triumph.

Steeler teammates saw Bettis as a leader. When quarterback Ben Roethlisberger was Pittsburgh's No. 1 draft pick in 2004, he was blown away when Bettis immediately befriended him to ease the comfort in Roethlisberger's rookie year. "I was kind of in awe," Roethlisberger said. "He was this super icon of a football player."

Bettis was blessed with an appropriate, colorful, and apt nickname and everyone seemed to enjoy using it. In a game against the Chicago Bears near the end of Bettis' career, played in a mix of wet snow and mud, Steeler Willie Parker watched Bettis plow through the line and yelled, "He's got his snow tires on! Ride The Bus!"

The big runner showed his devotion to Pittsburgh more than once. When he was a free agent he re-signed with the Steelers for less money than was available from other teams. To stay with the club late in his career Bettis took pay cuts. He liked the city, loved the fans, and didn't want to uproot himself and start over in a new place.

Bettis nearly retired after the 2004 season, but his Steeler teammates talked him into one more ride. It paid off, with the only Super Bowl game of his career, and a Super Bowl title, but the frosting on the cake was that it was played in his hometown of Detroit. When the Steelers were introduced, the team allowed Bettis to run out onto Ford Field by himself in the spotlight and he was greeted as a local son made good. "It was incredible," Bettis said. "It gave me a moment I'll never forget."

Bettis retired as the fifth ranked rusher in NFL history with 13,662 yards and 94 touchdowns. "I think The Bus' last stop is here in Detroit," said Bettis after the game when he was perhaps the happiest man on the planet.

Jerome Bettis, aka "The Bus," with the Vince Lombardi Trophy cradled under his arm like a regular football after the Steelers won their fifth Super Bowl on February 5, 2006.
Rick Chapman/Corbis

on the field and in the locker room, a high-character player who rushed for 1,000 yards or more each year.

Bettis, a Notre Dame product, was obtained from the St. Louis Rams in a trade three years into his 13-year career and was an instant hit in Pittsburgh. The bearded Bettis was a 243 pound handful, who surprised people with his quickness, but could barrel over tacklers. His nickname was "The Bus" and the only way to stop this bus was to hope it ran out of gas. Bettis was victimized by a Rams' coaching change.

"When a team makes a decision to go away from a player who once was one of their key players, they have to justify it," an angry Bettis said. "That was their justification, that I was a bad guy. They didn't try to say I wasn't the same player."

Bettis spent a decade proving the Rams were foolish. He always gained the hard yards on third-and-one or third-and-two, and took the handoffs inside the five for short-yardage touchdowns. Bettis imbedded himself in the community with charity work, and Pittsburgh fans showered him with affection. It was a two-sided love affair. Bettis became the NFL's fifth-leading all-time rusher, with 13,662 yards, performing the work he was celebrated for in Pittsburgh.

"The Steelers were all about tradition," Bettis said, "championships and passionate fans. They were like the Notre Dame of the NFL. If you go to the Pittsburgh International Airport you'll see a life-size mannequin of Franco Harris making the Immaculate Reception. There's even stories about Steelers' fans who are

Pittsburgh linebackers Joey Porter (55) and Clark Haggans (53) climb off Minnesota Vikings quarterback Brad Johnson after Porter tackled him in a 2006 pre-season game.
Jason Cohn/Reuters/Corbis

Quarterback Tommy Maddox of the Pittsburgh Steelers passes the ball during a game against the Seattle Seahawks.
Troy Wayrynen/Columbian/NewSport/ Corbis

buried wearing their black-and-gold pajamas, holding a TV remote, and having their legs covered by a Steelers' blanket. Now that's a city that loves its team."

The Steelers had the opportunities to draft high after their down years. In 1999, in accordance with the team's great tradition of selecting star linebackers, Pittsburgh grabbed Joey Porter out of Colorado State in the third round. Porter was a young man of undeniable talent and strong opinions. He did not walk softly and carry a big stick. He said anything that came to mind. At 6 feet 2 inches and 240 pounds, and after working mostly on special teams as a rookie, Porter became a throwback to the days of Jack Ham and Jack Lambert. In 2000, he recorded 10.5 sacks, a mark he matched in 2005. He played with a lot of emotion. "He gets us fired up," said linebacker Casey Hampton. "He's our emotional leader. He talks, but he backs it up."

Porter, a devastating hitter, once tried to convince Bill Cowher to use him on offense, too. "I thought I could help in goal-line situations," Porter said. "I petitioned coach, but he didn't see it that way."

Kordell Stewart, who had been nicknamed "Slash" for his ability to make game-breaking plays as a passer and receiver, but whose heart belonged to the quarterback's job, emerged as the starter, and led Pittsburgh to the playoffs in 2001. He was even selected to play in the Pro Bowl. But in 2002, Stewart started erratically and Cowher decided to give back-up Tommy Maddox a shot at the job.

Maddox was an amazing story. He played college football at UCLA and was the Denver Broncos' No. 1 draft in 1992. Maddox was relegated to the less-than-satisfying role of sitting behind future Hall of Famer John Elway. After two years in Denver he drifted to the Los Angeles Rams and New York Giants, again as a back-up. He was cut by the Atlanta Falcons in 1997 training camp. Then Maddox became a vagabond in fringe leagues, competing in the Arena Football League and the XFL. He made the Steelers roster in 2001, where he was viewed as an insurance policy.

However, when Stewart faltered and Maddox got a chance he shocked the football world by playing first-class ball. His 62.1 percent completion percentage accounted for 2,836 yards and 20 touchdowns. He had one eye-opener of a game, throwing for 473 yards against Atlanta. In 2003, he was the first-stringer and threw for 3,414 yards and 18 touchdowns.

In the early 2000s, the Rooneys decided to implement some housekeeping changes in the Steeler hierarchy. In 2003, president and chairman Dan Rooney made his son Art II the president while retaining the chairman's title. "I'm still going to be here," said Dan Rooney, who had just turned 71. "It's not like I'm not going to be here."

A Steelers fan shows his colors and his faith. The Steelers did exactly that, beating the seemingly unstoppable New England Patriots, 34–20, to end the Patriots' 21-game winning streak.
Pam Panchak/Reuters/Corbis

What followed was an injury-plagued 6–10 season, though Maddox was one of the few bright spots. Another was receiver Plaxico Burress, who had been the 2000 No. 1 draft choice and was now coming into his own. "The guy's just hungry," Burress said of Maddox. "The guy just has a never-say-die attitude. He's proven all the nay-sayers wrong, and that's what life's all about."

Maddox had a lock on the first-string job as the 2004 season began. Looking to the future, the Steelers drafted Ben Roethlisberger, a quarterback who had size and sturdiness akin to an ancient Roman pillar. Roethlisberger stood 6 feet 5 inches and weighed 240 pounds. He starred at Miami University of Ohio, so he had been a little bit under the radar on the national recognition scale. Roethlisberger would spend his rookie year on the bench backing up and studying Maddox, an avenue commonly taken for young NFL quarterbacks.

Roethlisberger was taken with the 11th choice of the first round. Fans who turned out at Heinz Field to watch the April 2004 draft liked what they heard, and cheered when Pittsburgh plucked the king-sized quarterback. "We think this kid's potential is unlimited," said Kevin Colbert, the Steelers' director of football operations.

That potential would be tested in a hurry when a Maddox injury knocked him out for the season after two games. The very inexperienced Roethlisberger, aka "Big Ben" was the surprised starter.

The groans emanating from the pain Maddox was suffering echoed through the locker room, to the fans, to the home viewers, to the media. There was trepidation that the season was lost. Roethlisberger was just 22 and only months removed from the Mid-America Conference. His biggest challenges had come facing Marshall University. Most of the football-watching country thought that MAC was a short name applied to a stranger in a bar, not the initials of a college football conference.

But a funny thing happened to the Steelers on the way to the NFL graveyard. Rallying around Roethlisberger, the 1–1 team started winning and kept winning. Cowher just asked Roethlisberger to play as error-free as possible and to hopefully make plays at critical times.

In Roethlisberger's fifth start, the Steelers upset New England, ending the Patriots' 21-game winning streak. By then NFL fans realized there was another Miami in Ohio, not just one on the Atlantic Ocean where they filmed "Miami Vice." "Everybody's antennas across the country are starting to go up a little bit," Burress said.

The fairy tale continued. Game after game, week after week, the astonishing Steelers steamrolled opposing teams, partying like it was 1975 all over again. Pittsburgh stomped its way to a 15–1 mark. Roethlisberger completed 66.4 percent of his passes, a

Right: Pittsburgh quarterback Ben Roethlisberger holds court during a media session for Super Bowl XLIII.
John G. Mabanglo/epa/Corbis

BEN ROETHLISBERGER

Quarterback
2004–

They call him "Big Ben" and Ben Roethlisberger is certainly that. The Steelers' 2004 No. 1 draft pick out of Miami of Ohio is 6 feet 5 inches and weighs 240 pounds. He is no dainty quarterback, rather a pillar in the pocket who is hard to knock down without a wrecking ball.

For all of the swings and misses in the draft, the selection of Roethlisberger, who was less heralded than other quarterback prospects, will go down in team lore as a major coup. As a rookie, Roethlisberger was expected to watch Tommy Maddox operate the offense, but when Maddox was injured, Roethlisberger led the Steelers to a 15–1 record. The next season he took Pittsburgh to a Super Bowl triumph.

"Run, block, whatever," said Roethlisberger of adapting when his throwing was off as Pittsburgh defeated Seattle to make him the youngest Super Bowl champion quarterback, aged 23. "We had to find different ways to get it done." And in his fifth season, Roethlisberger led Pittsburgh to another Super Bowl win.

It has been a lovely marriage between the Steel City and the strong-armed thrower who gains maturity each season, despite a 2006 motorcycle crash when the 24-year-old Roethlisberger bashed in his face—and was lucky to escape with relatively minor injuries. That scared the player and fans alike. Approaching the start of training camp that summer, Roethlisberger was subdued. "I know I'll say an extra prayer of thanks and be grateful just to be out there playing football again," he said. "I'm lucky to be alive."

The Pittsburgh defense prepares to rush the New England Patriots' offensive line and quarterback Tom Brady during a 2005 game at Heinz Field.
Greg Fiume/NewSport/Corbis

"It (focus) has to be on how you produce when your name is called and the ball is in your court."
—Versatile Antwaan Randle El, on his ability to break plays.

Bettis was touched by the gesture, only after spending time as one of a remarkable nine Steelers in the Pro Bowl in Hawaii did he change his mind. His teammates verbally worked him over for the week, cajoled and begged, and ultimately talked "The Bus" into one more ride.

Bettis stayed, but the diminutive, mouthy broadcaster Myron Cope retired after 35 years as a team radio man. The man who invented the Terrible Towel, popularized it, and saw to it that the proceeds went to charity, stepped down after 2004. Cope was so big in Pittsburgh that three different beer companies vied for the rights to put out Myron Cope commemorative cans, a distinction hard to rate next to Medal of Freedom-recognition, but nonetheless impressive.

The 2005 season was not a repeat fantasy campaign and the Steelers struggled far more often. Maddox was back and played some, but Big Ben was the No. 1 guy. Still learning, but adapting well, Roethlisberger threw for 2,385 yards while completing 62.7 percent of his passes. Bettis was mostly a short-yardage back, cheerfully backing up Duce Staley or Willie Parker, another remarkable find for the Steelers.

Parker attended North Carolina, but barely got off the bench in college. Someone miscalculated. He made the Pittsburgh roster as an undrafted free agent and although he saw limited action in 2004, he averaged 5.8 yards a carry. Parker rushed for 181 yards his senior year at North Carolina and rushed for 161 yards in his first pro game against Tennessee. "He's a very fast young man," Cowher said of the 5 foot 10 inch, 210 pound Parker, "a very powerful guy."

By 2005 Parker was established and rushed for 1,202 yards. Bettis tutored Parker, and tried to shorten his learning curve by telling him all that he knew about NFL defenses.

The Steelers finished 11–5. That was good enough to get them into the playoffs, but did not earn either a bye or a home game. They were very much long-shots to reach the Super Bowl and if they did so, they would have to do it the hard way, playing each game in someone else's stadium.

Pittsburgh's first-round opponent was the Cincinnati Bengals, who were enjoying a bit of a renaissance after being one of the NFL's worst teams

Broadcaster Myron Cope (left) shakes hands with Pittsburgh Steelers President Arthur J. Rooney II (right) as he is presented with a framed Pittsburgh Steelers jersey marking his 35 years of service with the team, at Heinz Field on October 31, 2005.
Sean Brady/NFL/Getty Images

Right: Willie Parker (39) scores a touchdown by running past Cincinnati Bengals linebacker Landon Johnson (on ground) and cornerback Deltha O'Neal (24) during a 2005 game.
Matt Sullivan/Reuters/Corbis

ridiculously good number for a rookie. He threw for 2,621 yards and 17 touchdowns.

Roethlisberger was selected as the Associated Press Offensive Rookie of the Year and *The Sporting News* Rookie of the Year. Could Big Ben really be this good? He was and the Steelers were. "We have a rookie who is playing tremendous," said linebacker Joey Porter.

Still, no one knew if Roethlisberger would stand up under playoff pressure. The Steelers had earned a first-round bye so that was a bonus—one less game was required to reach the Super Bowl. Then the Steelers outlasted the New York Jets, 20–17, setting up a confrontation with juggernaut New England. The Steelers couldn't handle the Tom Brady-led Patriots, who were at the peak of their game, and succumbed, 41–27, ending a glorious season that left the team full of hope.

Jerome Bettis, his body aching and aging, felt the best chance of his career to reach the Super Bowl had slipped away. He was 90 percent sure he would retire. Roethlisberger waylaid Bettis and immediately began working on his psyche, urging him to come back for one more try.

"This is really a dream come true. As a kid, watching Jerry Rice and Joe Montana and all those guys playing in the Super Bowl."
—*Steeler receiver Hines Ward, on getting to play in the 2006 Super Bowl.*

for years. The nearby Ohio rival took it on the chin, falling to the Steelers 31–17 after star quarterback Carson Palmer was injured. "When he got hurt, they were nervous," linebacker Joey Porter said of the Bengals. Roethlisberger presented Bettis with a game ball. He said it was going to be the first of four during those playoffs.

The task was mightier the next week. The Steelers traveled to Indianapolis, and the Colts, led by quarterback Peyton Manning, were clearly favored. As the clock ran down, the Steelers held a 21–18 lead. Pittsburgh needed one more first down to clinch the game. Cowher turned to Bettis. Bettis was a good bet to get the first down, but just as importantly, "The Bus" never fumbled. Opposing tacklers could not pry the ball out of his hands with a pair of pliers. Bettis had not fumbled once during the 2005 season.

Then, as Steeler Nation watched in horror, the handoff popped out of Bettis' hands. He couldn't believe it. The coaches couldn't believe it. The fans couldn't believe it. Even worse, the ball squirted into the air and was caught by Indianapolis defender Nick Harper, who began churning the other way.

Harper appeared on his way to a game-winning touchdown that would break Steeler hearts. Bettis thought his glorious career was ending on an inglorious mistake. "All my fault," he thought. Then, nearly as surprising as the fumble, came the miracle tackle. Roethlisberger, who likely hadn't tackled anyone since high school, except by accident, gave chase, dove, and made a shoestring tackle that tripped up Harper.

Still, the Colts had the ball, a minute to go, and were on their own 42-yard-line. With Manning, a master of late-game comebacks at the helm, the Colts might score a touchdown. And with only minor gains could at least provide Mike Vanderjagt, the most accurate field-goal kicker in the league that season, with a good chance. A 22-yard completion put the ball on the Steelers' 36. With 22 seconds left, the Colts lined up for a 46-yard field-goal try that would send the game into overtime. Only Vanderjagt missed. The best foot in the league missed at the worst time and the Steelers prevailed, moving on to the AFC title game at Denver.

Roethlisberger teased reporters for doubting his

team. "All the non-believers, you want to come in now?" he said.

Denver had upset New England, but the Steelers blasted the Broncos, 34–17. Roethlisberger was still only 23, but was playing like a veteran. "He's a second-year guy, but it's like he's been around forever," said Steelers' guard Kendall Simmons.

The Steelers were particularly happy that Jerome Bettis reached the Super Bowl. Bettis had never played in the NFL's showcase game, and even more thrilling was the fact that it would be contested in Ford Field in Detroit, where he grew up. The game between the Steelers and the Seattle Seahawks quickly became labeled "Jerome's game."

"I was treated like a king that week," Bettis said.

At the end of March, Art Rooney II further distinguished the family name by being selected as the NFL Executive of the Year by *The Sporting News*. And in June, the Steelers were invited to the White House for an audience with President George W. Bush. In a somewhat raucous gathering, the president said, "It sounds like some people have been drinking some Iron City beer here." As a Texan and a Dallas Cowboys fan, Bush said it was hard to admit that the rival Steelers were one of the league's great franchises. "And one of the reasons why is because of the Rooney family."

Bush, who had a 35-percent public approval rating at the time, took note that the Steelers were only 7–5 before winning their last four regular-season games and sweeping through the playoffs. "Halfway through the season, a lot of people counted the Pittsburgh Steelers out, said you don't have a chance," the president said. "I kind of know the feeling."

The Steelers had returned to glory on Cowher's watch, relying on freshly acquired stars like Ward at receiver, Roethlisberger at quarterback, guard Alan Faneca, a five-time All-Pro, and safety Troy Polamalu.

Polamalu, the 5 foot 10 inch, 210 pound destroyer, was becoming one of the best players in the league, an unstoppable defensive force given the green light to audible his own freelance tackling role at the line of scrimmage based on offensive formations. Soft-spoken, unpretentious, Polamalu, of Samoan background, could not blend into the scenery for two reasons: he was too good and he had the longest hair in the league. Polamalu's flowing hair could no more be contained

(continued on page 162)

"I just thought it was time."
—*Dan Rooney, on promoting his son Art Rooney II to the job of president of the Steelers.*

Left: Making the tackle of his life, Steelers quarterback Ben Roethlisberger (on ground) was able to pull down Indianapolis Colts defensive back Nick Harper (25) on a fumble return. The play saved the game in a 21–18 Steelers playoff win in 2006.
Don Larson/NFL/Getty Images

SUPER BOWL XL

On February 5, 2006, the Steelers defeated the Seahawks, 21–10. It marked a long-awaited Super Bowl triumph for Cowher and Bettis, but it was fulfillment of the quarter-century-old desire to win "one for the thumb," a fifth Super Bowl ring for the Steelers.

Receiver Hines Ward won the Most Valuable Player award with his five catches for 123 yards and a touchdown. The son of a Korean mother and black father, the international notoriety from his performance also led him to a post-season visit to South Korea for the first time, where he was embraced as a hero. Ward said he had always felt he was second-fiddle to Lynn Swann and John Stallworth, previous Pittsburgh receiving greats. "I never felt I belonged with those guys," he said. "Now I do."

For Bettis, it was the capstone of a great career, an ending almost too perfect to be true. "I came back to win a championship—mission accomplished," Bettis said. "With that I have to bid farewell."

Certainly, Cowher's satisfaction matched Bettis'. Succeeding the only coach to win four Super Bowls, Cowher had chased the elusive championship trophy for nearly a decade-and-a-half. When he got his hands on the Lombardi Trophy, he passed it to Steelers' chairman Dan Rooney.

"Mr. Rooney," said Cowher, "I've been waiting a long time to do this. This is yours, man."

Honors and recognition poured in for the Steelers. Only days after winning the fifth Super Bowl crown, an estimated 250,000 fans jammed into downtown Pittsburgh for a 58-vehicle parade along a 1.2-mile route. One fan waved a poster reading, "Feb. 5, 2006, The Best Day of My Life." The uniform of the day among fans was black-and-gold jerseys of favorite team members.

The next day, Roethlisberger, who had grown a beard for good luck after the Steelers won a game when he didn't shave, had it shaved off on *The Late Show with David Letterman*. "I don't really like the beard, you know," Roethlisberger said, "but we were winning, so I had to keep it going."

On the go. Pittsburgh running back Willie Parker dashes for a 75-yard touchdown, the longest in Super Bowl history, during the third quarter of Super Bowl XL. *John G. Mabanglo/epa/Corbis*

	Pittsburgh Steelers (AFC)			Seattle Seahawks (NFC)	
	21			**10**	

	1	2	3	4	Total
PIT	0	7	7	7	21
SEA	3	0	7	0	10

Left: Owner Dan Rooney displays the Lombardi Trophy as Steeler coach Bill Cowher looks on after Pittsburgh's 21–10 Super Bowl XL win.
Tomasso DeRosa/Corbis News Agency/Corbis

Right: Quarterback Ben Roethlisberger (center) celebrates with his teammates Max Starks (left) and Marvel Smith after Hines Ward caught a touchdown pass thrown by receiver Antwaan Randle El for a backbreaking play in Super Bowl XL.
Marc Serota/Reuters/Corbis

Above: Pittsburgh wide receiver Hines Ward leaps into the end zone to finish off a trick play for a touchdown in front of Seattle Seahawks cornerback Marcus Trufant (28). Ward caught a pass from teammate Antwaan Randle El. *Shaun Best/Reuters/Corbis*

Quarterback Ben Roethlisberger hands off to running back Willie Parker (39) in the third quarter of Super Bowl XL.
David Bergman/Corbis

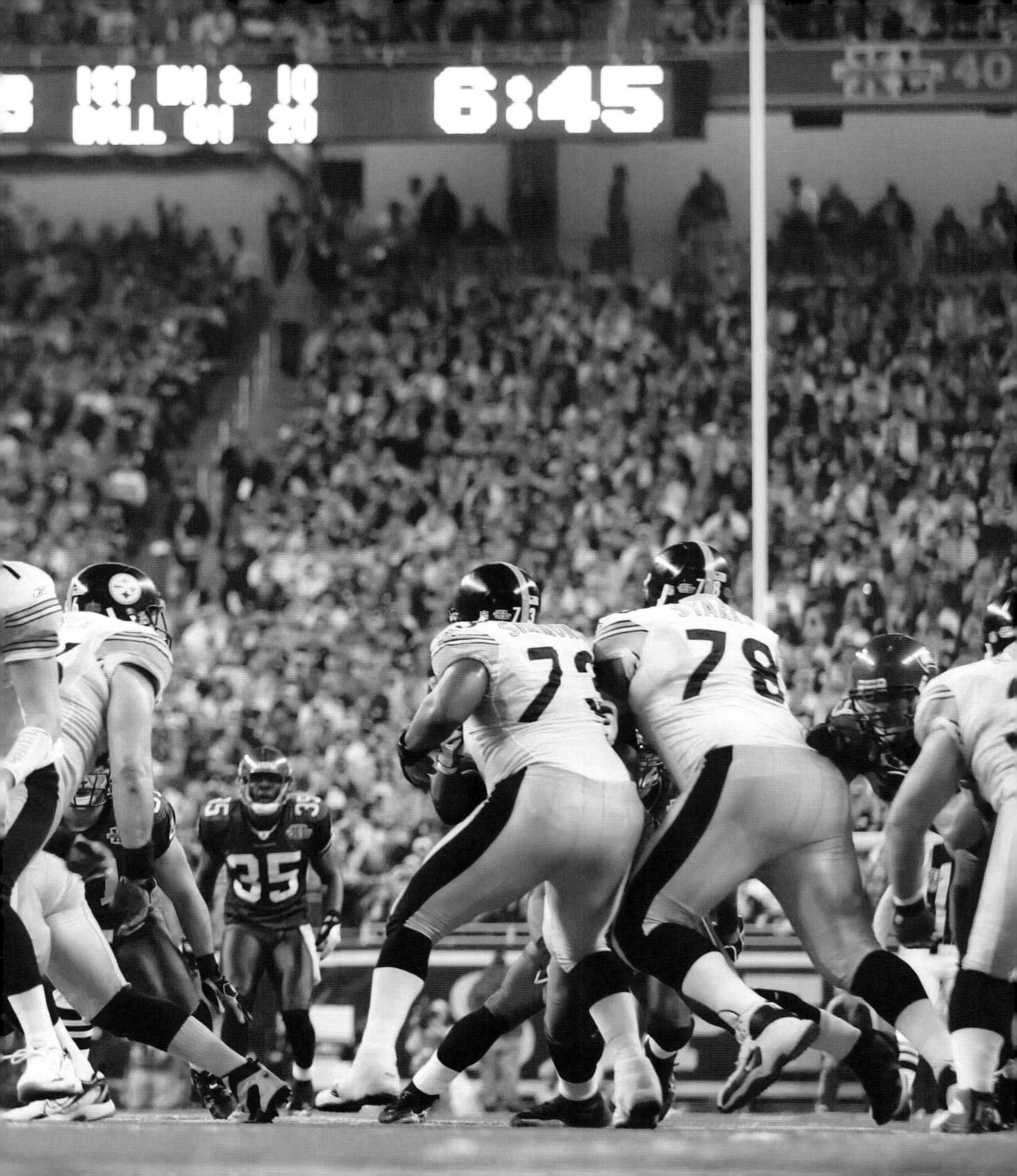
1ST DN & 10
BALL ON 20
6:45
78
35

Right: The opening play of Super Bowl XL between the Seattle Seahawks and the Pittsburgh Steelers (AFC) at Ford Field in Detroit, Michigan in 2006.
Katie Barnes/TSN/ZUMA/Corbis

Page 158: Pittsburgh Steelers quarterback Ben Roethlisberger (center) dives into the end zone for a touchdown during Super Bowl XL.
Shaun Best/Reuters/Corbis

Page 159: Pittsburgh Steelers head coach Bill Cowher argues with a referee at Ford Field during Super Bowl XL.
David Bergman/Corbis

HINES WARD
Wide receiver
1998–

When he was a youngster, Hines Ward wanted nothing more than to blend in with others. But with a black father and a Korean mother that was not going to happen easily. "I was a lost child," Ward said. "I wasn't accepted in the black community because I was Korean and I wasn't accepted in the Korean community because I was black." It took years, but Ward came to terms with his identity and his achievements playing football helped him gain contentment as a man.

In 1998, Ward, a wide receiver who attended the University of Georgia, was a Steelers third-round draft selection. He was a back-up as a rookie, caught 61 passes in his second season, and then blossomed into one of the top pass catchers in the league. In 2001, Ward caught 94 passes. A year later he grabbed 112. And in 2002 he caught 95. With good hands and shifty moves, he became a perennial All-Pro.

In college, Ward demonstrated considerable versatility. The Bulldogs just wanted to make sure he got the ball some way, because he had a nose for the end zone. The Steelers, who had some success with all-around talents like Kordell "Slash" Stewart and Antwaan Randle El, looked at Ward the same way. Coach Bill Cowher dubbed him "Slash II."

But Ward found a position where he could excel and stuck with it. Forget kick returns. He became too valuable catching the ball. In the autumn of 2005, with the Steelers revving up for a perceived Super Bowl run, Ward was a holdout. He felt he deserved big money. His teammate, Jerome Bettis, whom he had talked into playing one more year instead of retiring, got on the phone and urged him to get to training camp. Ward signed a five-year, $27-million-plus contract.

Ward caught 69 passes with 11 touchdowns that season, and came up even bigger in the Super Bowl against the Seattle Seahawks. That day Ward collected five passes for 123 yards. His 37-yard reception set up one Pittsburgh touchdown from the 1-yard-line and on a trick play he caught a 43-yard touchdown pass from Randle El. Ward was named MVP of the Super Bowl, an honor that left him giddy. "That was a great play call," Ward said of the connection with Randle El.

A few months after the Super Bowl, Ward, then 30, accompanied by his mother, Kim Young-hee, made his first trip to South Korea. They were treated royally, and Ward embraced and gained a fresh understanding of the Asian portion of his heritage. He and his mother were trailed by television crews, met the president, and Ward threw out the first pitch at a baseball game.

Ward had aligned himself with the Pearl S. Buck International Foundation in the United States, and in a homogenous society that treated him as a hero, he campaigned for warmer acceptance of mixed-race children. "If you can welcome me—a guy who doesn't speak the language—you can do it for them," Ward said.

Pittsburgh wide receiver Hines Ward during the Steelers' January, 2009 playoff game against the San Diego Chargers.
Jay LaPrete/Icon SMI/Corbis

Troy Polamalu is nearly as famous for his long, flowing hair as his outstanding strong safety play for the Steelers.
Bob Leverone/TSN/ZUMA/Corbis

TROY POLAMALU
Safety
2003–

The NFL doesn't keep records for players with the longest hair, but Troy Polamalu has Hall-of-Fame-length locks. Polamalu's black, flowing hair is an unrestrained 'do that makes Whoopi Goldberg's haircut preferences look like a crewcut.

It is a marvel that Polamalu, the Stealth bomber of a safety who destroys opponents who make incursions into his territory, does not have his hair pulled by foes in every pileup. But the 5 foot 10 inch, 207 pound alumnus of the University of Southern California may have intimidation on his side.

The hair gets mixed reactions. Seattle quarterback Matt Hasselbeck, who is going bald, ran his hand over his head and said, "I'm jealous. I'm really jealous."

The biggest question is how Polamalu, who is of Samoan heritage and grew up in Tenmile, Oregon, stuffs his hair into his Steelers helmet, though plenty of it is left over.

When long hair first became stylish in the 1960s, many pro sports coaches considered the fashion to be proof of defiance. Septuagenarian Steeler defensive coordinator Dick LeBeau laughed about Polamalu's hair. "As long as it doesn't slow him down, I don't care," he said. "He can grow it another foot if he can get another interception."

For a while, Polamalu's coiffure garnered more attention than his play, but those days are gone. His nickname is "The Tasmanian Devil" and that's a pretty accurate description of the way he flies around the field making hits. "I play football with a passion," Polamalu said.

He does not bring the same passion to visiting barber shops.

(continued from page 151)

by a football helmet than a tsunami could be contained by a shore.

The "Tasmanian Devil" said he was just as passionate reading the Bible or hanging with his wife at home as he was on the football field. "The greatest thing for me football-wise," Polamalu said, "is it's a test of will. When you overcome those obstacles within the game, that's when you become a better man."

For all of the post-season honors and accolades, the Steelers were just as content to get a break from public attention before training camp. But peace and quiet didn't last. Not long after the Steelers visited the White House, Roethlisberger suffered an unexpected and serious injury. Big Ben, not heeding the advice of team officials and friends, not only kept up his hobby of motorcycle riding, but also refused to wear a helmet because Pennsylvania law did not require it.

On a Monday morning, June 12, riding his Suzuki Hayabusa in Pittsburgh, Roethlisberger crashed into a car and was hurled to the ground over the front of the bike. Roethlisberger smashed in his face, breaking several bones, including a broken jaw and a broken nose, incurred a concussion, facial lacerations, loss of blood and teeth. He also injured both knees, but not seriously. He underwent seven hours of surgery at Mercy Hospital, where fans held a vigil in the street. Roethlisberger was told he could have bled to death at the scene of the accident if not for quick treatment.

Six weeks after the crash, a chastened Roethlisberger reported to training camp in Latrobe on time, surprising Steelers who had been worried about him. "A lot of players thought he was on his death bed," Hines Ward said.

Roethlisberger realized he was very lucky to still be able to play. "I do appreciate everything more now," he said. "I really do. I'm having a lot of fun. I still get mad if I do something wrong or make a mistake on the field. But when I'm not in that moment, and I'm off the field, I say, 'Wow, I'm playing football again.'"

The Steelers started playing football again, on schedule, in the fall of 2006, with the idea of a repeat, of winning a second Super Bowl trophy in a row. Things did

Running to daylight, Pittsburgh's Willie Parker bypasses a pile of Cleveland Browns defenders in a 2007 game.
Jason Cohn /Reuters/Corbis

> **"It's a dangerous thing, riding a motorcycle. I stay away from it. I don't have interest in it. I hope he's OK."**
> —*Giants' quarterback Eli Manning, after Steeler quarterback Ben Roethlisberger's 2006 motorcycle accident.*

not go well. Pittsburgh finished 8–8 and after 15 years Bill Cowher decided he needed a break from coaching.

It appeared that his offensive coordinator Ken Whisenhunt, or Russ Grimm, another assistant coach, would succeed him, but Dan and Art Rooney went outside the Steeler family to hire Mike Tomlin, the 34-year-old African-American defensive coordinator for the Minnesota Vikings. Whisenhunt got the job as head coach of the Arizona Cardinals and took Grimm with him.

Dan Rooney had chaired the NFL owners' diversity committee that studied ways to open more doors for black head coaches. When the committee decreed in 2003 that blacks must be interviewed for every head coaching opening, the policy was named "The Rooney Rule." The policy, and the man who helped establish what was viewed as an affirmative action step, lived by its precepts.

Although Tomlin was an unknown hire because he had no head coaching experience, his first Steeler team finished 10–6 and made the playoffs. In 2008, Tomlin's second season, the Steelers finished 12–4 and then polished off the San Diego Chargers and the Baltimore Ravens in the playoffs.

The Steelers, who had the NFL's toughest regular-season schedule, in shades of the old days, had the No. 1 ranked defense. They also had a grudge match rivalry going with the Ravens, who liked to believe they played the best defense in the league. Feelings are so intense between the Steelers and Ravens that Pittsburgh Mayor Luke Ravenstahl said he was changing his name to "Steelerstahl" for the day.

In a game played at Heinz Field in snow flurries and cold temperatures, the Steelers outlasted Baltimore, 23–14. Troy Polamalu killed any Raven comeback thoughts with a late interception for a touchdown. "I was just running for my life," said Polamalu of his 40-yard run with dreadlocks flying.

The victory sent the Steelers to Tampa for their seventh Super Bowl appearance and the chance to be the first franchise to win six rings, if they could top the underdog Arizona Cardinals—coached by Whisenhunt.

"We're opportunistic," said Tomlin, who became the third African-American NFL head coach to take a

Wearing throwback jerseys, Steeler kicker Jeff Reed (3) celebrates next to holder Mitch Berger (17) after kicking a field goal against the Baltimore Ravens in the first quarter of a 2008 game. Reed later won it with an overtime boot.
Jason Cohn/Reuters/Corbis

team to the Super Bowl since 2007, when Tony Dungy's Indianapolis Colts and Lovie Smith's Chicago Bears met. "We didn't start this journey to GET to Tampa. We've got some business to do."

Pittsburgh was working itself into a frenzy. In the lead-up to the February 1 game, a local television station ran a contest urging fans to write songs supporting their team and it evolved into a very humorous competition. Songs such as "Puttin' On the Blitz," "When Lombardi Comes Marching Home," and "Cardinals Roasting On An Open Fire," made their splashy debuts.

Several lyrics were worthy of preservation. The Pop Rocks' Steeler Song included the lines, "The Chargers wish they were us. The Ravens wish they were us." A singer named Mercedez sang "I love Black and Gold" to the tune of Joan Jett and the Blackhearts' "I Love Rock and Roll." In it, fans are told to "Grab your towels and wave 'em around." Those would be the Terrible Towels, and Myron Cope, who died at 77 in early 2008, would have loved the sentiment.

The Steelers would rely on Tomlin's wisdom, Big Ben's arm, Polamalu's reckless disregard for his own health, and a new star, linebacker James Harrison. Cut four times before he became a starter, Harrison was honored as the league's defensive player of the year. He, as much as Tomlin, represented the new generation of Steelers who sought a permanent link to the old Steeler greats. "Everybody wants to be

MIKE TOMLIN

Coach
2007–

When Bill Cowher stepped down as Steelers' coach after 15 years, the job had been in the hands of just two people for 38 years. It should have been no surprise that the Steelers' hierarchy brought the same viewpoint to hiring a new coach after the long, successful runs of Chuck Noll and Cowher.

Three weeks into 2007, the Steelers announced that their new coach would be Mike Tomlin, like the others before him a man with no head coaching experience. Tomlin was the defensive coordinator of the Minnesota Vikings. He had also been an assistant with the Tampa Bay Buccaneers.

Like his predecessors, too, Tomlin, at 34, was young for the position of responsibility. One difference was notable: Tomlin is black. In a league that had often been criticized for not giving chances to African-Americans (but that had been improving) Tomlin's hire was significant. "I think football is a tough man's game, an attrition game," Tomlin said.

Tomlin was given a four-year contract at rate of about $2.5 million per year and was a bit of a surprise hire. Steelers' assistant coaches Ken Whisenhunt and Russ Grimm were considered the frontrunners for the job.

"He's an impressive young guy," said Steeler president Art Rooney II of Tomlin, a former William & Mary college receiver. "Get in a room and spend two or three hours with Mike, you come away feeling this is a special person."

Within two seasons, Tomlin had won another Super Bowl for the Steelers.

"We're a team. There's no offense, there's no defense, there's no special teams. We're one."
—*Quarterback Ben Roethlisberger, on the Steelers before the 2009 Super Bowl.*

included in a group of elite people," Harrison said, "whether it's linemen, linebackers, or whatever it may be. You just want to come in and try to hold up the tradition."

The 2009 game was immediately hailed as a classic for its drama and theatrical turns, and made the Steelers the first franchise to win six Super Bowls. If the previous ring earned was "one for the thumb" this one might have to be a nose ring.

Tomlin at 36 became the youngest coach to win a Super Bowl title and joined Dungy as the second African-American to capture the biggest prize in football. "If I could win any way, it would be that way," said Tomlin of the last-minute heroics.

The Steelers display their Super Bowl booty—the Lombardi Trophy times six—in their headquarters for all to admire. After the heart-stopping triumph the office is due for redecorating.

PITTSBURGH
STEELERS
YEAR BY YEAR

2000	**9–7**
2001	**13–3**
2002	**10–5–1**
2003	**6–10**
2004	**15–1**
2005	**11–5**
2006	**8–8**
2007	**10–6**
2008	**12–4**
2009	**9–7**

Far left: Steeler coach Mike Tomlin gets his first taste of accepting trophies on the road to the Super Bowl as he holds up the Lamar Hunt Trophy following the Steelers' victory over the Baltimore Ravens in the AFC Championship game on January 18, 2009, in Pittsburgh. Next stop: Super Bowl XLIII.
Joe Robbins/Getty Images

Left: Troy Polamalu (43) is about to lower the boom on a Baltimore Ravens ball carrier during a January 2009 playoff game at Heinz Field. The 23–14 victory sent Pittsburgh to Super Bowl XLIII.
Rob Tringali/Sportschrome/Getty Images

SUPER BOWL XLIII

During Super Bowl XLIII James Harrison did, indeed, uphold the Steelers' tradition. The Steelers were clinging to a 10–7 lead, with time running out in the first half, and with the ball on their 1-yard-line before 70,000 fans at Raymond James Stadium. Cardinals quarterback Kurt Warner thought he saw an opening over the middle, but Harrison stepped in front of the receiver, clutched the ball to his chest on the goal-line and began a momentous, 100-yard weave downfield. The shocking play—the bookend Immaculate Interception to join the Immaculate Reception in Steeler legend—was the longest in Super Bowl history.

Although caught from behind as he crossed the goal line and the clock hit 00, Harrison's brilliant play counted as he tumbled into the end zone on his head. "I was just thinking I had to do whatever I could to get to the other end zone and get seven."

It seemed the spectacular play might be a spirit-crushing event, but behind Warner, the only quarterback to lead two franchises to a Super Bowl, and his All-World receiver Larry Fitzgerald, the resurgent Cardinals took the lead, 23–20, for the first time with 2 minutes, 37 seconds to go. All of the pressure rested on the Steelers, and Roethlisberger, who had rallied Pittsburgh to wins 17 times in the fourth quarter since 2004.

"I said, 'It's now or never,'" Roethlisberger told his huddle. "It's awesome we had to come out and do it the way we did."

Putting on a show for the ages, Roethlisberger repeatedly fired bullets to receiver Santonio Holmes. The slender, 5 foot 11 inch, 189 pound Holmes was a third-year player from Ohio State, who grew up poor in Belle Glade, Florida where as a youth he sold drugs to survive. With 35 seconds remaining, Holmes slithered into the far back right corner of the end zone and Roethlisberger lofted a pass over three defenders. Holmes leaped, snared the ball in both hands, and acrobatically made sure he landed with both feet in bounds. The magnificent play gave the Steelers a touchdown and the 27–23 victory. Holmes caught 9 passes for 131 yards and was voted the game's MVP.

"I knew it was a touchdown, 100 percent," said Holmes, who had urged Roethlisberger to keep throwing to him on the 78-yard drive. "I dared the team."

"The Immaculate Interception." Pittsburgh linebacker James Harrison (92) avoids being tackled by Arizona Cardinals wide receiver Larry Fitzgerald (11) before scoring on a Super Bowl record 100-yard interception return at Super Bowl XLIII. *John Angelillo/Corbis*

	Pittsburgh Steelers (AFC)			Arizona Cardinals (NFC)	
	27			**23**	
	1	2	3	4	Total
PIT	3	14	3	7	27
ARI	0	7	0	16	23

Pittsburgh Steeler players run onto the field prior to the start of of the game.
Tannen Maury/epa/Corbis

Previous page: Quarterback Ben Roethlisberger (7) leads the offense against the Arizona Cardinals during the 1st quarter of Super Bowl XLIII.
Justin Lane/epa/Corbis

Left: Santonio Holmes keeps both feet in the end zone as he beats Cardinals safety Aaron Francisco to catch the game-winning touchdown pass late in the fourth quarter.
Brian Snyder/Reuters/Corbis

Right: Quarterback Ben Roethlisberger celebrates with teammates after throwing the game-winning touchdown pass to Santonio Holmes in the fourth quarter of Super Bowl XLIII.
Paul Buck/epa/Corbis

Below left: Huddle up. The Pittsburgh Steeler defense tries to hold onto the lead in Super Bowl XLIII during the third quarter.
Chris Graythen/Getty Images

Below: In the traditional celebratory dousing, Pittsburgh coach Mike Tomlin is soaked with Gatorade at the end of Super Bowl XLIII.
Tannen Maury/epa/Corbis

BIBLIOGRAPHY

Books

Algeo, Matthew, *Last Team Standing*, Da Capo Press, New York, 2006.

Bettis, Jerome and Wojciechowski, Gene, *My Life In and Out Of A Helmet*, Broadway Books, New York, 2007.

Bleier, Rocky and O'Neil, Terry, *Fighting Back*, Bleier Edition, Pittsburgh, 1998.

Blount, Roy, Jr., *About Three Bricks Shy Of A Load…And the Load Filled Up*, University of Pittsburgh Press, Pittsburgh, 2004.

Bradshaw, Terry and Fisher, David, *It's Only A Game*, Pocket Books, New York, 2001.

Bradshaw, Terry and Martin, Buddy, *Looking Deep*, Berkley Books, New York, 1991.

Cope, Myron, *Double Yoi!*, Sports Publishing, Champaign, IL., 2002.

Fulks, Matt, *The Good, The Bad & The Ugly—Pittsburgh Steelers*, Triumph Books, Chicago, 2008.

Kowet, Don, *Franco Harris*, Coward, McCann & Geohegan, Inc., New York, 1977.

Mendelson, Abby, *The Pittsburgh Steelers Official Team History*, Taylor Trade Publishing, Lanham, Md., 2006.

O'Brien, Jim, *Steelers Forever*, Geyer Printing Company, Pittsburgh, 2002.

O'Brien, Jim, *The Chief—Art Rooney and His Pittsburgh Steelers*, Geyer Printing Company, Pittsburgh, 2001.

Pittsburgh Post-Gazette Staff, *Decade of Power: The Pittsburgh Steelers in the Cowher Era*, Triumph Books, Chicago, 2002.

Pittsburgh Steelers Staff, *Pittsburgh Steelers Media Guide 2006 and 2008.*

Pittsburgh Tribune-Review, *Tough As Steel: Pittsburgh Steelers 2006 Super Bowl Champions*, Sports Publishing, Champaign, IL., 2006.

Rooney, Dan, Masich, Andrew E., and Halaas, David F., *My 75 Years With the Pittsburgh Steelers,* Da Capo Press, New York, 2007.

Ross, Alan, *Steelers Glory*, Cumberland House, Nashville, 2006.

Russell, Andy, *A Steeler Odyssey*, Sports Publishing, Champaign, IL., 1998.

Silverman, Matthew (Ed.), *Total Football: The Official Encyclopedia of the National Football League,* HarperCollins, New York, 1999.

Sports Publishing Staff, *Roethlisberger: Pittsburgh's Own Big Ben*, Sports Publishing, Champaign, IL., 2004.

Toperoff, Sam, *Lost Sundays, A Season In the Life of Pittsburgh and the Steelers*, Random House, New York, 1989.

Vecsey, George, *Super Bowl*, Scholastic Books, New York, 1986.

Wexell, Jim, *Pittsburgh Steelers: Men of Steel*, Sports Publishing, Champaign, IL., 2006.

Web Sites

ESPN.com (http://espn.go.com/)
FoxSports.com (http://msn.foxsports.com/)
Pittsburgh Steelers (www.steelers.com)
SI.Co (http://sportsillustrated.cnn.com/)

Magazines

Black Sports Magazine.
Boxing World.
Coffin Corner.
Coronet Magazine.
Football Digest.
Inside Sports.
NFL GameDay.
Pro Football Weekly.
Pro Magazine.
Pro Quarterback.
Sport Magazine.
Sports Illustrated.
Steelers Digest.
Steelers Weekly.
Time Magazine.
USA Sports Weekly.

Other

Associated Press.
National Football League Yearbook.
Newspaper Enterprise Association.
Pittsburgh Steelers press releases.
Pro Football Hall of Fame press releases.
Pro Football Hall of Fame induction speeches.
Redskins Report.
United Press International.

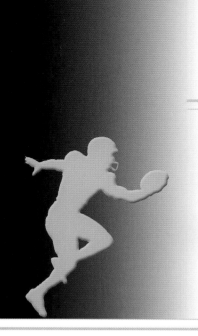

APPENDIX
STEELERS RECORD BOOK

STEELERS ALL-TIME PASSING LEADERS

Player	Att.	Comp.	Yds	Pct.	TDs	Int.	Rtg.
Terry Bradshaw (1970–83)	3,901	2,025	27,989	51.9	212	210	71.1
Kordell Stewart 1995–2002)	2,107	1,190	13,328	56.4	70	72	72.3
Neil O'Donnell (1990–95)	1,871	1,069	12,867	57.1	68	39	81.6
Ben Roethlisberger (2004–2007)	1,436	908	11,673	63.2	84	54	92.5
Bubby Brister (1986–92)	1,477	776	10,104	52.5	51	57	69.8
Bobby Layne (1958–62)	1,156	569	8,983	49.2	67	81	70.7
Jim Finks (1949–55)	1,382	661	8,854	47.8	55	88	48.5
Mark Malone (1980–87)	1,374	690	8,582	50.2	54	68	62.1
Tommy Maddox (2001–2005)	1,036	603	7,139	58.2	42	40	76.7
Mike Tomczak (1993–99)	973	546	6,649	56.1	37	42	72.0

STEELERS ALL-TIME RUSHING LEADERS

Player	Att.	Yds	Avg.	TDs
Franco Harris (1972–83)	2,881	11,950	4.1	91
Jerome Bettis (1996–2005)	2,683	10,571	3.9	78,
John Henry Johnson (1960–65)	1,025	4,383	4.3	26
Willie Parker (2004–2007)	945	4,198	4.4	19
Frank Pollard (1980–88)	953	3,989	4.2	20
Dick Hoak (1961–70)	1,132	3,965	3.5	25
Barry Foster (1990–94)	915	3,943	4.3	26
Rocky Bleier (1968, 1970–80)	928	3,865	4.2	23
Walter Abercrombie (1982–87)	842	3,343	4.0	22

STEELERS ALL-TIME SCORING LEADERS

Player	TDs	PATs	FGs	Pts.
Gary Anderson (1982–93)	0	416	309	1,343
Roy Gerela (1971–78)	0	293	146	731
Jeff Reed (2002–07)	0	293	146	731
Franco Harris (1972–83)	100	0	0	600
Jerome Bettis (1996–2005)	80	*1	0	482
Norm Johnson (1995–98)	0	137	105	452
Hines Ward (1998–2007)	66	**5	0	406

John Stallworth (1974–87)	#64	0	0	#384
Kris Brown (1999–2001)	0	98	80	338
Lynn Swann (1974–82)	+53	0	0	+318

*# Includes 1 rushing TD; + Includes 1 TD on Punt Return; *2-point conversions made*

STEELERS ALL-TIME RECEIVING LEADERS (RECEPTIONS)

Player	No.	Yds.	Avg.	TDs
Hines Ward (1998–2007)	719	8,737	12.21	65
John Stallworth (1974–87)	537	8,723	16.2	63
Louis Lipps (1984–91)	358	6.018	16.8	39
Lynn Swann (1974–82)	336	5,462	16.3	51
Elbie Nickel (1947–57)	329	5,133	15.6	37
Franco Harris (1972–83)	306	2,284	7.5	9
Plaxico Burress (2000–04)	261	4,164	16.0	22
Charles Johnson (1994–98)	250	3,400	13.6	15
Merril Hoge (1987–93)	241	2.054	8.5	13
Ray Mathews (1951–59)	230	3,919	16.1	34

STEELERS ALL-TIME INTERCEPTION LEADERS

Player	Ints.	Yds.	Avg.	TDs
Mel Blount (1970–83)	57	736	12.9	2
Jack Butler (1951–59)	52	827	15.9	4
Donnie Shell (1974–87)	51	450	8.8	2
Rod Woodson (1987–96)	38	779	20.5	5
Dwayne Woodruff (1978–85, 87–90)	37	689	18.6	3
Mike Wagner (1971–80)	36	491	13.6	0
Jack Harn (1971–82)	32	218	6.8	1
Darren Perry (1992–98)	32	574	17.9	1
Jack Lambert (1974–84)	28	243	8.7	0
Glen Edwards (1971–77)	25	652	26.1	1

STEELERS ALL-TIME SERVICE

Most Seasons

Mike Webster (1974–88)	15
Donnie Shell (1974–87)	14
John Stallworth (1974–87)	
Larry Brown (1971–84)	
Mel Blount (1970–83)	
Terry Bradshaw (1970–83)	
Ernie Stautner (1950–63)	
Tunch Ilkin (1980–92)	13
Joe Greene (1969–81)	
L .C. Greenwood (1969–81)	
Jon Kolb (1969–81)	
Sam Davis (1967–79)	
Ray Mansfield (1964–76)	
Gary Anderson (1982–94)	
Dermontti Dawson (1988–2000)	

Most Games

Mike Webster (1974–88)	220
Donnie Shell (1974–87)	201
Mel Blount (1970–83)	200
Gary Anderson (1982–94)	197
Ray Mansfield (1964–76)	182
Dermontti Dawson (1988–2000)	181
Joe Greene (1969–81)	
David Little (1981–92)	179
Jon Kolb (1969–81)	177
Tunch Ilkin (1980–92)	176
L.C. Greenwood (1969–81)	174
Ernie Stautner (1950–63)	173

Most Consecutive Games Played

Mike Webster (1974–85)	177
Dermontti Dawson (1988–99)	170
Ray Mansfield (1964–76)	168

MOST TOTAL POINTS

Career

Gary Anderson (1982–94), 416 PATs, 309 FGs	1,343
Roy Gerela (1971–78), 293 PATs, 146 FGs	731
Jeff Reed (2002–07), 211 PATs, 135 FGs	616
Franco Harris (1972–83), 100 TDs	600
Jerome Bettis (1996–2005), 80 TDs, 2-PT	482

Norm Johnson (1995–97), 116 PATs, 79 FGs ... 452

Hines Ward (1998–2007), 66 TDs, 5 2-PTs ... 406

John Stallworth (1974–87), 64 TDs ... 384

Season

Norm Johnson (1995), 39 PATs, 34 FGs ... 141

Gary Anderson (1985), 40 PATs, 33 FGs ... 139

Jeff Reed (2004), 40 PATs, 38 FGs ... 124

Kris Brown (2001) 34 PATs, 30 FGs

Roy Gerela (1973), 36 PATs, 29 FGs ... 123

Gary Anderson (1983), 38 PATs, 27 FGs ... 119

Roy Gerela (1972), 35 PATs, 28 FGs

Gary Anderson (1988), 34 PATs, 28 FGs ... 118

Jeff Reed (2005), 45 PATs, 24 FGs ... 117

Gary Anderson (1984), 45 PATs, 24 FGs

Game

Roy Jefferson (11/3/68 at Atlanta), 4 TDs ... 24

Ray Mathews (10/17/54 vs. Cleveland), 4 TDs ... 24

MOST TOUCHDOWNS

Career:

Franco Harris (1972–83) ... 100

Jerome Bettis (1996–2005) ... 80

Hines Ward (1998–2007) ... 66

John Stallworth (1974–87) ... 64

Lynn Swann (1974–82) ... 53

Louis Lipps (1984–91) ... 46

Ray Mathews (1951–59) ... 43

Kordell Stewart (1995–2002) ... 42

Buddy Dial (1959–63)

Elbie Nickel (1947–57) ... 37

Season

Willie Parker (2006) ... 16

Louis Lipps (1985) ... 15

Franco Harris (1976) ... 14

Jerome Bettis (2004) ... 13

Hines Ward (2002) ... 12

Franco Harris (1979)

Roy Jefferson (1968)

Buddy Dial (1961)

Game

Roy Jefferson (11/3/68 at Atlanta) ... 4

Ray Mathews (10/17/54 vs. Cleveland)

Hines Ward (10/22/06 at Atlanta) ... 3

Jerome Bettis (1/1/06 vs. Detroit)

Jerome Bettis (9/12/04 vs. Oakland)

Richard Huntley (9/12/99 at Cleveland)

Charles Johnson (11/1/98 vs. Tennessee)

Yancey Thigpen (12/7/97 vs. Denver)

Jerome Bettis (11/30/97 at Arizona) (OT)

Bam Morris (11/19/95 at Cincinnati)

Erric Pegram (11/5/95 at Chicago) ... 3

Barry Foster (9/27/93 at Atlanta)

Merril Hoge (10/29/90 vs. L.A. Rams)

Eric Green (10/14/90 at Denver)

Merril Hoge (11/26/89 at Miami)

Walter Abercrombie (12/13/86 at N.Y. Jets)

Weegie Thompson (11/2/86 vs. Green Bay)

Louis Lipps (9/8/85 vs. Indianapolis)

John Stallworth (11/25/84 vs. San Diego)

John Stallworth (11/4/84 vs. Houston)

Jim Smith (9/28/80 vs. Chicago)

Rocky Bleier (12/5/76 vs. Tampa Bay)

Steve Davis (9/22/74 at Denver)

Franco Harris (10/29/72 at Buffalo)

Earl Gros (12/21/69 vs. New Orleans)

John Henry Johnson (10/10/64 at Cleveland)

MOST FIELD GOALS

Career

Gary Anderson (1982–94) ... 309

Roy Gerela (1971–78) ... 146

Jeff Reed (2002–07) ... 135

Norm Johnson (1995–98) ... 105

Kris Brown (1999–2001) ... 80

Quarterback Ben Roethlisberger reads the defense during Super Bowl XLIII.
Tom Hauck/Getty Images

Season

Norm Johnson (1995)	34
Gary Anderson (1985)	33
Kris Brown (2001)	30
Roy Gerela (1973)	29
Jeff Reed (2004)	28
Gary Anderson (1993)	
Gary Anderson (1992)	
Gary Anderson (1988)	
Roy Gerela (1972)	
Gary Anderson (1983)	27

Game

Jeff Reed (12/1/02 vs. Jacksonville)	6
Gary Anderson (12/23/88 vs. Denver)	

STEELERS ALL-TIME YARDS FROM SCRIMMAGE
Career

Franco Harris (1972–83)	14,234
Jerome Bettis 1996–2005)	11,377
Hines Ward (1998–2007)	9,163
John Stallworth (1974–87)	8,834
Louis Lipps (1984–91)	6,406
Lynn Swann (1974–82)	5,534
Dick Hoak (1961–70)	5,417
John Henry Johnson (1960–65)	5,197
Merril Hoge (1987–93)	5,169
Rocky Bleier (1968, 1970–80)	5,159

Season

Barry Foster (1992)	2,034
Jerome Bettis (1997)	1,775
Willie Parker (2006)	1,716
Jerome Bettis (1996)	1,553
Willie Parker (2007)	1,480
Franco Harris (1979)	1,477
Hines Ward (2002)	1,471
Franco Harris (1975)	1,460
Jerome Bettis (2000)	1,438
Willie Parker (2005)	1,420

STEELERS ALL-TIME RUSHING
MOST YARDS RUSHING
Lifetime

Franco Harris (1972–83)	11,950
Jerome Bettis (1996–2005)	10,571
Willie Parker (2004–08)	4,987
John Henry Johnson (1960–65)	4,383
Frank Pollard (1980–88)	3,989

Season

Barry Foster (1992)	1,690
Jerome Bettis (1997)	1,665
Willie Parker (2006)	1,494

Jerome Bettis (1996)	1,431
Jerome Bettis (2000)	1,341

Game yards

Willie Parker (12/7/06 vs. Cleveland)	223
John Fuqua (12/20/70 vs. Philadelphia)	218
Willie Parker (11/12/06 vs. New Orleans)	213
John Henry Johnson (10/10/64 vs. Cleveland)	200
Barry Foster (9/13/92 vs. N.Y. Jets)	190

100-YARD RUSHING GAMES
Career

Jerome Bettis (1996–2005)	50
Franco Harris (1972–83)	47
Willie Parker (2004–08)	25
Barry Foster (1990–94)	20
John Henry Johnson (1960–65)	15

Season

Barry Foster (1992)	12
Jerome Bettis (1997)	10
Jerome Bettis (1996)	10
Willie Parker (2007)	8
Willie Parker (2006)	7
Jerome Bettis (2000)	
Franco Harris (1972)	

MOST RUSHING ATTEMPTS
Career

Franco Harris (1972–83)	2,881
Jerome Bettis (1996–2005)	2,683
Willie Parker (2004–08)	1,154
Dick Hoak (1961–70)	1,132
John Henry Johnson (1960–65)	1,025

Season

Barry Foster (1992)	390
Jerome Bettis (1997)	375
Jerome Bettis (2000)	355
Willie Parker (2006)	337
Willie Parker (2007)	321

Game

Franco Harris (10/17/76 vs. Cincinnati)	41
Willie Parker (12/31/06 vs. Cincinnati)	37
Amos Zereoue (11/10/02 vs. Atlanta)	37
Jerome Bettis (12/18/04 vs. NY Giants)	36
Jerome Bettis (11/30/97 vs. Arizona)	36

MOST RUSHING TOUCHDOWNS
Career

Franco Harris (1972–83)	91
Jerome Bettis (1996–2005)	78
Kordell Stewart (1995–2002)	37

Terry Bradshaw (1970–83)	32
John Henry Johnson (1960–65)	26
Barry Foster (1990–94)	26

Season

Franco Harris (1976)	14
Willie Parker (2006)	13
Jerome Bettis (2004)	13
Five players with 11	

Game

Jerome Bettis (3 times, last 1/1/06 vs. Detroit)	3
Also six others with 3.	

HIGHEST RUSHING AVERAGE

Career (Minimum 1,500 yards)

Kordell Stewart (1995–2002)	5.23
Terry Bradshaw (1970–83)	5.05
Bill Dudley (1942, 1945–46)	4.39
Willie Parker (2004–08)	4.31
Barry Foster (1990–94)	4.28

Season

Kordell Stewart (2001)	5.8
Franco Harris (1972)	5.6
Sidney Thornton (1979)	5.0
John Fuqua (1970)	5.0
Dick Hoak (1968)	4.9

STEELERS ALL-TIME PASSING
MOST YARDS PASSING

Career

Terry Bradshaw (1970–83)	27,989
Kordell Stewart (1995–2002)	13,328
Neil O'Donnell (1990–95)	12,867
Ben Roethlisberger (2004–07)	11,673
Bubby Brister (1986–92)	10,104
Bobby Layne (1958–62)	8,983
Jim Finks (1949–55)	8,854
Mark Malone (1980–87)	8,582
Tommy Maddox (2001–05)	7,139
Mike Tomczak (1993–99)	6,649

Season

Terry Bradshaw (1979)	3,724
Ben Roethlisberger (2006)	3,513
Tommy Maddox (2003)	3,414
Terry Bradshaw (1980)	3,339
Neil O'Donnell (1993)	3,208
Ben Roethlisberger (2007)	3,154
Kordell Stewart (2001)	3,109
Kordell Stewart (1997)	3,020
Ed Brown (1963)	2,982
Neil O'Donnell (1995)	2,970

Game

Tommy Maddox (11/10/02 vs. Atlanta)	473
Ben Roethlisberger (11/5/06 vs. Denver)	433
Bobby Layne (12/13/58 vs. Chicago Cardinals)	409
Ben Roethlisberger (12/4/05 vs. Cincinnati)	386
Neil O'Donnell (11/19/95 at Cincinnati)	377
Mark Malone (9/30/85 vs. Cincinnati)	374
Terry Bradshaw (11/25/79 vs. Cleveland)	364
Neil O'Donnell (10/19/95 vs. Cincinnati)	359
Neil O'Donnell (10/24/93 at Cleveland)	355
Bubby Brister (10/14/90 at Denver)	353

MOST 300–YARD PASSING GAMES

Career

Tommy Maddox (2001–05)	6
Neil O'Donnell (1990–95)	5
Ben Roethlisberger (2004–07)	4
Terry Bradshaw (1970–83)	4
Mike Tomczak (1993–99)	3
Kordell Stewart (1995–2002)	3
Bubby Brister (1986–92)	3
Jim Finks (1949–55)	3
Mark Malone (1980–87)	2

Season

Tommy Maddox (2003)	4
Neil O'Donnell (1995)	4
Terry Bradshaw (1979)	3
Ben Roethlisberger (2006)	2
Tommy Maddox (2002)	2
Kordell Stewart (1997)	2
Bubby Brister (1988)	2

MOST PASSING ATTEMPTS

Career

Terry Bradshaw (1970–83)	3,901
Kordell Stewart (1995–2002)	2,107
Neil O'Donnell (1990–95)	1,871
Bubby Brister (1986–92)	1,477
Ben Roethlisberger (2004–07)	1,436
Jim Finks (1949–55)	1,382
Mark Malone (1980–87)	1,374
Bobby Layne (1958–62)	1,156
Tommy Maddox (2001–05)	1,036
Mike Tomczak (1993–99)	973

Season

Tommy Maddox (2003)	519
Neil O'Donnell (1993)	486
Terry Bradshaw (1979)	472
Ben Roethlisberger (2006)	469
Kordell Stewart (1998)	458
Kordell Stewart (2001)	442
Kordell Stewart (1997)	440

Mark Malone (1986)	425
Terry Bradshaw (1980)	424
Neil O'Donnell (1995)	416

Game

Tommy Maddox (12/8/02 vs. Houston)	57
Neil O'Donnell (12/24/95 at Green Bay)	55
Ben Roethlisberger (11/5/06 vs. Denver)	54
Neil O'Donnell (10/19/95 vs. Cincinnati)	52
Joe Gilliam (9/22/74 at Denver)	50
Bobby Layne (12/13/58 vs. Chicago Cardinals)	49
Jim Finks (11/5/55 at Chicago Cardinals)	49
Kordell Stewart (12/13/97 at New England)	48
Mark Malone (9/15/86 vs. Denver)	48
Tommy Maddox (9/14/03 at Kansas City)	47
Tommy Maddox (9/28/03 vs. Tennessee)	47

MOST PASSES COMPLETED
Career

Terry Bradshaw (1970–83)	2,025
Kordell Stewart (1995–2002)	1,190
Neil O'Donnell (1990–95)	1,069
Ben Roethlisberger (2004–07)	908
Bubby Brister (1986–92)	776
Mark Malone (1980–87)	690
Jim Finks (1949–55)	661
Tommy Maddox (2001–05)	603
Bobby Layne (1958–62)	569
Mike Tomczak (1993–99)	546

Season

Tommy Maddox (2003)	298
Ben Roethlisberger (2006)	280
Neil O'Donnell (1993)	270
Kordell Stewart (2001)	266
Ben Roethlisberger (2007)	264
Terry Bradshaw (1979)	259
Kordell Stewart (1998)	252
Neil O'Donnell (1995)	246
Kordell Stewart (1997)	236
Tommy Maddox (2002)	234

Game

Ben Roethlisberger (11/5/06 vs. Denver)	38
Neil O'Donnell (11/5/95 at Chicago)	34
Neil O'Donnell (12/24/95 at Green Bay)	33
Tommy Maddox (9/28/03 vs. Tennessee)	31
Joe Gilliam (9/22/74 at Denver)	31
Tommy Maddox (12/8/02 vs. Houston)	30
Terry Bradshaw (11/25/79 vs. Cleveland)	30
Neil O'Donnell (10/19/95 vs. Cincinnati)	30
Ben Roethlisberger (12/4/05 vs. Cincinnati)	29
Terry Bradshaw (9/19/82 vs. Cincinnati)	29

Most Consecutive Passes Completed

Ben Roethlisberger (11/26/07 vs. Miami)	15
Bubby Brister (10/1/89 at Detroit)	15
Bill Nelson (12/18/66 at Atlanta)	13
Bill Nelson (9/17/67 vs. Chicago)	13
Tommy Maddox (10/27/02 at Baltimore)	11
Bubby Brister (12/27/92 vs. Cleveland)	11
Neil O'Donnell (10/11/92 at Cleveland)	11
Mark Malone (11/25/84 vs. San Diego)	11

HIGHEST COMPLETION PERCENTAGE
Career (Minimum 500 Attempts)

Ben Roethlisberger (908–1,436, 2004–07)	63.2%
Tommy Maddox (603–1,036, 2001–05)	58.2%
Neil O'Donnell (2,025–3,901, 1990–95)	57.1%
Mike Tomczak (546–973, 1993–99)	56.1%
Kordell Stewart (1,190–2,107, 1995–2002)	56.4%
Bubby Brister (776–1,477, 1986–92)	52.5%
Terry Bradshaw (2,025–3,901, 1970–83)	51.9%
Mark Malone (690–1,374, 1980–87)	50.2%
Bobby Layne (569–1,156, 1958–62)	49.2%
Jim Finks (661–1,382, 1949–55)	47.8%
Dick Shiner (245–513, 1968–69)	47.8%

Season (Minimum 250 Attempts)

Ben Roethlisberger (196–295, 2004)	66.4%
Ben Roethlisberger (264–404, 2007)	65.3%
Ben Roethlisberger (168–268, 2005)	62.7%
Tommy Maddox (234–377, 2002)	62.1%
Kordell Stewart (266–442, 2001)	60.2%
Ben Roethlisberger (280–469, 2006)	59.7%
Neil O'Donnell (185–313, 1992)	59.1%
Neil O'Donnell (246–416, 1995)	59.1%
Kordell Stewart (160–275, 1999)	58.2%
Terry Bradshaw (165–286, 1975)	57.7%
Bubby Brister (223–387, 1990)	57.6%
Tommy Maddox (298–519, 2003)	57.4%
Neil O'Donnell (212–370, 1994)	57.3%
Terry Bradshaw (207–368, 1978)	56.3%
Neil O'Donnell (270–486, 1993)	55.6%

Game (Minimum 20 Attempts)

Ben Roethlisberger (18–21, 11/26/07 vs. Miami)	85.7%
Kordell Stewart (22–26, 11/24/02 vs. Cincinnati)	84.6%
Ben Roethlisberger (16–19, 10/15/06 vs. Kansas City)	84.2%
Ben Roethlisberger (21–25, 10/17/04 at Dallas)	84.0%
Neil O'Donnell (21–25, 9/19/93 vs. Cincinnati)	84.0%
Ben Roethlisberger (14–17, 12/5/04 at Jacksonville)	82.5%
Mark Malone (18–22, 11/25/84 vs. San Diego)	81.8%
Mike Tomczak (22–27, 10/27/96 at Atlanta)	81.5%
Kordell Stewart (22–28, 11/15/98 at Tennessee)	78.6%
Neil O'Donnell (25–32, 10/11/92 at Cleveland)	78.1%
Bubby Brister (21–27, 10/1/89 at Detroit)	77.8%
Neil O'Donnell (24–31, 11/19/95 at Cincinnati)	77.4%

Ben Roethlisberger (16–21, 10/10/04 vs. Cleveland)	76.2%
Neil O'Donnell (19–25, 9/27/93 at Atlanta)	76.0%
Bubby Brister (22–29, 9/15/91 vs. New England)	75.9%

MOST TOUCHDOWN PASSES

Career

Terry Bradshaw (1970–83)	212
Ben Roethlisberger (2004–07)	84
Kordell Stewart (1995–2002)	70
Neil O'Donnell (1990–95)	68
Bobby Layne (1958–62)	67
Jim Finks (1949–55)	55
Mark Malone (1980–87)	54
Bubby Brister (1986–92)	51
Tommy Maddox (2001–05)	42
Mike Tomczak (1993–98)	37

Season

Ben Roethlisberger (2007)	32
Terry Bradshaw (1978)	28
Terry Bradshaw (1979)	26
Terry Bradshaw (1980)	24
Terry Bradshaw (1981)	22
Kordell Stewart (1997)	21
Ed Brown (1963)	21
Tommy Maddox (2002)	20
Bubby Brister (1990)	20
Bobby Layne (1959)	20
Jim Finks (1952)	20

Game

Ben Roethlisberger (11/5/07 vs. Baltimore)	5
Mark Malone (9/8/85 vs. Indianapolis)	5
Terry Bradshaw (11/15/81 at Atlanta)	5
Ben Roethlisberger (10/21/07 at Denver)	4
Ben Roethlisberger (9/9/07 at Cleveland)	4
Tommy Maddox (11/10/02 vs. Atlanta)	4
Bubby Brister (12/23/90 vs. Cleveland)	4
Bubby Brister (10/29/90 vs. L.A. Rams)	4
Bubby Brister (10/14/90 at Denver)	4
Mark Malone (11/25/84 vs. San Diego)	4
Terry Bradshaw (9/28/80 vs. Chicago)	4
Terry Bradshaw (11/4/79 vs. Washington)	4
Dick Shiner (11/24/68 vs. San Francisco)	4
Ed Brown (10/27/63 vs. Dallas)	4
Jim Finks (10/17/54 vs. Cleveland)	4
Jim Finks (11/30/52 vs. N.Y. Giants)	4
Jim Finks (11/16/52 at Cleveland)	4

MOST PASSES HAD INTERCEPTED

Career

Terry Bradshaw (1970–83)	210
Jim Finks (1949–55)	88
Bobby Layne (1958–62)	81

Kordell Stewart (1995–2002)	72
Mark Malone (1980–87)	68

Season

Jim Finks (1955)	26
Terry Bradshaw (1979)	25
Terry Bradshaw (1970)	24
Ben Roethlisberger (2006)	23
Terry Bradshaw (1971)	22
Terry Bradshaw (1980)	22

Game

Tommy Wade (12/12/65 vs. Philadelphia)	7
Mark Malone (9/20/87 at Cleveland)	5
Terry Bradshaw (11/18/79 at San Diego)	5
Terry Bradshaw (10/30/77 at Baltimore)	5
John Gildea (12/1/35 at Boston)	5
Ben Roethlisberger (10/29/06 at Oakland)	4
Mike Tomczak (12/18/99 at Kansas City)	4
Neil O'Donnell (9/25/94 at Seattle)	4
Kordell Stewart (12/30/01 at Cincinnati)	4

Hines Ward seems to jump for joy after scoring a game–clinching touchdown during the fourth quarter of Super Bowl XL.
Albert Dickson/TSN/ZUMA/Corbis

HIGHEST PASSER RATING (AMONG QUALIFIERS)

Career

Ben Roethlisberger (2004–07)	92.5
Neil O'Donnell (1990–95)	81.6
Tommy Maddox (2001–05)	76.7
Kordell Stewart (1995–2002)	72.3
Mike Tomczak (1993–99)	72.0
Terry Bradshaw (1970–83)	71.1
Bobby Layne (1958–62)	70.7
Bubby Brister (1986–92)	69.8
Bill Nelsen (1963–67)	67.0

Season

Ben Roethlisberger (2007)	104.1
Ben Roethlisberger (2005)	98.6
Ben Roethlisberger (2004)	98.1
Terry Bradshaw (1975)	87.8
Neil O'Donnell (1995)	87.7
Tommy Maddox (2002)	85.2
Terry Bradshaw (1978)	84.8
Terry Bradshaw (1981)	84.0
Neil O'Donnell (1992)	83.6

STEELERS ALL-TIME PASS RECEIVING
MOST RECEPTIONS

Career

Hines Ward (1998–2007)	719
John Stallworth (1974–87)	537
Louis Lipps (1984–91)	358
Lynn Swann (1974–82)	336
Elbie Nickel (1947–57)	329
Franco Harris (1972–83)	306
Plaxico Burress (2000–04)	261
Charles Johnson (1994–98)	250
Merril Hoge (1987–93)	241
Ray Mathews (1951–59)	230
Buddy Dial (1959–63)	229
Yancey Thigpen (1992–97)	222
Bennie Cunningham (1976–85)	202
Roy Jefferson (1965–69)	199
Eric Green (1990–94)	198

Season

Hines Ward (2002)	112
Hines Ward (2003)	95
Hines Ward (2001)	94
Yancey Thigpen (1995)	85
Hines Ward (2004)	80
John Stallworth (1984)	80
Yancey Thigpen (1997)	79
Plaxico Burress (2002)	78
John Stallworth (1985)	75
Hines Ward (2006)	74
Andre Hastings (1996)	72

Hines Ward (2007)	71
John Stallworth (1979)	70
Hines Ward (2005)	69
Roy Jefferson (1969)	67

Game

Courtney Hawkins (11/1/98 vs. Tennessee)	14
Hines Ward (11/30/03 vs. Cincinnati)	13
J.R. Wilburn (10/22/67 vs. Dallas)	12
Hines Ward (12/2/07 vs. Cincinnati)	11
Hines Ward (11/10/02 vs. Atlanta)	11
Yancey Thigpen (10/26/97 vs. Jacksonville)	11
John Stallworth (9/30/85 vs. Cincinnati)	11
Roy Jefferson (11/3/68 at Atlanta)	11
Hines Ward (11/17/02 at Tennessee)	10
Hines Ward (12/9/01 vs. N.Y. Jets)	10
Yancey Thigpen (9/24/95 vs. Minnesota)	10
Yancey Thigpen (11/5/95 at Chicago)	10
Andre Hastings (9/18/95 at Miami)	10
Dick Compton (10/7/67 at Cleveland)	10
Elbie Nickel (12/14/52 at Los Angeles)	10
Val Jansante (10/30/49 vs. Philadelphia)	10

MOST YARDS RECEIVING

Career

Hines Ward (1998–2007)	8,737
John Stallworth (1974–87)	8,723
Louis Lipps (1984–91)	6,016
Lynn Swann (1974–82)	5,462
Elbie Nickel (1947–57)	5,133
Buddy Dial (1959–63)	4,723
Plaxico Burress (2000–04)	4,164
Ray Mathews (1951–59)	3,919
Roy Jefferson (1965–69)	3,671
Yancey Thigpen (1992–97)	3,641

Season

Yancey Thigpen (1997)	1,398
John Stallworth (1984)	1,395
Hines Ward (2002)	1,329
Plaxico Burress (2002)	1,325
Yancey Thigpen (1995)	1,307
Buddy Dial (1963)	1,295
John Stallworth (1979)	1,183
Hines Ward (2003)	1,163
Louis Lipps (1985)	1,134
John Stallworth (1981)	1,098
Roy Jefferson (1969)	1,079
Roy Jefferson (1968)	1,074
Plaxico Burress (2001)	1,008
Charles Johnson (1996)	1,008
Hines Ward (2001)	1,003

Game

Plaxico Burress (11/10/02 vs. Atlanta)	253
Buddy Dial (10/22/61 vs. Cleveland)	235
Jimmy Orr (12/13/58 vs. Chicago Cardinals)	205
Elbie Nickel (12/14/52 at Los Angeles Rams)	202
Roy Jefferson (11/3/68 at Atlanta)	199
Yancey Thigpen (10/26/97 vs. Jacksonville)	196
Jeff Graham (12/19/93 vs. Houston)	192
Lynn Swann (12/2/79 vs. Cincinnati)	192
Elbie Nickel (12/4/48 at Chicago)	192
Louis Lipps (9/2/84 vs. Kansas City)	183

MOST 100–YARD RECEIVING GAMES

Career

John Stallworth (1974–87)	25
Hines Ward (1998–2007)	16
Louis Lipps (1984–91)	16
Plaxico Burress (2000–04)	11
Lynn Swann (1974–82)	10
Yancey Thigpen (1992–97)	10

Season

John Stallworth (1984)	7
Yancey Thigpen (1997)	6
Louis Lipps (1989)	5
Hines Ward (2005)	4
Hines Ward (2002)	4
Plaxico Burress (2002)	4
Charles Johnson (1996)	4
Yancey Thigpen (1995)	4
Louis Lipps (1985)	4
John Stallworth (1981)	4
Theo Bell (1980)	4

MOST RECEIVING TOUCHDOWNS

Career

Hines Ward (1998–2007)	65
John Stallworth (1974–87)	63
Lynn Swann (1974–82)	51
Buddy Dial (1959–63)	42
Louis Lipps (1984–91)	39
Elbie Nickel (1947–57)	37
Ray Mathews (1951–59)	34
Roy Jefferson (1965–69)	29
Eric Green (1990–94)	24
Jim Smith (1977–82)	24
Ron Shanklin (1970–75)	24

Season

Hines Ward (2002)	12
Louis Lipps (1985)	12
Buddy Dial (1961)	12
Hines Ward (2005)	11
John Stallworth (1984)	11

Lynn Swann (1978, 1975)	11
Roy Jefferson (1968)	11
Hines Ward (2003)	10
Ron Shanklin (1973)	10
Louis Lipps (1984)	9
Jim Smith (1980)	9
John Stallworth (1978)	9
Roy Jefferson (1969)	9

Game

Roy Jefferson (11/3/68 at Atlanta)	4
Hines Ward (10/22/06 at Atlanta)	3
Charles Johnson (11/1/98 vs. Tennessee)	3
Yancey Thigpen (12/7/97 vs. Denver)	3
Eric Green (10/14/90 at Denver)	3
Weegie Thompson (11/2/86 vs. Green Bay)	3
Louis Lipps (9/8/85 vs. Indianapolis)	3
John Stallworth (11/4/84 vs. Houston)	3
John Stallworth (11/25/84 vs. San Diego)	3
Jim Smith (9/28/80 vs. Chicago)	3
Ray Mathews (10/17/54 vs. Cleveland)	3

Most Consecutive Games Caught Pass

Hines Ward (11/9/98 vs. Green Bay to present)	145
John Stallworth (10/9/72 vs. Houston to 12/2/82 vs. Buffalo)	143

STEELERS ALL-TIME PUNTING
MOST PUNTS

Career

Bobby Walden (1968–77)	716
Josh Miller (1996–2003)	574
Craig Colquitt (1978–81, 1983–84)	429
Harry Newsome (1985–89)	375
Mark Royals (1992–94)	259

Season

Mark Royals (1994)	97
Josh Miller (2000)	90
Mark Royals (1993)	89
Harry Newsome (1986)	86
Josh Miller (1999)	84
Josh Miller (2003)	84
Craig Colquitt (1981)	84
Harry Newsome (1989)	82
Josh Miller (1998)	81
Craig Colquitt (1983)	80
Pat Brady (1953)	80

Game

Josh Miller (10/15/00 vs. Cincinnati)	12
Mark Royals (12/5/93 vs. New England)	11
Mark Royals (11/6/94 at Houston)	11
Harry Newsome (11/9/86 at Buffalo)	10
Harry Newsome (9/16/85 at Cleveland)	10

Bobby Walden (12/7/69 vs. Dallas)	10

HIGHEST PUNTING AVERAGE

Career

Bobby Joe Green (1960–61)	45.7
Pat Brady (1952–54)	44.5
Josh Miller (1996–2003)	42.4
Chris Gardocki (2004–06)	42.1
Mark Royals (1992–94)	41.5

Season

Bobby Joe Green (1961)	47.0
Pat Brady (1953)	46.9
Josh Miller (1999)	45.2
Bobby Walden (1970)	44.2
Bobby Walden (1971)	43.9

Longest Punt

Joe Geri (11/20/49 at Green Bay)	82
Josh Miller (12/2/99 at Jacksonville)	75
Bobby Joe Green (1960)	75
Craig Colquitt (12/7/81 at Oakland)	74
Bob Cifers (1947)	74

STEELERS ALL-TIME PUNT RETURNS
MOST PUNT RETURNS

Career

Rod Woodson (1987–96)	256
Antwaan Randle El (2002–05)	167
Theo Bell (1976, 1978–80)	139

Willie Parker carries the ball during Super Bowl XLIII.
Timothy A. Clary/AFP/Getty Images

Louis Lipps (1984–91)	107
Glen Edwards (1971–77)	99
Jim Smith (1977–82)	98
Andre Hastings (1993–96)	87
Hank Poteat (2000–02)	76
Rick Woods (1982–86)	70
Lynn Chandnois (1950–56)	66

Season

Louis Lipps (1984)	53
Andre Hastings (1995)	48
Antwaan Randle El (2003)	45
Theo Bell (1979)	45
Antwaan Randle El (2005)	44
Paul Skansi (1983)	43
Antwaan Randle El (2004)	41
Rod Woodson (1993)	41
Lynn Swann (1974)	41
Rod Woodson (1994)	39
Theo Bell (1976)	39

Game

Theo Bell (12/16/79 vs. Buffalo)	10

MOST YARDS PUNT RETURNS

Career

Rod Woodson (1987–96)	2,362
Antwaan Randle El (2002–05)	1,594
Theo Bell (1976, 1978–80)	1,259
Louis Lipps (1984–91)	1,212
Glen Edwards (1971–77)	941
Bill Dudley (1942, 1945–46)	838
Hank Poteat (2000–02)	788
Ray Mathews (1951–59)	779
Lynn Swann (1974–82)	739
Jim Smith (1977–82)	737

Season

Louis Lipps (1984)	656
Lynn Swann (1974)	577
Antwaan Randle El (2003)	542
Andre Hastings (1995)	474
Hank Poteat (2000)	467
Antwaan Randle El (2005)	448
Louis Lipps (1985)	437
Walt Slater (1947)	435
Rod Woodson (1990)	398
Theo Bell (1976)	390

MOST TOUCHDOWNS PUNT RETURNS

Career

Antwaan Randle El (2002–05)	4
Louis Lipps (1984–91)	3
Ray Mathews (1951–59)	3

Season

Antwaan Randle El (2005)	2
Antwaan Randle El (2003)	2
Louis Lipps (1985)	2
Ray Mathews (1952)	2

Game

Several, last time by	
Santonio Holmes (12/17/06 at Carolina)	1

Highest Punt Return Average
Career

Bobby Gage (1949–50)	14.9
Bill Dudley (1942, 1945–48)	14.4
Courtney Hawkins (1997–99)	12.8
Ray Mathews (1951–59)	12.8
Lynn Swann (1974–78)	12.3
Larry Anderson (1978–81)	10.4
Hank Poteat (2000–02)	10.3
Santonio Holmes (2006)	10.2
Antwaan Randle El (2002–05)	9.5
Glen Edwards (1971–77)	9.5
Jon Staggers (1971)	9.5

Season

Bobby Gage (1949)	16.0
Walt Slater (1947)	15.5
Ray Mathews (1951)	15.4
Lynn Swann (1974)	14.1
Hank Poteat (2000)	13.0

Longest Punt Returns

Brady Keys (9/20/64 vs. N.Y. Giants)	90
Antwaan Randle El (10/26/03 vs. St. Louis)	84t
Brady Keys (9/22/63 vs. N.Y. Giants)	82
Antwaan Randle El (1/1/06 vs. Detroit)	81t
Rod Woodson (10/25/92 at Kansas City)	80t
Roy Jefferson (11/10/68 at St. Louis)	80t
Louis Lipps (11/19/84 at New Orleans)	76t
Andre Hastings (9/10/95 at Houston)	72t
Louis Lipps (11/10/85 at Kansas City)	71t
Ray Mathews (10/19/52 vs. Washington)	70t
Ray Matthews (10/26/52 at Chicago Cardinals)	70t

STEELERS ALL-TIME KICKOFF RETURNS
MOST KICKOFF RETURNS
Career

Rod Woodson (1987–96)	220
Larry Anderson (1978–81)	122
Dwight Stone (1987–94)	109
Lynn Chandnois (1950–56)	92
Will Blackwell (1997–2001)	78
Ernie Mills (1991–96)	76
Antwaan Randle El (2002–05)	75

Gary Ballman (1963–66)	64
Preston Pearson (1970–74)	52
Rich Erenberg (1984–86)	49

Season

Ernie Mills (1995)	54
Rod Woodson (1991)	44
Henry Odom (1983)	39
Allen Rossum (2007)	38
Rod Woodson (1988)	37
Larry Anderson (1978, 1981)	37
Rod Woodson (1989)	36
Rod Woodson (1990)	35
Larry Anderson (1979)	34
Antwaan Randle El (2002)	32
Lee Mays (2002)	32
Will Blackwell (1997)	32

Game

Rich Erenberg (9/2/84 vs. Kansas City)	7
Jack Deloplaine (9/26/76 vs. New England)	7

MOST YARDS KICKOFF RETURNS
Career

Rod Woodson (1987–96)	4,894
Larry Anderson (1978–81)	2,866
Lynn Chandnois (1950–56)	2,720
Dwight Stone (1987–94)	2,086
Will Blackwell (1997–2001)	1,772
Ernie Mills (1991–96)	1,753
Antwaan Randle El (2002–05)	1,727
Gary Ballman (1963–66)	1,711
Jim Butler (1965–67)	1,191
Preston Pearson (1970–74)	1,177

Season

Ernie Mills (1995)	1,306
Rod Woodson (1989)	982
Larry Anderson (1978)	930
Allen Rossum (2007)	885
Rod Woodson (1991)	880
Rod Woodson (1988)	850
Ike Taylor (2003)	831
Larry Anderson (1981)	825
Will Blackwell (1997)	791
Rod Woodson (1990)	764

MOST TOUCHDOWNS KICKOFF RETURNS
Career

Lynn Chandnois (1950–66)	3
Larry Anderson (1978–81)	2
Will Blackwell (1997–2001)	2

Season

Lynn Chandnois (1952)	2

Game

Several, last time by	
Allen Rossum (9/23/07 vs. San Francisco)	1

HIGHEST KICKOFF RETURN AVERAGE

Career

Lynn Chandnois (1950–56)	29.6
Gary Ballman (1963–66)	26.7
Mel Blount (1970–83)	25.8
David Dunn (1998)	25.0
Brady Keys (1961–67)	23.8
Larry Anderson (1978–81)	23.5
Allen Rossum (2007)	23.3
Ernie Mills (1991–96)	23.1
Will Blackwell (1997–2001)	22.7
Antwaan Randle El (2002–05)	22.6

Season

Lynn Chandnois (1952)	35.2
Lynn Chandnois (1951)	32.5
Mel Blount (1970)	29.7
Lynn Chandnois (1953)	29.0
Will Blackwell (2000)	28.1
Larry Anderson (1980)	27.1
Quincy Morgan (2005)	25.3
Larry Anderson (1978)	25.1
David Dunn (1998)	25.0
Allen Rossum (2007)	23.3

Longest Kick Returns

Don McCall (11/23/69 at Minnesota)	101t
Antwaan Randle El (10/13/02 at Cincinnati)	99t
Allen Rossum (9/23/07 vs. San Francisco)	98t
Will Blackwell (12/24/00 at San Diego)	98t
Will Blackwell (10/9/97 at Baltimore)	97t
Billy Wells (10/13/57 vs. Chicago Cardinals)	96t
Larry Anderson (11/25/79 vs. Cleveland)	95t
Mike Collier (10/26/75 at Green Bay)	94t
Jim Butler (10/30/66 at Dallas)	93
Gary Ballman (11/17/63 at Washington)	93
Lynn Chandnois (10/3/53 vs. N.Y. Giants)	93
Lynn Chandnois (10/12/52 at Philadelphia)	93

STEELERS ALL-TIME INTERCEPTIONS

Most Interceptions

Career

Mel Blount (1970–83)	57
Jack Butler (1951–59)	52
Donnie Shell (1974–87)	51
Rod Woodson (1987–96)	38
Dwayne Woodruff (1979–85, 1986–90)	37

Mike Wagner (1971–80)	36
Darren Perry (1992–98)	32
Jack Ham (1971–82)	32
Jack Lambert (1974–84)	28
Glen Edwards (1971–78)	25
Howard Hartley (1949–52)	25

Season

Mel Blount (1975)	11
Jack Butler (1957)	10
Howard Hartley (1951)	10
Bill Dudley (1946)	10
Rod Woodson (1993)	8
Mike Wagner (1973)	8
Johnny Sample (1961)	8
Willie Williams (1995)	7
Darren Perry (1994)	7
Donnie Shell (1980, 1985)	7
Dean Derby (1959)	7
Paul Cameron (1954)	7
Art Jones (1941)	7

Game

Jack Butler (12/13/53 at Washington)	4
Many with 3; last time by	
Darren Perry (9/11/94 at Cleveland)	3
Several with 2; last time by	
Troy Polamalu (11/14/04 vs. Cleveland)	2

MOST INTERCEPTION RETURN YARDS

Career

Jack Butler (1951–59)	827
Rod Woodson (1987–96)	779
Mel Blount (1970–83)	736
Dwayne Woodruff (1979–85, 1987–90)	689
Glen Edwards (1971–78)	652
Darren Perry (1992–98)	505
Mike Wagner (1971–80)	491
Donnie Shell (1974–87)	450
Chad Scott (1997–2004)	368
Dewayne Washington (1998–2003)	311

Season

Bill Dudley (1946)	242
Chad Scott (2001)	204
Glen Edwards (1973)	186
Tony Compagno (1948)	179
Dewayne Washington (1998)	178

MOST TOUCHDOWNS ON INTERCEPTIONS

Career

Rod Woodson (1987–96)	5
Chad Scott (1997–2004)	4
Jack Butler (1951–59)	4

Dwayne Woodruff (1979–85, 1986–90)	3
Tony Compagno (1946–48)	3
Deshea Townsend (1998–2007)	2
Dewayne Washington (1998–2003)	2
Donnie Shell (1974–87)	2
Sam Washington (1982–85)	2
Mel Blount (1970–83)	2

Season

Chad Scott (2001)	2
Dewayne Washington (1998)	2
Rod Woodson (1994)	2
Jack Butler (1954)	2
Tony Compagno (1947)	2

Game

Dewayne Washington (11/22/98 vs. Jacksonville; 78, 52)	2
Several, last time by	
Ike Taylor (12/20/07 at St. Louis)	1

MOST CONSECUTIVE GAMES INTERCEPTING A PASS

Mel Blount (1975)	6

LONGEST INTERCEPTION RETURNS

Martin Kottler (9/27/33 vs. Chicago Cardinals)	99t
Glen Edwards (9/30/73 at Houston)	86t
Tony Compagno (11/7/48 vs. Green Bay)	82t
Russ Craft (10/17/54 vs. Cleveland)	81
Dewayne Washington (11/22/98 vs. Jacksonville)	78t
Deon Figures (9/27/93 at Atlanta)	78
Dwayne Woodruff (12/18/88 vs. Miami)	78t
John Rowser (12/15/73 at San Francisco)	71
Harvey Clayton (10/10/83 at Cincinnati)	70t
John Rowser (11/21/71 vs. N.Y. Giants)	70t

STEELERS ALL-TIME SACKS
MOST QUARTERBACK SACKS

Career

Jason Gildon (1994–2003)	77.0
L .C. Greenwood (1969–81)	73.5
Joe Greene (1969–81)	66
Joey Porter (1999–2006)	60
Keith Willis (1982–87, 1989–91)	59
Greg Lloyd (1988–97)	53.5
Dwight White (1971–80)	46
Ernie Holmes (1972–77)	40
Aaron Smith (1999–2007)	36.5
Kevin Greene (1993–95)	35.5
Gary Dunn (1977–87)	35
Steve Furness (1972–80)	32
Clark Haggans (2001–07)	31.5
Chad Brown (1993–97, 2006)	31
Mike Merriweather (1982–87)	31

Season

Mike Merriweather (1987)	15
Kevin Greene (1994)	14
Keith Willis (1983)	14
Jason Gildon (2000)	13.5
Chad Brown (1996)	13
Kevin Greene (1993)	12.5
Jason Gildon (2001)	12
Keith Willis (1986)	12
Ernie Holmes (1974)	11.5
Jason Gildon (1998)	11
L .C. Greenwood (1973)	11

Game

Joe Greene (12/10/72 at Houston)	5
Chad Brown (10/13/96 vs. Cincinnati)	4.5
L .C. Greenwood (11/25/79 vs. Cleveland)	4.5
Joey Porter (10/14/01 at Tampa Bay)	4
Jerrol Williams (12/22/91 vs. Cleveland)	4
Edmund Nelson (9/16/84 vs. LA Rams)	4

Most Consecutive Games With a Sack

Greg Lloyd (1994)	6
Joe Greene (1974)	6
Ernie Holmes (1974)	6
Jason Gildon (1998)	5
Dwight White (1972)	5

STEELERS ALL-TIME FUMBLE RECOVERIES
Career

Ernie Stautner (1950–63)	23
Jack Ham (1971–82)	21
Donnie Shell (1974–87)	19
Carnell Lake (1989–98)	16
Joe Greene (1969–81)	16
Jack Lambert (1974–84)	15
Robin Cole (1977–87)	14
L .C. Greenwood (1969–81)	14
Greg Lloyd (1988–97)	14
Mel Blount (1970–83)	11
Mike Wagner (1971–80)	11

Season

Jack Lambert (1976)	6
Carnell Lake (1989)	5
Donnie Shell (1978)	5
Joe Greene (1978)	5
L .C. Greenwood (1971)	5
John Reger (1955, 1957)	5
Gary Glick (1957)	5

STEELERS ALL-TIME OPPONENT RECORDS
TOP 10 RUSHING PERFORMANCES
Game

Fred Taylor (11/19/00 vs. Jacksonville)	30–234–3
O .J. Simpson (9/28/75 vs. Buffalo)	23–227–0
Steve Van Buren (11/27/49 at Philadelphia)	27–205–0
John David Crow (12/18/60 at St. Louis)	24–203–0
Joe Morris (12/21/85 at N.Y. Giants)	36–202–0
O .J. Simpson (10/29/72 at Buffalo)	22–189–0
Emmitt Smith (9/4/94 vs. Dallas)	31–179–1
Curtis Martin (12/14/03 at N.Y. Jets)	30–174–0
Terry Allen (12/20/92 vs. Minnesota)	33–172–0
Gary Anderson (12/11/88 at San Diego)	26–170–0

TOP 10 RECEIVING PERFORMANCES
Game

Qadry Ismail (12/12/99 vs. Baltimore)	6–258–3
Eddie Brown (11/6/88 at Cincinnati)	7–216–2
Carl Pickens (10/11/98 at Cincinnati)	13–204–1
Terry Glenn (12/6/98 vs. New England)	9–193–1
Otis Taylor (10/18/71 at Kansas City)	6–190–2
Rob Moore (11/30/97 at Arizona/OT)	8–188–0
Steve Watson (12/30/84 at Denver)	11–177–1
Torry Holt (10/26/03 vs. St. Louis)	7–174–1
Kellen Winslow (12/22/80 at San Diego)	10–171–0
Marques Colston (11/12/06 vs. New Orleans)	10–169–0
James Lofton (9/11/83 at Green Bay)	5–169–3

TOP 10 PASSING PERFORMANCES
Game

Doug Williams (9/11/88 at Washington)	52–30–430–2–1
Dan Marino (1/6/85 at Miami)	32–21–421–4–1
Steve Bartkowski (11/15/81 at Atlanta)	50–33–416–2–2
Bernie Kosar (11/23/86 at Cleveland)	46–28–414–2–1
Jon Kitna (12/30/01 at Cincinnati)	68–35–411–2–1
Boomer Esiason (11/22/87 at Cincinnati)	53–30–409–0–3
Rich Gannon (9/15/02 vs. Oakland)	64–43–403–1–2
Tom Brady (12/9/07 at New England)	46–32–399–4–0
Drew Brees (11/12/06 vs. New Orleans)	47–31–398–1–0
Gifford Nielson (12/20/81 at Houston)	37–24–377–3–2

STEELERS TEAM RECORDS
Games Won
Season: 15 (2004)
Most Consecutive: 16 (2004–05)
Most Consecutive (One Season): 14 (2004)

SCORING
Most Points
Game: 63 (11/30/52 vs. N.Y. Giants)
Season: 416 (1979)

Most Points Allowed
Game: 54 (12/8/85 at San Diego; 11/23/41 at Green Bay)
Season: 421 (1988)

Fewest Points
Game: 0 (many times, last time 11/26/06 at Baltimore)
Season: 51 (1934 – 12 games)
202 (1965 – 14 games)
263 (1998 – 16 games)

Fewest Points Allowed
Game 0 (many times, last time 11/26/07 vs. Miami)
Season: 117 (1946 – 11 games)
138 (1976 – 14 games)
195 (1978 – 16 games)

Most Points, Combined
Game: 98 (12/8/85, San Diego 54, Pittsburgh 44)
Season: 757 (1988)

Fewest Points, Combined
Game: 0 (10/22/33, Pittsburgh 0, Cincinnati 0)
Season: 238 (1940 – 11 games)
339 (1957 – 12 games)
480 (1976 – 14 games)
524 (1992 – 16 games)
Most Touchdowns
Game: 9 (11/30/52 vs. N.Y. Giants)
Season: 52 (1979)

Most Touchdowns Allowed
Game: 8 (12/8/85 vs. San Diego; 11/23/41 vs. Green Bay)
Season: 50 (1969; 1968)

Fewest Touchdowns Allowed
Game: 0 (several times, last time 11/26/07 vs. Miami)
Season: 14 (1976 – 14 games)
22 (1978 – 16 games)

Most Rushing Touchdowns
Game: 5 (9/20/81 vs. N.Y. Jets; 11/7/76 at Kansas City)
Season: 33 (1976)

Most Rushing Touchdowns Allowed
Game: 6 (10/24/53 vs. Green Bay; 10/14/34 at Boston)
Season: 20 (1988; 1947)

Fewest Rushing Touchdowns Allowed
Game: 0 (many times, last 12/20/07 at St. Louis)
Season: 5 (2001; 1997)

Most Passing Touchdowns
Game: 5 (11/5/07 vs. Baltimore, 10/22/06 at Atlanta, 11/3/96 vs. St. Louis; 9/8/85 vs. Indianapolis; 11/5/81 at Atlanta; 10/7/79 vs. Washington; 11/30/52 vs. N.Y. Giants)
Season: 34 (2007)

Most Passing Touchdowns Allowed
Game: 6 (9/8/91 vs. Buffalo)
Season: 34 (1962)

Fewest Passing Touchdowns Allowed
Game: 0 (many times, last 11/26/07 vs. Miami)
Season: 9 (1990; 1976; 1975; 1972)

Most Defensive Touchdowns
Game: 3 (10/10/83 vs. Cincinnati)
Season: 7 (1987; 1983)

Most Points After Touchdown
Game: 9 (11/30/52 vs. N.Y. Giants)
Season: 45 (2005; 1984)

Most Points After Touchdown Allowed
Game: 7 (9/8/91 at Buffalo)
Season: 49 (1969; 1968)

Most Field Goals
Game: 6 (10/23/88 vs. Denver; 12/11/02 at Jacksonville)
Season: 34 (1995)

Most Field Goals Allowed
Game: 7 (9/24/67 vs. St. Louis)
Season: 29 (2000; 1997)

FIRST DOWNS
Most First Downs
Game: 36 (11/25/79 vs. Cleveland)
Season: 344 (1995)

Most First Downs By Opponents
Game: 35 (11/23/86 at Cleveland)
Season: 344 (1995)

Most First Downs, Combined
Game: 58 (11/25/79; Pittsburgh 36, Cleveland 22)
Season: 641 (1981)

Most Rushing First Downs
Game: 21 (11/7/76 at Kansas City)
Season: 163 (1976)

Most Rushing First Downs Allowed
Game: 18 (11/9/69 vs. Chicago Bears)
Season: 122 (1965)

Most Passing First Downs
Game: 21 (three times: 11/5/06 vs. Denver; 10/22/06 at Atlanta; 12/13/58 vs. Chicago Cardinals)
Season: 201 (2006)

Most Passing First Downs Allowed
Game: 22 (12/5/48 vs. N.Y. Giants)
Season: 194 (1991)

Most First Down Penalties
Game: 6 (10/16/05 vs. Jacksonville; 11/16/86 vs. Houston; at Oakland 10/25/70)
Season: 34 (1995; 1978)

Most First Down Penalties By Opponents
Game: 9 (10/30/77 at Baltimore)
Season: 40 (1978)

NET YARDS
Most Net Yards Gained
Game: 683 (12/13/58 vs. Chicago Cardinals)
Season: 6,258 (1979)

Fewest Net Yards Gained
Game: 53 (9/10/89 vs. Cleveland)
Season: 3,354 (1965)

Pittsburgh Steelers running back Gary Russell (second from left) celebrates with teammates after rushing for a touchdown against the Arizona Cardinals in Super Bowl XLIII.
John G. Mabanglo/epa/Corbis

Most Net Yards Gained By Opponent
Game: 559 (11/6/88 at Cincinnati)
Season: 5,805 (1988)

Fewest Net Yards Gained By Opponent
Game: 40 (9/12/99 at Cleveland)
Season: 3,074 (1974 – 14 games)
4,115 (1990 – 16 games)

RUSHING
Most Yards Gained Rushing
Game: 361 (10/7/79 at Cleveland)
Season: 2,971 (1976)

Fewest Yards Gained Rushing
Game: 7 (10/30/66 at Dallas)
Season: 1,092 (1966)

Most Yards Gained Rushing By Opponents
Game: 426 (11/4/34 at Detroit)
Season: 2,193 (1954)

Fewest Yards Gained Rushing By Opponents
Game: –33 (10/2/43 vs. Brooklyn)
Season: 1,125 (1953 – 12 games)
1,377 (1967 – 14 games)
1,195 (2001 – 16 games)

Fewest Yards Rushing Allowed (Per Game)
Season: 74.7 (2001)

Most Rushing Attempts
Game: 60 (10/3/50 vs. Boston)
Season: 653 (1976)

Fewest Rushing Attempts
Game: 11 (11/26/06 at Baltimore)
Season: 368 (1954 – 12 games)
375 (1966 – 14 games)
394 (1991 – 16 games)

Most Rushing Attempts By Opponents
Game: 64 (10/18/36 at Chicago Bears)
Season: 449 (2003)

Fewest Rushing Attempts By Opponents
Game: 6 (10/31/04 vs. New England)
Season: 357 (2004)

PASSING
Most Yards Gained Passing
Game: 472 (12/13/58 vs. Chicago Cardinals)
Season: 4,093 (1995)

Fewest Yards Gained Passing
Game: 16 (10/17/65 vs. St. Louis)
Season: 652 (1945 – 11 games)
1,711 (1972 – 14 games)
2,178 (1989 – 16 games)

Most Yards Gained Passing By Opponents
Game: 422 (9/11/88 vs. Washington)
Season: 3,941 (1988)

Fewest Yards Gained Passing By Opponents
Game: –28 (12/7/58 at Washington)
Season: 1,466 (1974 – 14 games)
2,394 (1978 – 16 games)

Most Passes Attempted
Game: 57 (12/19/93 vs. Houston Oilers; 12/8/02 vs. Houston Texans)
Season: 554 (1997)

Fewest Passes Attempted
Game: 0 (11/13/49 vs. Los Angeles; 11/16/41 vs. Brooklyn)
Season: 277 (1976 – 14 games)
358 (2004 – 16 games)

Most Passes Attempted By Opponents
Game: 68 (12/30/01 at Cincinnati OT)
Season: 573 (2002)

Fewest Passes Attempted By Opponents
Game: 8 (12/14/74 vs. Cincinnati; 12/1/57 at Philadelphia)
Season: 162 (1946 – 11 games)
339 (1974 – 14 games)
442 (1978 – 16 games)

Most Passes Attempted, Combined
Game: 95 (12/19/93; Pittsburgh 57, Houston 38)
Season: 1,124 (2002)
Most Passes Completed
Game: 38 (twice: 11/5/06 vs. Denver; 11/1/98 vs. Tennessee)
Season: 350 (2002)

Fewest Passes Completed
Game: 0 (11/13/49 vs. Los Angeles; 11/16/41 vs. Brooklyn)
Season: 42 (1941 – 11 games)
140 (1973 – 14 games)
198 (1987 – 16 games)

Most Passes Completed By Opponents
Game: 43 (9/15/02 vs. Oakland)
Season: 336 (2002)

Fewest Passes Completed By Opponents
Game: 3 (several times; last time on 12/8/02 vs. Houston)
Season: 64 (1946 – 11 games)

147 (1974 – 14 games)
221 (1978 – 16 games)

SACKS

Most Sacks
Game: 10 (4 times, last time on 10/21/01 at Tampa Bay)
Season: 55 (2001, 1994)

Most Sacks Allowed
Game: 12 (11/20/66 vs. Dallas)
Season: 52 (1983; 1969)

INTERCEPTIONS

Most Interceptions
Game: 7 (10/13/74 at Kansas City; 11/30/52 vs. N.Y. Giants)
Season: 37 (1973)

Fewest Interceptions
Game: 0 (several times, last time on 12/30/07 at Baltimore)
Season: 9 (1994)

Most Interceptions By Opponents
Game: 9 (12/12/65 vs. Philadelphia)
Season: 35 (1965)

Fewest Interceptions By Opponents
Game: 0 (several times, last time on 12/20/07 at St. Louis)
Season: 9 (2000; 1994)

Most Yards Interceptions Returned
Game: 147 (10/17/54 vs. Cleveland)
Season: 673 (1973)

Fewest Yards Interceptions Returned
Game: –1 (12/15/02 vs. Carolina)
Season: 96 (1964 – 14 games)

Most Yards Interceptions Returned By Opponents
Game: 172 (12/12/65 vs. Philadelphia)
Season: 535 (1969)

Fewest Interception Return Yards By Opponents
Game: 0 (many times, last time on 10/21/07 at Denver)
Season: 47 (1975 – 14 games)

Most Touchdowns On Interceptions
Game: 2 (11/22/98 vs. Jacksonville; 10/1/95 vs. San Diego; 12/18/88 vs. Miami; 10/1/84 vs. Cincinnati; 10/10/83 at Cincinnati; 9/30/73 at Houston; 10/17/54 vs. Cleveland)
Season: 5 (1987)

Most Touchdowns On Interceptions By Opponents
Game: 3 (9/29/68 vs. Baltimore; 12/12/65 vs. Philadelphia)
Season: 6 (1965; 1964)

PUNTING

Most Punts
Game: 12 (10/15/00 vs. Cincinnati)
Season: 97 (1994)

Fewest Punts
Game: 0 (3 times, last time on 12/26/04 vs. Baltimore)
Season: 6 (1965; 1964)

Fewest Punts By Opponents
Game: 0 (9/17/89 at Cincinnati)
Season: 54 (1960)

Highest Punting Average
Season: 47.0 (1961)

Highest Punting Average By Opponents
Season: 46.4 (1959)

PUNT RETURNS

Most Punt Returns
Game: 10 (12/16/79 vs. Buffalo)
Season: 71 (1976)

Most Punt Returns By Opponents
Game: 10 (12/5/93 vs. New England)
Season: 51 (1970)

Most Yardage By Punt Returns
Game: 178 (11/29/42 vs. Brooklyn)
Season: 774 (1974)

Most Yardage By Punt Returns By Opponents
Game: 166 (10/24/93 at Cleveland)
Season: 678 (1993)

Most Touchdowns By Punt Returns
Game: 1 (several times, last time 1/1/06 vs. Detroit)
Season: 2 (2005; 2003; 1952)

Most Touchdowns By Punt Returns By Opponents
Game: 2 (10/24/93 at Cleveland; 11/1/59 at Chicago Cardinals)
Season: 3 (1993; 1959)

KICKOFF RETURNS

Most Kickoff Returns
Game: 8 (12/8/85 at San Diego)
Season: 74 (1988)

Most Kickoff Returns By Opponents
Game: 9 (12/8/85 at San Diego)
Season: 88 (1995)

Most Kickoff Return Yardage
Game: 266 (11/17/68 vs. Cleveland)
Season: 1,575 (1988)

Highest Kickoff Return Average (per game)
Season: 28.9 (1952)

Most Kickoff Return Yardage By Opponents
Game: 259 (12/18/04 at N.Y. Giants)
Season: 1,671 (2002)

Most Touchdowns By Kickoff Returns
Game: 1 (last time on 9/23/07 vs. San Francisco)
Season: 2 (1988; 1952)

Most Touchdowns By Kickoff Returns By Opponents
Game: 1 (many times, vs. Cleveland, 11/11/07)
Season: 2 (1988; 1952)

PENALTIES
Most Penalties
Game: 17 (10/30/77 at Baltimore)
Season: 122 (1977)

Most Penalties By Opponents
Game: 13 (12/18/05 at Minnesota; 10/27/02 at Baltimore; 11/17/85 at Houston)
Season: 120 (2005)

Most Penalties Combined, Both Teams
Game: 25 (12/18/05 at Minnesota)
Season: 219 (2005; 1984)

Fewest Penalties Combined, Both Teams
Game: 0 (11/10/40 vs. Philadelphia; 10/28/34 at Brooklyn)
Season: 98 (1941; 1962; 1965)
Most Penalty Yards
Game: 154 (9/17/89 at Cincinnati)
Season: 1,005 (2003)

Most Penalty Yards By Opponents
Game: 134 (10/1/95 vs. San Diego)
Season: 960 (1981)

Most Penalty Yards Combined, Both Teams
Game: 239 (10/25/70 at Oakland)
Season: 1,897 (1978)

Fewest Penalty Yards Combined, Both Teams
Game: 0 (11/10/40 vs. Philadelphia; 10/28/34 at Brooklyn)
Season: 858 (1941 – 11 games)
941 (1965 – 14 games)
1,322 (2001 – 16 games)

FUMBLES
Most Fumbles
Game: 10 (10/9/43 vs. N.Y. Giants)
Season: 47 (1979)

Most Fumbles By Opponents
Game: 9 (12/23/90 vs. Cleveland)
Season: 42 (1976)

Most Fumbles Lost
Game: 7 (10/14/79 at Cincinnati)
Season: 29 (1950 – 12 games)
28 (1977 – 14 games)
26 (1979 – 16 games)

Most Fumbles Lost By Opponents
Game: 8 (12/23/90 vs. Cleveland)
Season: 24 (1976)

NET YARDS
Most Shutouts
Season: 5 (1976)

Most Shutouts Against
Season: 6 (1934)

Consecutive Quarters Without Scoring a TD* 9 (9/23/90 – 10/7/90)

Consecutive Quarters Without Allowing a TD* 22 (10/10/76 – 11/21/76)

* Since 1970

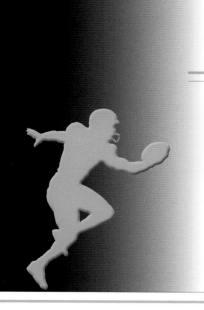

INDEX